NICHIVÓ

NICHIVÓ

LIFE, LOVE AND DEATH
ON THE RUSSIAN FRONT

GIORGIO GEDDES

CASSELL&CO

Cassell & Co
Wellington House, 125 Strand
London WC2R 0BB

The author would like to thank Giuse Ballerini
and Leslie Buskirk for their patience and dedication
in helping to organise the various episodes which
make up this chronicle of the years 1941–43.

A catalogue record for this book is available from the British Library

ISBN 0-304-35926-2

Printed and bound in the UK by Creative Print and Design (Wales)

CONTENTS

FOREWORD

IT WAS THE MONTH of April 1942 and I was in Florence on a short leave. I had just taken a course in German military terminology at the Military Academy of Modena, as preparation for joining the Intelligence Service (the R.I.E.) in the war zone, as a second lieutenant in the artillery.

The telephone rang and I heard the voice of Colonel Marchetti of the Army General Staff, calling me from the Ministry of War in Rome. The Colonel had to find two officers who spoke perfect German for assignments in Africa and Russia. He had immediately thought of me, and gave me five minutes to make my choice. I thanked him for letting me choose and decided on Russia, thinking that at least this way I would be able to clear up some of the mysteries that had surrounded the Soviet regime in my mind since my days as a student.

After an eleven-day journey in a troop train through Austria, Poland and White Russia, I arrived in the Ukraine. A year before, Italy had sent an expeditionary force of almost 75,000 men to Russia, called the CSIR (*Corpo di Spedizione Italiano in Russia*), under the command of General G. Messe. However, Mussolini, carried away by the success of the German *blitzkrieg* in the first months of the invasion of Russia, went against the better judgement of our General Staff and decided to increase the Italian contingent from three to ten divisions, transforming the CSIR into the ARMIR (*Armata Italiana in Russia*), consisting of about 225,000 men under the command of General Italo Gariboldi.

Relations between Hitler and Mussolini were very close at that time. This was reflected in our good collaboration with the *Wehrmacht* which, although aided by two Romanian armies, a Hungarian one, an Italian one and thousands of Finnish, French, Spanish and Croatian volunteers, still accounted for ninety per cent of the forces fighting on the Eastern front. Once I was in service there, however, I noticed how the relations between the German and Italian officers were gradually deteriorating.

Our weapons and equipment were totally inadequate, not only in the face of the stronger numbers of a well-armed adversary who were equipped with a huge amount of tanks and armoured vehicles, but also to withstand the severe climate. It was only through courage and the spirit of emulation, and at the cost of heavy losses, that our soldiers managed to achieve some exceptional military exploits, for which the Germans eventually showed their appreciation.

My knowledge of the German language and mentality was a great help in resolving some very tense situations with *Wehrmacht* soldiers, often only possible by showing the same stubbornness that they showed us. As an Intelligence officer with the R.I.E., I was constantly on the move along the Southern front, co-ordinating missions with the German command and solving the day-to-day problems that arose. This is how I got to know the Russian people who were silently making history on the front and behind the lines.

I chose to entitle this book with the Russian word '*nichivó*', which means 'nothing', because it was an expression used constantly by the Ukrainian and Russian population to express their profound resignation to the events of the war that so deeply affected their lives but over which they had no control. Also, I believe that these episodes that tell the story of the lives and suffering of these people are nothing in the context of the most horrifying and bloody war of all time. Perhaps the human events that I relate here can, for the first time, shed some light on what nobody until now has really spoken of. The countless books that have been written on the great 'patriotic war' waged by the Russians ignore the appalling suffering of the common people in their daily fight for survival. The Russian people had to travel for hundreds of miles on foot in search of wheat or flour, challenging freezing weather conditions, land mines and bandits ready to take everything they had made such sacrifices to obtain. At the same time, they had to be on their guard against the Ukrainian Militia who abused the authority it had acquired from the German army and sequestered their hard-earned bread. This all took place against the unpredictable backdrop of the war, where the battling armies could not neglect the operational matters of the conflict to worry about the fate of civilians.

Another of the risks run by civilians seeking bread was to be captured by the German army who needed them to dig trenches to halt the advance of enemy tanks. However, perhaps the highest risk for the younger generation was to be deported to Germany for forced labour in one of the hundreds of weapons factories.

Amongst these people fighting to survive there were some who took advantage of their position as collaborators with the Germans, the 'liberators' of the Ukraine, and were sometimes even more ruthless than the occupying forces.

This is why in *Nichivó* I have narrated little about the fighting of the war, although I did have first hand experience of it during missions when I was sent to the front line, where I shared in the sacrifices, the hardship and the awful tragedies suffered by our troops.

A few weeks after my return to Italy, the Armistice was signed with the British and American allies on the 8th September 1943, and thus we became Germany's enemies. I was imprisoned in a concentration camp, but I managed to escape with two companions and decided to join the Liberation Units that were springing up all over Italy. The aim was to get the Germans out of our cities as soon as possible so that the Allies would have no reason to bomb them.

So as not to be caught in the city and forced to enlist with the Army of the Fascist Republic of Salò, I took refuge in a farm owned by my family in the Apennine region of Toscana-Romagna, on the Gothic line. I had to hide there from the *republicchini* for a few weeks, and I spent this time organising my recollections of Russia. This is how I began the first draft of this book, although in the first version I omitted any criticisms of the Germans so as to avoid any risks in case the manuscript were sequestered.

Today I can say that we became embroiled in the tragic events in Russia in the hope of participating in a German peace, an idea with which Germany and the apparently invincible Führer had won over Mussolini. Of so many battles, so many dead, displaced, imprisoned and invalided, nothing is left but the memory of a poorly planned adventure that was carried out with no forethought of the immense sacrifices we would have to bear in order to sit at the peace table, beside a German super-power that would never have rewarded us. Even as partners in its victory, we would have been nothing but a Mediterranean pawn in the German game.

The following figures concerning the Russian front in the Second World War come from the book *The Road to Berlin* by Professor John Erickson of the University of Edinburgh. During the 1,320 days of the German/Soviet war the Red Army destroyed or disabled 506.5 German Divisions, while the German allies lost a further 100 Divisions. The Germans lost 10 million soldiers. In the same period, the Soviets lost over 20 million men. The Red Army in this period destroyed 48,000 tanks and almost 77,000 enemy aircraft.

The Italian contingent in Russia came to 230,000 men. Of these 170,000 died or were lost in action, which works out at about 74 per cent of the total.

Today's wars, however bloody and horrible, are comparatively very small. The Second World War was – and the figures do not lie – the biggest massacre in history.

GIORGIO GEDDES DA FILICAIA *Florence, 31 March 1999*

NB: the names of all the characters – apart from those
that are of historical renown – are fictitious.
Many of them are still alive, and I prefer to respect their privacy.

BEHIND THE BASTION

T HE COLISEUM THEATRE was rebuilt under the Italian authority's initiative after the city of Rikovo in the Donets basin was occupied. Just one month after its creation the theatrical company, with its orchestra, chorus drama and opera group, and a large corps de ballet with solo artists and acrobats, already had over seventy members, young and old, male and female, all full of enthusiasm although they were mostly inexperienced on the stage.

Maestro Zeiss, an excellent musician who had reaped the rewards of glory and acclaim both in the times of the tsar and of the soviets, knew how to infuse them with such enthusiasm that this peculiar company turned out to be truly harmonious and professional. As for *gospodin* Mugilov, former mathematics professor from the industrial school, he was achieving the reputation of a great director, encouraged by the success of Katia, ex-ballerina from the Stalino theatre and now the tireless teacher of the Coliseum's corps de ballet. Even *gospodin* Guernikov, who was protected from the Germans and acted as the steadfast under-secretary of Training and Performances in the province, congratulated himself on this initiative. He spared no efforts in promoting it every-where, even at communication lines near to the front, with posters designed to attract the *muzhiks*, who were lovers of the theatre and had grown wealthy from the black market sale of food.

The theatre was always full to the brim, despite the fact that at the time the Russian Army was kept at bay by only a few Italian and German divi-sions just 9 miles away. The company continued to improve and before long they were working with ease and enthusiasm; new numbers, dances, music and songs were added to the show, and the artists, with the right to the same rations as the Italian military corps, were rebuilding their strength. Those who performed badly were easily replaced, as there was no lack of candidates for such a sought-after position, with food, freedom and an exemption from labour deportation to Germany included.

Volodia Grishkievich, an accomplished 20-year-old pianist, was the subject of gossip amongst the troops that flocked from the front and seized the occasion to go to the theatre. The same was true for violinist Lumienko, as her artistic talents were in perfect harmony with the Italian and Russian musical tastes. Everyone knew the melodies played by the trio of balalaikas and guitar by heart, and the dance troupe had legs that captivated the audience, causing quite a few minds to wander. The German song 'Lilli Marlene' was increasingly requested, and ended up reaching the front and being adopted by the Red Army itself. The Coliseum's corps de ballet tapped their shiny black shoes on the stage, kicking up a dense cloud of dust from the boards like the hoofs of wild horses.

Niusia, with her golden locks, especially attracted the public's eye. Her round face, with blue eyes and tiny, round, full mouth, held a placid and smiling expression that won the hearts of the spectators. A garland of tiny flowers encircled her head with multicoloured ribbons that spilled down her shoulders and back; a white blouse and a little skirt with a pretty apron covered her nimble, gymnastic body. With a few variations in colour, the costumes of the other dancers were the same. Rosa, the smallest and youngest (she was only just 17), danced just as well as the rest. Marta, tall and dark, had the best figure and a mischievous look twinkled in her eye. It was glorious to see them. Ana, the oldest (21!), was the most serious. When Katia was not there she would take over as teacher. And Katia was often absent, at the request of a German captain, fervently in love, whose official girlfriend she was. Little Vera, an understudy, would only occasionally come out on stage; she would stay behind the scenes in case she had to act as a replacement for a colleague who was too tired, or perform during the encores that the public would keep calling for. When Ana and Katia danced the Kaukaski Danz, Vera replaced Ana in the corps de ballet and shared the public's applause with her companions.

The Coliseum theatre was a dull building. Its architecture, in an attempt at blending modernism with the Russian style, had given birth to a bastard work of undeniable bad taste. The ticket office was to the left of the main entrance and to obtain a ticket you had to queue in the open air. The inside walls, smooth and grey, lacked any decoration and the colour reminded one of the high walls of the metallurgical factory to which the auditorium belonged. This did not stop a heterogeneous public of soldiers and civilians from filling the hall. And what unaffected happiness radiated from the faces in that unusual horde of spectators, unexpected and perhaps the only one so close to the front! The scene of the 'drunken Cossack' for example, drinking incessantly from his bottle of vodka, aroused an almost childish mirth. The candour of that mixed public of Ukrainians and Italian and German soldiers, so ready and willing to be touched, excited, and to forget, revealed the absurdity of that historic period that we were having to live through.

During the small breaks we sometimes heard the rumble of the artillery and the windows even shook. But the public took it without concern. They were indifferent to whatever was happening outside of those grey walls, as long as it did not have a direct and immediate effect on the stage action.

In the intervals we danced; men, women, girls and boys became entwined, with no discrimination of sex or aesthetic desire. A tall, fat woman would be held around the waist by a skinny, fragile little man; next to them two well-built men fit for service (who knows why they were exempt) did not seem to be at all perturbed by the gender of their dance partner; a pretty girl, and a bearded *muzhik* who lifted her masterfully, wriggled under the impatient gazes of whoever had not found a space on the dance floor and awaited their turn with resignation, following the devilish rhythms of the band with their hips and thighs. The strangest medley of tunes were played in succession: Italian ballads brought over by our soldiers, old dance numbers of international renown retrieved from the dusty treasure chest of memories, impish Russian compositions and nostalgic and melancholic French songs that mentally transported us to some soirée or another, like the ones that take place in any popular district of a large city. The only relief from the monotony of haunting grey-green military uniforms was the bright colours of light summer dresses worn by some of the young women. The civilians wore their best clothes, and showed off their suits manufactured in a limited supply of standard sizes by the proletariat with cheap material in a mammoth factory in the Urals or Siberia. Very few Ukrainian or Caucasian blouses were seen. The fashionable young men and women's inclination to dress as Westerners and abandon the (secular) tradition of their regional dress was evident.

Despite the years of scientific proletarianization, a group of a select few was seated separately in a row above the stalls. This was the court of *Starosta* Didienko, extolled to the position of Mayor due to the persecution he suffered under the Stalinist dictatorship. Tall, dressed in a dignified black suit, he personified the perfection of Russian intellectuals hounded for years by the regime's police. His tie was also black, with a large knot closing the badly cut collar of his white shirt. At his side sat his wife, with painted lips and nails, wearing an elaborate dress that showed off her shapely young body. Some ladies and gentlemen, new courtesans, surrounded the couple; this was the select court that had emerged after the expulsion of the Bolsheviks, replacing the bigwigs of the Red Star who were the unconditional arbiters of the town until the German Army brought down Communism.

I was deep in these thoughts when the music stopped and the spectators started to clear the hall. Muzhikov took the opportunity to take me down a narrow passage between the wings backstage to an almost invisible door that led into a shared dressing room where the girls from the corps de ballet were already taking off their make up and regional dress. He presented them to me one by one with lavish praises. The truth is that offstage they were not as confident as they seemed from the stalls. Up close, they seemed more like healthy fair country lasses than real dancers. Rosa was the only one with truly fine features. The others, especially Marta, had splendid ruddy complexions, but little more; their hands betrayed their origins and a childhood given over to physical labour.

We accompanied them to their homes, far away in the urban area of unpaved streets that melted into the immensity of the steppe like rivers in an estuary. There they lived, very close to one another, in modest little houses with walls made of mud, straw and wood. To see them off the stage, entering those miserable dwellings, brought down the fascination of the performance. Before crossing the threshold they took their boots off in order not to tread on the wooden floor in them. We spoke briefly and formally; their Italian was minimal and we did not linger for long, but promised that we would return to the theatre as soon as we could.

The days passed by and we did not fulfil our promise. A short while after, poor Muzhikov was struck down by a burst of '*katiusha*' on his way to the Coliseum. His death deeply affected me and took away the desire to return to see those four dancers he had introduced me to. Others did not pass up the opportunity, however. An Italian superior officer took a fancy to Niusia while watching her dance. He courted her for fun and ended up being seduced by the girl's charm. She thus achieved a coveted superiority over her companions. Of course, the officer had quite a lot of authority in the garrison and later became a major. This was not why Niusia left the corps de ballet, but the jealous protection of her admirer distanced her from her companions. Marta and Rosa refrained from such dangerous relationships, whereas Ana went and fell in love with an Italian officer. She was lucky enough to be replaced by another dancer and awaited the end of the war in order to be able to marry and move to Italy.

The company followed the course of the war, with a few tours to other cities, good box-office takings and assured success with the public. Chernikov, who was married to an Iranian and had a child by her, fell hopelessly in love with the first soprano, and any pretext whatsoever was a valid one to move the whole chorus and flee the marital nest. One day, he and another man were arrested by the police, accused of previous militancy in the Communist Party, and of subsequently professing their convictions in secret. During the arrest several other accusations were added, that both of them, but especially Chernikov, harboured spics and secret agents from the Bolshevik Secret Service in the theatre. Whether this was true or false, the accusation appeared to have good grounds. The Coliseum's theatre company had become very famous and many people regarded it as a kind of oasis away from trouble. In-depth investigations were carried out objectively and a few days later they were both declared innocent and were released.

The outcome revived the company, and they set up frequent exchanges with actors from other theatres. Not even the great German winter offensive managed to interrupt the performances. For many soldiers, subjected to the rigour of terrible fighting, the Coliseum's show was a means of escape. The Red Army's energetic counter-offensive in March 1943 re-emphasized the threat to the Coliseum's home town, and those who feared the return of the political commissars made haste in their bid to escape. Niusia and Ana also ended up leaving. Thanks to their acquaintances, it seems they managed to get out towards the Dnieper in a truck in which there were places for civilians in very awkward positions due to collaboration with the occupying authorities. They got to Golta on the banks of the Bug in order to reach Odessa where, through the influence of a superior officer, they managed to obtain safe conduct passes to Italy. In that same column was Chernikov, with the beautiful Katia and his Iranian wife. Trustees of more than 70,000 roubles in the company cash register, Chernikov and his Katia slipped away and disappeared from my horizons.

In April of 1943, when I had the opportunity to return to Rikovo and spend the day at the Coliseum, everything had changed. It was almost another place altogether. The Teutonic mark was evident, and the purge carried out by the German command had relieved the Italians from the theatre's management once the Russian offensive had been contained. Now the civilian attendance to the show was restricted to two days per week; on the other five days the theatre was exclusively reserved for the members of the armed forces.

The artistic cast had to adapt to their new audience and endeavoured to get by with the German language in order to satisfy the spectators. Of the corps de ballet the only ones left were Marta and Rosa, but their days were also numbered; they were born in 1924 and 1925 respectively, and due to a new provision from the German command, there were no longer any exemptions, even for the Coliseum's troupe. In May 1943 the theatre's audience had undergone a radical change. The dance in the interval was a thing of the past and those faces that had made such an impression on me with their ability to distance themselves from the drama that the war had created in their lives, were far-off and faded memories.

The corps de ballet was no longer the same either. None of its brilliance remained, nor did it raise that delirious applause simply by stepping out onto the stage. Niusia and Ana had gone to Italy; Vera, the understudy, had been victim to an incendiary bomb on leaving the theatre on a Sunday in March. Marta and Rosa had already been handed their summons to leave for Germany; they continued to dance, but were preparing their escape. Where to? They wanted to go to Italy, but they did not have an influential officer to turn to for help.

Maestro Zeiss, who kept his position as director of the orchestra, told me that on the days reserved for civilians the audience was sparse, if not absent. Everyone was scared of Inspector Schmidt who had carried out raids, even on Sunday afternoons, with the house full to the brim. I had the feeling that an eternity had passed. With a powerful thrust, the first line had advanced to the banks of the Don, and beyond the Don the Germans had fought next to the Volga, in the streets and houses of Stalingrad. From Stalingrad to the Volga, the Don and the Donets, the front had been re-established almost up to the Dnieper, where some of the lost ground had been regained. At that moment the war on the front continued a few miles to the north-east.

Zeiss, who had also directed the orchestra in the time of the

Bolsheviks, asked me what I thought about the war. I wanted to know what luck had come his way, that in little over a year the area had passed through the hands of the Soviet, Italian and German authorities. First, a period of concerts had run for the big metallurgical factory during which thousands of workers had attended the shows to alleviate the deadening monotony of the workshops in Svierdlov Street. Then, after a brief interval of Italian occupancy, life was revived in the area; work was resumed and thousands of soldiers came to see the show to forget the horrors of the war. Next, a rapid relief of troops, general angst, furious fighting, a break of a few weeks and then concerts and shows again for the newly arrived German troops come to garrison the area.

Another bar of silence followed, as we waited in suspense.

Then the Russians conquered the Donets basin.

Some of the escaped civilians explained that the revolutionary tribunal of the political commissary was held on the stage of the Coliseum's theatre. Nothing further was known of Zeiss and his musicians. It was rumoured that they were hiding in a mine, waiting for the 'storm' to pass. Their destiny would probably already have been decided, for better or worse, by the political commissary on duty: either a pardon or the firing squad.

THE *FINSKI PULEMIOT*
AND THE
PARTISAN PISTOL

FRANZ BENDER, commander of the *Wehrmacht*'s *Feldpolizei* in the Stalino/Gorlovka district, promised one day to give me a partisan pistol in return for a few litres of Italian wine. I had no idea what kind of firearm this was, but did not want to admit my ignorance before such an old hand at all things Russian. Bender then said: 'And, if you can save my girlfriend from being deported to Germany, I'll get you a *Finski Pulemiot!*'

Once again, I could not bring myself to ask what those strange words meant, but I now had a morbid curiosity about these unknown weapons.

The second promise was the first to be kept. Bender came to me one day with a rusty object, half iron, half wood. I had managed to save his *baryshnia*, his girlfriend, from deportation by finding her a job as interpreter in an Italian command post, and he was overcome with gratitude, so he brought me this kind of 'shotgun'.

'With this contraption,' he told me, 'you needn't be afraid of anybody. And I pity the poor fellow who dares to come at you with a partisan pistol when you're armed with this!'

I took it to a gun repair workshop to have all the rust cleaned off and its crude mechanism oiled, so that even its wooden butt, soiled from being buried underground for so long, recovered its shiny red hue. What infuriated the workman the most was the magazine that held almost eighty shots and had a spiral spring that kept popping out. He did finally manage to dominate this rebellious mechanism though: however typically Russian it was, it saw reason and succumbed.

From then on the *Finski Pulemiot* accompanied me everywhere I went. I learned how to use it as skilfully as the Russians had in the birch forests of Finland, where it got its name, famous for its performance in close-fought struggles in the thick woodland. It was quite crudely constructed, and this was the first example of the Soviet weaponry industry that had fallen into my hands, the first I could examine in detail. 'These

Russians sure are smart,' I thought. Two pieces of iron slapped together, joined by a simple pin; a simply cast trigger with no aesthetic pretensions; a rough handguard big enough to hold a medium-calibre barrel; the simplest spring trigger device that seemed as if it could have been made for a toy gun, and a roughly planed wooden butt with a little metal panel fastened by two screws that could be opened to store a swab.

I loved the simplicity, easy handling and firepower of this gun. Despite the drawback of its greed for ammunition, it took the place of my old rifle, a 1891/41 model that had already reached retirement age.

A few days later, Bender brought me the partisan pistol as promised. His eyes were sparkling with joy as he unwrapped it from the oil-paper packaging. I took hold of it cautiously, but immediately realized that this was just an ordinary calibre 9 semi-automatic Tokarev, but reduced to a minimum. The butt and the barrel were smaller, and all that was left was a few inches of the explosion chamber.

As I did not look too convinced, Bender urged me to try the gun to see how well it worked. The kickback was so violent when I fired it that I had to grip it tightly in order for it not to jump out of my hands. Bender told me that it was with this very same gun that partisans had tried to shoot him, adding even more significance to his gift. I repeated my offer of wine, and Bender enthusiastically accepted so that he could take it with him on leave to Germany.

Unlike the *Finski Pulemiot*, the partisan pistol was relegated to the bottom of my army trunk to keep the Moschetto 91 company. I did not even know how to use it – that is, until the day I saw a partisan captured. Then I understood.

It took place in a cafe packed full of civilians and reeking with the usual smell of Russian public houses, hermetically sealed during the winter months to keep the cold out. It was so impregnated with smoke from the *papirosy* that it was hard to breathe. Some regulars from the Ukrainian Militia saw me arrive and moved over to leave me space, but due to the cramped surroundings, one of them bumped against somebody on the next table and nudged a bulge in his jacket. The militiaman immediately guessed just what that bulge was and tried to grab him, but the man resisted, making a sudden movement, and without a weapon in his hand he somehow managed to fire a shot. Luckily it did not hit anybody.

During the fracas that followed, the partisan tried to make for the door, but another soldier made a catlike leap, stopped him in his tracks and dealt him a blow that brought him straight to the ground. The soldiers cleared the room of civilians and held the man down. They got a knife and cut through his thick fur jacket to reveal the weapon, cleverly fastened to his chest by a system of belts that held it in two different positions: vertical when unused, which hid its bulk, especially in winter under a heavy fur jacket; or in the firing position, where a shot could be fired by making a simple arm movement. Although the partisan pistol was a semi-automatic, it could only fire a single shot, but a lethal one if its owner positioned himself right. After a brief interrogation, we left the partisan for the Ukrainian Militia to deal with.

After this experience, the *Finski Pulemiot* gained popularity amongst a great many of my comrades. One of them asked if he could borrow it for a special mission and I never got it back.

I soon got myself another one now that I knew how to use it. This one was a more recent model, which clearly showed the progress being made in the Soviet industry, in spite of the battles lost.

A few weeks later, the dirt tracks that passed for roads in the area were obstructed with all sorts of wreckage: the carcasses of dead horses along with the metal frames of burnt trucks and overturned cannon. The corpses of dead soldiers lay in the bloodstained snow, thrashed by the relentless wind that blew with a menacing whistle. Freezing tears pierced our eyes; our lips were chapped from the cold and our gums bleeding from the lack of vitamins. We felt the end was near. Amongst the cadavers surrounding us I caught sight of a sub-machine gun with a fine leather belt. Further on I saw another, and yet another, all *Finski Pulemiots*, enough to equip a whole battalion.

The sun was setting behind the white horizon and a frozen greyish twilight seemed to reflect the death that surrounded us on all sides. A group of civilians, muffled up to the eyes in their cloaks, suddenly appeared from behind the curve of the ditch. They were bent over, with their heads to the ground like bloodhounds in pursuit of the quarry. Behind them came a bony horse pulling a freight sleigh.

They had come among the dead in search of anything they could find to sell in the marketplace. They were prying into everything. From the wrecked machinery they were taking any usable parts: magnetos, carburettors, tyres, copper wires and so on. Protruding from a photoelectric cell, overturned and abandoned by the soldiers in their retreat, was a heavy copper ring, shining like gold. A gang of boys ran over to it and started to hack at it furiously, trying to detach it from its heavy base.

To touch the weapons of fallen soldiers was strictly prohibited, under pain of death, but nobody seemed to care.

Night fell, and the following day, as dawn broke, the first weak light revealed ten dead men tied up together by their feet.

The first to pass by looked furtively in their direction, as if gripped by a grave terror. '*Partisanen kaput*,' pronounced an old shoemaker, sniffing a pinch of tobacco with indifference, as if he had seen too much of the world, and even of life itself.

A group of disbanded Italians, Germans and Romanians arrived on the dirt track. One of them had a heavy machine gun slung over his shoulder, and he struggled along under its weight, determined not to stop, while the others dragged themselves along in his footsteps. Two German soldiers from the *Feldgendarmerie* came forward, and halted them to check their documents and send them to the refugee centre. The man with the machine gun tried to ignore them and continue on his way, but the police insisted and a quarrel started. The disbanded soldiers suddenly found energy from somewhere and started to shout insults, accusing the Germans of ambushing them. Other police arrived at the sound of their cries and there was nothing they could do but obey. However, the man with the machine gun refused to give up, and without even taking the time to position the gun on the ground, he let out a spray of gunfire and shot the two Germans down. He was ready to carry on his way, as if nothing had happened ; but one of the disbanded soldiers of the *Wehrmacht*, who had seen the offence, shot down the murderer with his machine pistol, ending the incident, so that they could continue as planned to the improvised refugee camp, where everything was supposed to start again from the beginning.

As they turned to leave, one of the disbanded soldiers, ravaged by hunger and fatigue, ripped the Edelweiss emblem of the German alpine troops off his uniform, and angrily flung it onto the ill-fated dead. This gesture was copied by the others, and the guards could do nothing to prevent it, so they just pretended not to see, busily herding them towards the refugee zone, where they would have to restore them not just with their uniforms, but also arms and discipline, and above all the faith that they had lost for ever amongst the ruins of the industrial zone on the outskirts of Stalingrad.

THREE MEN
AND A FACTORY

As STALIN LAUNCHED incessant appeals to the people from the halls of power in Moscow, the Russian Army in its retreat methodically destroyed almost all the factories to the west of the Donets, from the most colossal in size to the most modest, using tonnes and tonnes of explosives, so that nothing would remain standing that could be of possible use to the enemy in either the short or the long term. The Germans were to find nothing more than a pile of rubble remaining from Soviet industrial development. These were the orders. However, the *Wehrmacht* offensive was tremendous, and not all of the orders could be followed. There were those who did not have time to carry out their duty, there were cowards and traitors who ran in sudden flight, and there were saboteurs of Bolshevism who served in the party's own ranks in order to boycott it.

This is why in Krivoi Rog, Mariupol, Rostov, Konstantinovka and Kramatorsk part of the destroyed industry could be revived for production in a relatively short time. When the order was received in Voroshilovsk, Jarkov and Taganrog to transport all of the factory equipment to the Urals and Siberia, there was only just enough time for the workers to flee towards the east with the principal machinery, the smelting ingots and the precious raw materials that would obviously soon become scarce, so that the Germans could not seize much of the large mineral supplies.

The objective of the Nazi high command in their victories along the eastern front of the Donets basin was to obtain an inexhaustible supply of raw materials for the service of the homeland in its war effort. In the rich subsoil of the immense plains of wheat and sunflowers that the thousands of army vehicles ploughed through during their onslaught, they were expected to extract as much iron, manganese, tungsten, carbon and mercury as they could, at whatever cost. Germany's destiny was riding on this supreme fight. What did it matter that, in those invaded fields, the crops were scarce and the steppe was scattered with disused farm machinery, that many mines had been destroyed and many complex industries had been converted into a pile of rubble? The promised land of Eastern Europe was opening up to the penetration of the Axis alliance, and the steamroller of the Third Reich would flatten whatever obstacle stood in its way, in order for Germany to be free to gather the fruits of triumph and never more to be defeated.

Hitler ordered a titanic industrial reconstruction from a consortium led by Hermann Goering himself. Russia's industrial and mineral resources would have to pay for the armed forces during their march and for future war operations, and to make up for the serious damage incurred by the Reich's industry through the air raids carried out by the English and North Americans. Due to their resolve and unbending will to triumph, the top leaders of German industry would devote themselves with unprecedented fanaticism to the cause and lay out the most appropriate guidelines.

In June 1942, pushing the Russians further back in their retreat, beyond the Volga to the Urals, seizing petroleum from the Caucasus and reaching the western coast of the Caspian Sea, the Germans prepared to launch their second offensive: 'Operation Barbarossa'.

It was during those days, serving in a counter-espionage section of the Italian Eighth Army, that I had the opportunity to see how the Germans carried out the restoration of one of the biggest steelworks on the Donets coalfield, near Stalino. The circumstances that led me to witness this effort, through my contacts with the German authorities, enabled me to admire the incredible difficulties they overcame, their achievements and outright failures, and also to see how ineffectual many projects can be, however resolutely man may embark upon them and however steadfast the ideas that uphold them may seem.

Four companies of engineers from the German Army were ready to leave. Trucks of all shapes and sizes filled the avenues in the industrial sector of Rikovo in a somewhat disorderly fashion. Half-naked children were helping the soldiers in their final preparations, loading crates of munitions, provisions, metal beds, tables, chairs and miscellaneous objects. Out of curiosity, some civilians stood by to watch, maybe asking themselves where the convoy was going or whether its departure was perhaps a sign that the war was about to end. Lovesick couples could be seen hiding in the shadows of the large acacia trees and through the wrought-iron gates of the characteristic wooden fences around the little houses, adding a note of contrast to the context of war. While I stood contemplating the scene, Captain Rudek, commander of Company 10a, appeared.

'We are going to the Caucasus,' he said, greeting me in a cordial fashion and anticipating my curiosity. 'We have received new orders and one of the priorities is the reconstruction of the oil refineries in Maikop and Krasnodar.'

These units were not normal companies from the Engineering Corps, but special sections of technicians made up of specialized personnel, picked from different sectors of the mechanical and electrical industries. Their skills were expected to complement each other, in order to carry out a co-ordinated job. Rudek's company, for example, specialized in building and repairing electric generators; that of Lieutenant Tebelihanns, a renowned engineer from Berlin, was in charge of blast furnaces; Lieutenant Wiek's unit was made up of Martin converter workers; and Milch had a unit of laminators from Krupp of Essen. The four of them had been sent to the Eastern front in the rearguard of a front line unit, with the mission to start immediately the first reconstruction work of any industrial complex where, despite the destruction, possibilities existed of resuming production, however limited.

A short while later the other three officers arrived, completing the meagre but efficient outfit. The command and administration were Rudek's responsibility, with the help of an older sergeant.

'We are fenced in,' said the captain seriously, 'but in order to win the war, nobody can abandon the front. I have been in Russia with my men since the campaign began, but the commanders do not get leave until the subordinates have taken it. You can now see how difficult it is for Captain Rudek, a former soldier of the First World War who got as far as Rostov in 1917, to be granted permission to see his wife and son. Provided his son has not been enlisted, that is, because he has just turned 17.'

He finished what he was saying with a deep sigh, and as an afterthought he added that it was a fanciful idea on behalf of the generals who commanded the war from the great halls of Berlin to promise two or three weeks' leave for each year spent at the front.

'Pure fantasy!' he repeated sarcastically, looking towards the east where the imposing black chimneys of the steelworks stood erect, intact amongst the ruins that were no less impressive. 'There lies our almost completed job,' he added, more reassured; 'those who come after us will find that reconstruction has been started, but in order to complete the renovation they will have to sacrifice their lives and bring their families to this inhospitable country. I hope that Hermann Goering's consortium does not make the mistake of sending older men; those of my generation are affected by a dangerous and incurable disease, which is very contagious: pessimism. It is new men that are needed; people who have no memories of what seems now to be a thing of the past, but which still haunts us like a recurrent nightmare that poisons everything. You understand what I mean.'

The old captain had confided in me, and I was contemplating his words when a sharp order was rapped out in a typically Prussian manner, ending our conversation. The vehicles had already formed an imposing column along the cobbled avenue that led to the main entrance of the factory.

The other three commanders, sitting in their respective vehicles, waited for Rudek, their senior officer, to give the order to leave. The first vehicle started up and the others followed at a regimental distance, wobbling along on the uneven cobbles. The women, waving their multi-coloured handkerchiefs in the bright sunshine on that July day in 1942, gave their send-off a folkloric note. 'There must be something good in this world,' commented Rudek, as he watched those outstretched arms waving goodbye. 'Eternal love! Or rather, eternal sexual attraction!'

Those were his last words before bidding us farewell. I saw that his small Opel, at the rear of the moving column, stopped a few yards further on in front of a half-open wooden gate, where the figure of a woman stood, dressed in white.

I spent a moment longer on the deserted avenue to admire the grandiose edifice of the factory, dauntless in its deadly silence. The smokeless chimneys, the smashed up blast furnaces, the enormous sunken platforms void of their machinists, under that intense blue sky, like a counterpoint to the last words of the old captain, 'Eternal love! Eternal sexual attraction!' A young couple crossed the avenue in front of the broken railings of the steelworks, wrapped up in their happiness, detached from it all; those mountains of ruins, the end of a world and of an era, did not detract at all from their physical magnetism. I thought of Rudek's long column on the road to the line of fire and of the dangerous and contagious illness called pessimism.

One of the consortium's men was sick with pessimism. He was the Lieutenant Engineer Dr Rasch, arrived from the steelworks at Krivoi

Rog in order to manage the factory for the teams under the command of Rudek, Tebeljhanns, Wiek and Milch. They had summoned him from Stalino's *Wirtschaft Kommando* to take charge of an extremely important mission in reward for his success at Krivoi Rog.

'You will run the reconstruction of the number 5 steelworks, as the technical companies that were moved here had to stop work because they were needed in other vitally important sectors to aid the final victory. Although the basic reconstruction is substantially under way, there is much left to do. At the moment you will not have more than two engineers and an administrator. That is all. Recruit the rest of your co-workers from the Russian civilian population and manage as best you can with the local resources for your basic needs. Look for Russian engineers; you will find quite a few hiding amongst the machinists. For transport, make use of the vehicles found in the Soviet depot that need repairing, and make do with them. Recover anything useful from the vast ruins, taking into account that Germany is expecting a lot from you, the *Sonderführer*, as men of the reconstruction. But due to serious obligations under way, the fatherland is not able to help you further in your titanic efforts without making enormous sacrifices.'

These were, in general terms, the orders that the high official of Goering's consortium rapped out to Dr Rasch, who came out of his office overwhelmed by what had been said to him. From his eight months of effort in Krivoi Rog he knew perfectly well how much creative work awaited him and the enormity of the responsibilities that he was taking on. Even supposing that what the official had said, emanating from the orders of the war's high governing powers, could be realistic in terms of practical application, which he doubted, did he really feel up to the task? Could he, at over 50 years of age, however expert an engineer he might be, rely on his physical and moral endurance in order to persevere in such an immense task, without faltering? His first Russian winter, from 1941 to 1942, living amongst the ruins of Krivoi Rog, always on his feet come rain or shine, amidst designated Russian workers who were undernourished, tired and sluggish in their forced labour, conjured up images in his mind of intrepid sea captains facing ferocious gales in the north seas. Nevertheless, how far removed this image was from his own experience: at sea the storm lasts for hours or days at the most, and each man on board does his best to stay alive and save the ship. Whereas he, in Russia, was forced to face an eight-month persistent gale, with the knowledge that it would perhaps last for years.

The captain alone, thrown about in this Russian squall, was the only one trying to save both the ship and himself from perishing, in face of the sailors' desire to be shipwrecked in the faint hope of liberation.

He was about to walk back into the high official's office to tell him, 'Doctor, I appreciate the confidence you have invested in me, but on second thoughts, I do not consider myself up to the mission. I am from another generation, a man for whom the memory of the past is like a poisonous nightmare. I have a contagious and incurable disease: pessimism. Give the task to new blood, from the generation that has not been through the other war; tough, persistent men with faith.' But thirty years of impeccable conduct, dedicated to serving his country in his work, made him fall into apathy. There was no choice. With the fatherland at war, the young and able men went to the front. Germany would gain nothing by replacing him, a 50-year-old reservist, with an inexperienced young man. On the contrary, they would be losing the advantage of his greater experience. A gust of warm wind encircled him when he stepped out into the street. He had a car waiting to transfer him to his new destiny, its white fenders painted with the anagram of the number 5 steelworks.

A long freight train slumbered on a dead rail track in Ordzhonikidze station. Standing on the platform, judging by the fuss being made, Dr Rasch was holding an animated and heated argument with three other German officers. The two taller men were Dr Ploke, a Prussian through and through, and Dr Weimann, a jovial Viennese man. With them was Rolfe, chief inspector of the labour office, leaving no doubts over what the discussion was about: 'human merchandise'. And it smelled pretty bad, judging by the fumes given off by those livestock wagons. If you were able to stomach it, and ignore the weak groans that could be heard, by looking through the shadows you could make out human forms entwined like snakes, the faces of women, children and men, mixed up in a shapeless heap, with bags of household goods of all kinds. Recorded in the departure log of Stalino's *Transport Kommandantur*, shipment number 55 would be described as 'human material'; and in a summary calculation of ages, genders and numbers it was obvious that this was made up of entire families.

The bitter discussion between the four German officers was focused on the cargo of convoy number 55 from Mariupol, via Jasinovataya, made up of 800 human beings, dispatched by the German labour office for the attention of Dr Rudek for reconstruction of the Ordzhonikidze factory. The merchandise had been gathered and loaded by Inspector Gustav, with the transport costs seen to by Stalino's *Transport Kommandantur*, anticipating possible damage or loss due to the vicissitudes of the transit across the war zone, apart from other unforeseen consequences due to the physical health of those being transported.

It was more than understandable that Dr Rasch, building up the courage to look into those wagons, was having a bad time of it and was swearing at Gustav, who was convinced that he had fulfilled his duty. This useless sacrifice of human lives, that paid such a meagre service to the German cause, weighed upon Rasch's conscience. It was regrettable that there were so many officials like Gustav, performing orders to the letter rather than with their intelligence. If Inspector Gustav, when ordered to send a few hundred workers from the qualified and skilled workforce of the devastated Mariupol factory, had said that it was impossible because 80 per cent of the plant workers had escaped to the Urals and the remaining 20 per cent were almost entirely taken up with other jobs, then Dr Rasch would not have found himself in this predicament, having to give food and shelter to that contingent of substitutes for workers that were more of a hindrance than a help. Prussian to the hilt, Dr Ploke listened to his superior without contradicting him, until he had finished. Then he put forward his own opinion in complete opposition to his two colleagues. In his view, Rasch was faint-hearted, and young Weimann was driven by his Austrian, or to be precise, Viennese idiosyncrasy.

The problem with the Mariupol consignment was resolved in part by collecting more workers from other districts of the Ukraine, and soon the factory had a 6,000-strong workforce, both male and female; but thousands more were needed to meet their objectives. Meanwhile, twenty Russian engineers were retrieved and the work advanced at a good pace; those pyramids of ruins, of blocks of reinforced concrete and all kinds of pieces of machinery, were cleared up and made use of. Of the six thermoelectric generators, three were working; one of the six blast furnaces was repaired and the plant started generating energy, linked to the Don-Energo, the big hydroelectric network of the Donets. It was at this point that the Reich's Minister of Armaments and Munitions, Dr Speer, arrived, with an entourage of experts and politicians from Berlin. In a matter of months, they had to start the manufacturing of rails and had a project under way to reconvert certain sections to produce artillery projectiles and other war equipment. The Minister

and the committee held a meeting in one of the large rooms recon-
verted by Dr Rudek in the former offices of the Soviet command. They
presented several projects to each other, accompanied by models and
plans and, each in their own field of expertise, the three engineers of the
factory explained the enormous difficulties that arose each day. Finally
Dr Rasch intervened to recapitulate in realistic terms:

'Gentlemen, with my two tireless co-workers, I have spent three
months, day and night, striving to meet the objectives within the dead-
line set by our superiors. The factory that used to run with 35,000 select
workers under the Bolsheviks has re-embarked upon production with
only 6,000 mediocre ones, with great difficulty.

'Believe me, it is much more difficult and takes longer to rebuild
ruins than to start from scratch. In addition, the workforce is undernourished (the supplies department tells us that the armed forces con-
sume the best part of the resources), poorly clothed and badly housed.
We have suffered three air raids, which luckily did not flatten the efforts
of the past months; but we will need more German engineers, a great
number of specialists, supplies, clothes, blankets, glass to replace broken
windows in the workers' houses due to the effects of the Russians blowing up the factory before abandoning it, and anti-aircraft batteries for
defence so that the factory can function smoothly.'

Rasch's speech fell on the committee like cold water. If the chief engineer had presented a satisfactory overview of the situation, the meeting
would have ended with the usual 'Heil Hitler!' and he would have had
to face the consequences. However, such a realistic explanation, and
from such a trustworthy source, could not allow the issues to be
avoided. 'Cursed country, Russia!' Everything had worked out so well at
the beginning… and now the situation was becoming more and more of
a mess. They had to agree on a reconstruction plan that would mitigate
the insufficiencies that had been outlined.

In the evening, after the meeting, and very well satisfied by developments, Ploke confided in me, telling me his most personal desire. When
the war was over, he was going to bring his family to Ordzhonikidze;
since Dr Rasch was already old and Weimann was a frivolous man and
Austrian besides, Ploke was sure that he would get the post of chief
engineer. He was already building a little house that he invited me to
take a look at. In surroundings like these the luxury and the relatively
good taste of its decor startled me. The electricity was already function-
ing and the walls had been freshly plastered. It had a modern bathroom

and furniture in the bedrooms and the living room, with attention paid to the detail. He admitted to me that the factory workers were happy to do anything in order to avoid spending the whole day amongst the rubble of the factory.

Subsequent to the agreements that had been reached, ten technicians soon arrived, recruited from different parts of Germany, to reinforce Rasch's meagre team. They arrived in a truck from the *Wehrmacht*, although they were dressed in peasant clothing and carried no arms. It was their decision to live together in a house, barricading themselves in with all the arts of medieval fortifications. They must have heard tales about the partisans, as they insisted on having a good machine gun and some rifles, and would not be satisfied until poor Rasch supplied them. They also asked him for a course in the handling of these firearms, a mission which, despite the language difficulties and their immense pedantry, a Ukrainian sergeant carried out with the patience of a saint. At least the factory had ten first class technicians at its disposal, which consequently relieved Rasch and gave a notable thrust to the reconstruction effort. No more workers arrived because by then the Germans had already expended the entire available workforce; however, they did not improve the rationing, nor did they install anti-aircraft batteries.

The Russian air force intensified their nightly visits, dropping bombs everywhere, and although they mostly hit their mark, the industrial complex was such an indeterminate target and the ruins so extensive compared to the renovated parts, that in the morning it was difficult to tell where the bombs had fallen. Nevertheless, the danger persisted during the air raids, as the possibility of a more accurate 'discharge' was not to be ruled out, because overnight they could destroy all that had been rebuilt with such effort and in which so much hope had been vested. When the first repaired blast furnace went into operation, enormous red flames shot up into the night sky, showing the resurrection of the great steelworks for miles around. This was a fire that brought an enemy with the will to put it out with a violent bombing campaign. Fortunately they did not always hit their targets, and the damage was minimal: two sheds collapsed. However, the worst was suffered by the Russian workers on night duty who, on trying to evacuate the presumed target, ran straight into the zone where the bombs fell.

The manufacturing of the rails was programmed to start in March 1943 and, strangely enough, the first to be ready was the Viennese engineer who, despite his apparently 'frivolous' approach, proved the most efficient. However, in order to begin production, a large amount of steel was needed. Day and night, hundreds of workers lined up next to furnace number 2 for which trains and trains of tonnes of coke were not enough to keep it going. Since the smelting was six months behind schedule, Weimann made use of the situation to ask for leave in order to go to Vienna to get married. He managed to get it, and left on Christmas Day.

The Russian counter-offensive had already started, with the consequent collapse of the Don front. Despite its violence, the battles were taking place too far away to trouble seriously the tranquillity of the factory; even so, the repercussions definitely started to be felt, and the workers smelled the gunpowder in the air. The most decisive and undisciplined of them, said Ploke, started sporadic absenteeism from work. The punishments, such as imprisonment of resistants and the sending of repeat offenders to a forced labour camp annexed to the factory itself, were impossible to apply: the Ukrainian police, the only armed forces that the German engineers had, were easy to get around, and even more so when they could see a possible change in the situation and had to worry about their future position. According to Rasch's philosophy there was no other choice but to resign oneself to absenteeism and even to marvel at the fact that it was not more acute. However, it was not long before the situation at the front worsened, and when Mijerovo fell, the roads of the rearguard saw the first defeated German troops pass. Emaciated faces, tattered uniforms, without either officers or discipline, tortured by the ice, hungry, and terrified by battles of one against ten. The workers in the great factory witnessed this and before long they heard about the havoc of the tremendous battles from the mouths of the defeated, coming to the logical conclusion that the battles taking place less than 125 miles away were being won by the Soviet army.

In the factory, however, work continued as usual, until one day there was a telltale sign that led us to understand how rapidly the situation was deteriorating. The ten civilian technicians were urgently transferred to Dniepropetrovsk. The transportation of raw materials by train was interrupted in favour of the rail transfer of troops, resulting in a shortage of the indispensable coke needed for production, and the workers were relegated to cleaning the miles of avenues within the factory. The ten specialists went to a more secure area to the west of the Dnieper, carried away in a heavy truck, along with their equally heavy baggage, to the delight and scorn of those who had looked after them.

THREE MEN AND A FACTORY

Once again, there were three men at the head of the factory. Meanwhile, the recently married Weimann's leave had expired, and he was due back any moment. Instead, a letter arrived from Briest-Litovsk, where the troop train in which he was travelling had been blocked. He said that he regretted having had to interrupt his journey and hoped to resume it promptly.

In the meantime the situation worsened. The news from the front, which drew closer each day, was grave and discouraging. It spoke of unprecedented superior numbers, of extraordinary Siberian troops entering into battle, magnificently equipped for winter combat, and the huge deployment of armoured equipment. Stalingrad was the beginning of the end for the myth of the invincible *Reich*; the contagious disease Captain Rudek had spoken of spread like wildfire, and not only amongst the elderly men. Kamensk fell, and the evacuation of Voroshilovgrad led to the disbanding of units, filling the roads with trucks, rusty cannons and columns and columns of cars and horses. Nothing seemed able to resist the powerful Soviet offensive, which was hardly slowed by a few meagre divisions sent in great haste from France.

I found myself passing through Ordzhonikidze, and it occurred to me to drop in on the directors of the factory to see if they were still there, although I thought it highly unlikely. It was quite late when I found them there, gathered in a circle, deep in conversation. They were very happy to see me, and even more so with the prospect of receiving my updates on the current situation. Dr Rasch, despite his apparent calmness, did not hold back his tongue against the bigwigs of Berlin, whose visit to the 'consortium's' factories consisted of flying above Russia in an aeroplane or looking out of a car window. The true Russia, with conditions of minus 40 degrees Celsius, of titanic battles across thousands of miles, could hardly even be known to them through hearsay; if it had been, at least they could have made the effort of giving consistent orders: was it a lot to ask them to take charge of the situation personally? Then, breathlessly he added, 'there are just three of us Germans and 5,000 Russian workers, and we know what setbacks we are suffering, and they are realizing our vulnerability.'

In a nutshell, the Russians were 50 miles away. I explained my point of view, which matched his pessimism and contrasted with Ploke's opinion since, as any good Prussian would, he resented giving up the party for lost. He continued to live in an illusion with his pretty little house, prepared to receive his wife, and he would not give up the idea of

31

finishing the colossal renovation of the factory and being appointed chief engineer. Of course, Rasch was a man of the past, and Ploke was new blood: they were unbridgeable seas apart. The 1914–1918 war weighed like a ton of bricks on the whole existence of the first man, while the second was spurred on by his longing for revenge and his confidence in victory.

We said our goodbyes that evening with great sadness, fearing that this would be the last time we would be seeing each other. 'Three men and a factory,' I thought as I went on my way. Three Germans, 5,000 Russian workers and a huge factory in which a man could disappear without anyone even noticing. Three men and 5,000 enemies entrenched in an absurd factory, with the Russian army on an unstoppable offensive less than 50 miles away. The strength and weakness of Germany at once.

Having left Ordzhonikidze far behind me, I found out that the advancing Russian troops had passed the city and skirted around the factory without even daring to take it, believing that it was well defended.

I wanted to make the most of a warm April day to return there. I arrived in the middle of the day and found Engineer Ploke working quietly in Rasch's office. We greeted each other cordially, happy to receive news about friends in common. The first thing he told me was that Weimann had not come back. In Briest-Litovsk he had not tried very hard to find a means to return to the factory and one day he had been stripped willingly of his military uniform, enlisted in a battalion of non-commissioned officers and trained somewhere in Poland. Once the course was finished they would send him to the front, and there, after a few months demonstrating his worth, he could pass examinations to become an officer. As for Rasch, he had gone on leave to Germany, but given his advancing years he was unlikely to return to such a difficult task. Ploke was covering his post and awaited new co-workers for the restructuring of the small administrative staff. For the moment they had assigned a civilian to the position of chief technician, a man named Hofer, who some years before had installed some German machinery ordered by the Bolsheviks in that very factory. He had a typist and secretary, a 30-year-old lady whose husband, a medical officer of the *Wehrmacht*, had been sent to serve in France. They had indeed held the Russians at their gates, but since neither he nor Rasch had been ordered to blow up the factory, they put up with difficult moments, turning up to work without fail, and the workers did not dare to go against them.

There had been absenteeism, but in general everything on the front had stabilized, so the plan was to resume reconstruction as soon as new trains of coke and raw materials arrived. He went back to building castles in the air, or rather his dream house, and waited for the grey-green and silver-braided leaders quickly to sign and seal his commission of director in chief.

However, everything seemed to me inexorably changed and obscure. Perhaps more than obscure: precarious, because on the surface the changes were not obvious. Of course the factory was laced with mines, and a simple switch would have sufficed to blow up the whole lot, with no possibilities of rebuilding. The timetable in which the lamination department was due to start work to produce rails had been postponed by four months, the time the great winter battle had lasted; but it was not an obvious setback, because, as the new director explained, everything was going according to plan with the ten-year project, and the *Wehrmacht*'s summer offensive would secure the front far enough away and finally aim that long-awaited decisive blow at the enemy. Ploke thought that the danger of the Russians, less than 12 miles from the factory, would remain at a distance, and insisted on the excellent prospects of a counter-offensive, rejecting my scepticism on the subject.

I was transferred to the north and a short while later I received a letter from Ploke in Germany where he was recovering in hospital from a cranial fracture received in a car accident near the steelworks. He said that he would do his utmost to return to Russia as soon as his health permitted. In another card sent to me at the beginning of August he told me that he had returned to his post. This was during the crucial days in which the Russians, with triumph after triumph, regained the Donets basin. From that moment on, the Ordzhonikidze factory and Ploke fell into a deadly silence.

Never-ending columns of people in tatters fled in disorder, driven by their fear of reprisals from the commissars, overcome by supernatural terror. They filled the roads like a mass exodus racing before the wall of fire that was raging through the steppe and forcing the Germans to retreat. The ruins of total destruction piled on top of the older ruins of the previous devastation. What happened to Ploke and all of the engineers like him? There were those who died with their factory, like a captain who goes down with his ship, and there were others who preferred to save themselves if there was any way of doing so without losing their honour as a man, a chief and a soldier.

I close my eyes and I can see the cobbled avenue that leads to the factory's main entrance. Captain Rudek's Opel engine starting up, behind the long column of trucks, then stopping a few yards down the road in front of a half-open gate where the slender figure of a woman is standing. A young couple crosses the avenue and, although it is a fleeting vision, and I am deep in thought, I recognize them: it is Ploke and his wife. Behind them, above their heads, on all sides, stands the huge factory. Suddenly the piles of rubble begin to collapse noiselessly, in slow motion, like a backdrop falling to pieces, leaving nothing but the vast, rolling steppe, and the young couple, melting into the horizon. Where once, in years gone by, the immense factory had stood erect, now there stood three hazy silhouettes.

SCHWARZ AND NAGARIANSKI AT THE LIBERATION PARTY

IT WAS THE SUMMER of 1942. The civilian and military authorities had arranged to meet in the factory canteen to celebrate the first anniversary of Gorlovka's liberation from Bolshevism, with a real feast of a banquet. The two big halls were packed with people. The place was decorated with white tablecloths, lamps, garlands of flowers and multicoloured paper. Pamphlets were handed out in Ukrainian, German and Italian that read: *On the first anniversary of liberation from Bolshevism, we all exclaim: 'Long live the liberators!'* On the walls were portraits of Hitler and Mussolini, surrounded by laurel wreathes and posters reading: '*Long live the Ukraine free from Bolshevism*'.

In the morning there had been the prize-giving ceremony for the first agricultural year under the aegis of the Nazis. It was a lavish ceremony with the audience full of *muzhiks* and on the stage was a large table covered by a big green cloth, and on it were bottles of water and a glass for each conference member. Monumental chairs were set out for the committee. There were also Ukrainian janissaries in uniform, not that they were needed, but because they served a decorative role on the sides and the centre of the proscenium, giving the act a military air. Dominating over all was the imposing figure of the host to whom homage was being paid, *Kreislandwirtschafter* Schwarz. A diploma and an envelope of money were handed to the *starostas* of the most outstanding *kolkhozes* for their performance over the previous twelve months... although the first prize could not be given to the *starosta* of Korsiun, Igor Salimakov. His absence was explained as due to the fact that he had been arrested the evening before, accused of illicit partisan involvement. The winner's 10,000 roubles stayed in the deposit box of the *Landwirtschaft Abteilung* because Schwarz could not bring himself to admit that his best co-worker could be guilty of such a serious crime.

Once the ceremony was over, most of the participants went on to the workers' restaurant where *Sonderführer* Schwarz had organized a lunch with no expense spared. This was laid on to compensate for the effort made by the guests, especially the Germans, who had travelled long distances in order to emphasize the importance of the event.

Despite the restrictions imposed by the war, our powerful host did not run the risk of making a poor impression with this lavish feast. He had 200,000 thousand acres of fertile land under his command. The vodka was provided by the Ukrainian Militia, who brought it from the confiscation warehouses, or perhaps, a more likely scenario, from their own clandestine distillery that supplied civilians and speculators.

The tobacco smoke made it difficult to breathe, but the girls wearing little white aprons continued to serve tasty dishes and pour vodka. There was a mixture of *Wehrmacht* uniforms and civilian dress, regional or Caucasian blouses and the khaki uniform of the heads of the Ukrainian Militia: a blend of the liberators and the liberated. They were all more or less drunk and some excessively so, to the point of being grotesque, unbecoming to their dignity and office. Schwarz himself had turned a purple red colour and was sweating from every pore. He had undone his tunic and shirt, showing off a tuft of blonde fuzz on his chest that was not at all aesthetically pleasing. His appearance was somewhat unedifying.

He came straight up to me, making an ambiguous gesture that could have been either reproach or satisfaction at my having turned up late, followed by *Starosta* Koniev, the accountant Zeinmuzzer, secret agent Nagarianski and others who did not know me. In the blink of an eye I was lifted up in the air and deposited onto a chair that Schwarz had reserved for me and had forbidden anyone else to sit in. Their stinking breath was revolting and their incomprehensible exclamations, that must have been greetings, congratulations and playful comments, were deafening. While humming fashionable tunes, they filled a row of glasses to the brim with the strangest drinks and pushed them towards me, insisting with exaggerated hospitality and pestering me to drink up. A repulsive fog of tobacco smoke created a strange atmosphere and on the tablecloth, already covered with a multicoloured pattern of food and drink, there was a large provision of German cigarette boxes lying open. To one side, there was a little Ukrainian orchestra that strained to make themselves heard over that rabble, the players either blowing into their wind instruments, plucking at their balalaikas, or languidly drawing their bows across the violin and viola strings. It seemed more as if they were playing pretend instruments or we were watching a silent film. The dishes continued incessantly to land on the tables: yogurt with Russian salad, slices of roast beef British style, roast duck, chicken, stewed veal, little rolls made from flour and milk, pickled cucumbers, green tomatoes soaked in brine and all kinds of desserts...

Some couples had livened up and started to dance but their lack of balance stopped them from following the rhythm. The 'ladies' were nothing special: quite a few *Volksdeutsche*, interpreters and employees of the German territorial administration. Some seemed decent, and did not deserve to have to put up with their uncouth drunken partners. The dancing also got Schwarz on his feet. He danced with exaggerated delight, glued to his interpreter, a large lady in her thirties, fat and clumsy just like him. Bender, the elegant *Sonderführer* from Morozov, a graceful and friendly man, was holding a beautiful blonde, perhaps his girlfriend, around the waist. Even skinny old Nagarianski, a reliable source for our counter-espionage, temporarily exonerated from his assignment as an investigator and informer, was having a fling. His well-cut uniform failed to hide the lean constitution of that bag of nerves, though. His eyes were like two pinheads, almost invisible, sunken behind his cheekbones and his exaggerated forehead with its bushy grey eyebrows. Hanging from his belt was a heavy *nagan*, which also surrendered itself to the grotesque, clumsy dance.

It was in fact Nagarianski upon whom my attention was focused that day, as I contemplated him and *Kreislandwirtschafter* Schwarz, rapidly thinking of different possible theories from the information I had on them already. The story in which they held the chief roles had been going on for some time and had culminated in the arrest of Igor Salimakov, *starosta* of Korsiun. The inspection of his home turned up a meagre shotgun, two hand grenades and a couple of other irrelevant objects, but the powerful *starosta* ended up in prison like a vulgar criminal. Schwarz found out by word of mouth as the German police thought it better not to inform him that his right-hand man had been reported to them. According to rumour, the informer had been the secret agent, Nagarianski, who was in fact the *éminence grise* of Kalinin's Ukrainian police. To put it plainly, this meant that he was officially under orders of the 'Third Group'. He was a spy capable of outwitting any civil servant and, if it came to it, bringing him down with accusations that nobody could check up on.

The crafty Nagarianski made use of informers motivated by the attractive rewards he provided. I did not know, but I wondered if he was not a double agent. It was not my responsibility to investigate the situation, although it was my job to puzzle out any intrigues that could compromise our military objectives. It was Nagarianski who handled the investigation on the *starosta* of Korsiun, and who had declared Igor Salimakov free of all suspicion. Nevertheless, the German command decided to go further, based on a number of anonymous testimonies and letters that stated the opposite and accused him of hiding partisans, supplying them with provisions and arms and using violence against whoever did not give in to his demands. Faced with this new investigation Nagarianski understood that he could no longer cover up for his friend and, changing tactics, it was he who advised them to arrest him. With this, his 'friend' Nagarianski sought Salimakov's ruin, and Schwarz, who had chosen Salimakov as the number one prize-winner for his admirable management of the land in his district, had to swallow the bitter pill and reflect on his mistaken choice. From jail, Igor Salimakov prepared his own defence, and in support of his innocence he blamed others for his crimes – taking care not to implicate Nagarianski, assuming he was a friend and the only one who could save him. How many times had he loaded the sleigh with sacks of wheat taken from Schwarz's silos, how much gold had he given him in exchange for weapons? A lot of wheat, a lot of milk, a lot of honey, butter and sunflower oil, too many shady dealings had passed between them for the powerful Nagarianski to forget his friend in trouble.

Salimakov's allegations only served to have the other accomplices detained and thus to lead the *Schutzpolizei* to check the information meticulously. If Nagarianski thought he had rid himself of Salimakov, Schwarz had lost all hope of saving him.

So this was the relationship between Schwarz and Nagarianski, both in an identical condition of inebriation, dancing and euphoric, and seemingly the most powerful and carefree at the party. The lieutenant of the *Schutzpolizei*'s attitude intrigued me, as he stood to one side, not missing a single detail of the events.

After the liberation party Schwarz, who had done his utmost for his right-hand man, continued to put the pressure on. One morning his protégé returned to his office, but Schwarz's triumph was ephemeral. The *Schutzpolizei* was convinced that, in good faith, Schwarz had been tricked by Salimakov, so they arrested him again, this time telling

Salimakov that he had been reported to them by Nagarianski. Salimakov did not believe them, and thought it was a trap.

The truth prevailed in the end, however, when the *starosta* of Korsiun wrote the equivalent of a death sentence for the man who had betrayed him in order save his own skin. In his confession, Salimakov explained that Nagarianski traded wheat, sold arms and munitions, handled false permits in order to help Russian spies to disappear, acted as a spy for the Germans, used horses and sleighs for trafficking, and became wealthy in the process. Nagarianski was alerted to his imminent arrest so, without wasting time, he stopped by at his house to pick up his family and fled.

They thought they had made it, when the Ukrainian police caught up with them. The fugitive would not give up easily and, in the skirmish that followed, he and his family members lost their lives. This did not prevent the police from hanging Nagarianski from the gallows in the marketplace after he had already been dead for hours. Igor Salimakov was hanged next to him, not having managed to save himself by selling the skin of his former friend and accomplice.

Schwarz had to choose another *starosta* but he did not know how to take the blow: despite all the evidence of the crimes committed, he refused to believe it and put it down to envy, because the land that the hanged man had managed was the most productive.

The two corpses hung ominously from two gallows in the marketplace on that November morning. Nagarianski and Salimakov had ended their days. The civilians who came to the marketplace could read the following words written in Cyrillic on rudimentary wooden boards at the base of the gallows: '*Igor Salimakov, Starosta of Korsiun, hanged for taking advantage of his office to rob civilians, speculate and commit acts of violence*' and '*Nagarianski, head of the Third Group, hanged for robbing civilians, harassing them unjustly, speculating and helping spies and partisans*'. There was no mention of the other three crimes: informer for Russia to the detriment of the Germans, for Germany to the detriment of the Russians and for the Germans to the detriment of his colleagues in the police.

KURT HOFFMANN,
SONDERFÜHRER
AND SOLDIER

THE HEAD of the Agriculture, Mining and Industry Department of 'liberated' Ukraine, Mr Kurt Weil, received me in his spacious office in the Economy building, the *Wirtschaftkommando* in Dniepropetrovsk. He was going to bring me up to date with the duties assigned to a category of militarized civil servants called *Sonderführer*, special head administrators. Apart from the standard photograph of Hitler on the wall behind his seat, the room was virtually covered with maps of the Ukraine, divided into areas called *raiony*, each clearly numbered and entrusted to a select group of *Sonderführer*.

I wanted to know how the gigantic peace machine worked, conceived by the Germans in order to revitalize the agriculture, mining and industry that had been sabotaged by the Russian Army in its precipitated retreat after Germany's 'Operation Barbarossa' on 22 June 1941. The high ranking civil servant greeted me cordially, knowing that our Eighth Army now garrisoned Dniepropetrovsk after having contributed to the occupation of the Donets basin region, an exceptionally fertile area rich in agriculture, mining and industry. Kurt Weil explained that a *raion* comprised an area of 90,000 hectares of crops, industrial plants often covered 20 hectares and a mine could produce millions of tonnes of coal. Stressing the fact that Germany's allies had to collaborate so that all of the agricultural produce, the coal and steel and however many resources the Ukraine offered would contribute to the victory, he explained how the organization of all this was run. He also emphasized the importance of Germany's policy of weaning the Ukraine from dependence on Russia, thus winning the support of the population which believed that the *Sonderführer* were going to rebuild all that the Russian Army had destroyed during its retreat.

After this preliminary discourse, Weil then entered into detail on the complex identity of the *Sonderführer*, excellent engineers and, in some cases, valiant former officers, non-commissioned officers or soldiers from the German Army, many of whom had had to abandon their units or an important post in Germany in order to devote themselves to the revival of the immense Ukraine.

'The *Sonderführer*,' he said, 'wear a uniform that is almost identical to the *Wehrmacht*'s, although they are not part of the army itself. Their assignment is to be self-sufficient with their resources, recruiting as much available workforce as there is in their areas to rebuild the industries, regenerate the agriculture and resume the mining production. At times it is just as dangerous a job as fighting on the front. They are no more than a handful of Germans in charge of thousands of Soviets, facing the risk of partisan attacks. Despite this, they are not considered as front line soldiers, worthy of the honours bestowed on the heroes of the *Wehrmacht*.'

Weil's words emphasized the position of inferiority felt by these *Sonderführer* in relation to the soldiers and he urged me at the same time to forewarn our troops to respect them, because it was on this militarized organization that the maximum production relied, which would allow the economic battle to be won, and thus, naturally, the war.

Before bidding me farewell Weil gave me a confidential list with the names of all of the *Sonderführer* in charge within the area of the Southern Armies, pointing out that the loyal collaboration with these brave civil servants might, furthermore, allow me to obtain provisions for our own Italian forces in Russia.

I opted to follow his advice and a few days later I decided to visit the well-known *Sonderführer* Kurt Hoffmann, who, according to what Weil had told me, had just miraculously survived a partisan attack. A colleague of mine who knew him told me all the details of the attack. He had received two upward pistol shots, but fortunately they were oblique and just chipped his frontal bone. The four perpetrators of the attack on his car must have really been after him, because they repeated the act the following day in the same place, again without success, although this time the victim was his Russian chauffeur. Hoffmann, sitting in the passenger seat, once again miraculously unharmed and with the dead man at the wheel, acted without hesitation. He took hold of the wheel, keeping the car from overturning, and drove at high speed to the nearby *kolkhoz* at Krestovka, garrisoned by a German infantry detachment. Determined to put an end to these four partisans, he explained everything to the commanding officer and convinced him to take his men to the ambush site immediately. It was on a deserted bleak plateau where the four individuals would not have had time to go far or to hide themselves anywhere. Although it was not plain sailing between the *Wehrmacht* officers and the *Sonderführer*, and despite the usual distrust of the soldiers for these 'peasants dressed as officers', the lieutenant agreed to go.

In any case, however impressionable the *Sonderführer* might be, the windscreen riddled with bullet holes and the driver's corpse spoke for themselves. The modest punitive expedition, led by Kurt Hoffmann, arrived at the scene of the ambush and began the search for the partisans, who were soon located by a 'Stork' that had been called upon to help. Having been discovered in the ravine where they were hiding, after trying in vain to shoot down the little plane, they entrenched themselves, ready to put up a fight. The *Wehrmacht*'s lieutenant, having assumed the responsibility of the operation without reporting to his commander, was not prepared to risk the lives of his men. He was aware that if something went wrong he would be in serious trouble with his superiors. He gave cautious orders to attack, firing a small mortar bomb on the partisans, who responded with powerless sprays of semi-automatic rifle fire. One of the resistants tried to make a run for it and was shot down by a spray of machinegun fire. Hoffman, displaying more courage than the soldiers, approached the enemy with a hand grenade, ordering them to give themselves up. He was greeted with gunfire and two bullets skimmed the top of his head. At this point he threw the grenade and the target was blown into the air, ending the lives of the other three partisans.

Justice had been done and Hoffmann was proud of his wound that was soon taken care of and bandaged. Furthermore, he wanted to keep one of those partisan pistols that had nearly killed him three times. The lieutenant and his platoon returned to their base without casualties, congratulating the *Sonderführer* on this initiative.

Some time after, on entering his office to meet him and explain a serious problem with mined areas, I saw his bandaged head and I made a gesture to withdraw again. Instead, he stopped me from leaving, beckoning me to enter. He found it difficult to speak, but he introduced me to his interpreter, Annie, a *Volksdeutsche* from Shevchenko who was also his secretary. She would take note of the matter since, especially in these days while he was convalescing, she was helping him to carry out his duties.

They were delighted to accept the cigarettes that I offered them, which would help to lift the *Sonderführer*'s spirits. Annie explained:

'The German government doesn't supply us with cigarettes. We have to make do, smoking acacia leaves like the countryfolk, since we don't like to buy them secretly from the troops in transit or on the black market at astronomical prices.'

At this point I pulled out a carton of Italian cigarettes, since our government tobacco monopoly kept us in supply. The same friend who told me Hoffmann's story had advised me that in order to get off to a good start with the agricultural *Sonderführer*, failing cognac or wine, I should take a small reserve of cigarettes. It was important to have a good relationship with those civil servants in agriculture who enjoyed unlimited power within their areas and could decide at will what to do with those immense agricultural riches abandoned by the Russian army in the *kolkhozes* and *sovkhozes*. It was very important to have them as 'friends', as Kurt Weil had recommended. Hoffman insisted that Annie tell me about the skirmish with the partisans in detail and I had to listen to the story a second time. I congratulated him on his bravery and good fortune on having escaped a worse fate, noticing how proud he felt, with his wound, to be not only a *Sonderführer* but also a soldier.

It was undeniable that when the German soldiers ran into one of those Russian cars, solid old rust-buckets, driven by a civilian, they knew that there was a German *Sonderführer* inside with his interpreter. For them, the car and the uniformed civil servant were an unfair symbol of privilege. At the same time, a *Sonderführer*, seeing the soldiers, no doubt thought that he was physically just as fit as them for service and could be fighting the war (some, in fact, were former servicemen) as an officer. However, the government had decided that, due to their noteworthy technical and farming expertise, the *Sonderführer* would be of more use towards the victory using their professional knowledge than their military capabilities. So these men, who had perhaps served in the campaigns of Poland, France or Norway, one day received an order to leave for Russia and there they found themselves, in that black land of the Ukraine before thousands and thousands of hectares to cultivate, abandoned farm machinery, *kolkhozes* destroyed by the Russian Army in retreat, half-deserted villages and, of course, memoranda from the *Landwirtschaft Gruppe* for the development of agricultural production. Their commanding authorities were demanding and unwilling to take into consideration the continual difficulties faced by the *Sonderführer*, their sole order from the supreme command being: '*Germany has sent you to Russia not so that you can ask for help, but so that you can provide the means to help the Homeland*'. They were indeed a privileged class compared to those who faced the enemy. To be living in Russia without fighting was already a lot. However, deep down, the *Sonderführer* felt an intense sense of loss for the camaraderie of the front. With his exploits in facing the partisans, Kurt Hoffmann had lifted a weight off his conscience and could look at anyone with his head held high: *he* had overcome this complex.

I explained the problem that I had come to consult him about and he referred me to the central office to speak to Mr Dutz or his assistant Mr Schnitzler. I had to travel 20 miles on an odious, dusty track to reach the 'castle' of the powerful Dutz. During the journey I pictured this man Dutz as a powerful feudal lord, and Hoffmann as his modest vassal. However, what I saw on my arrival were not strong battlements, but a small hamlet, whose buildings were blackened by coal dust, and the towering chimneys of the steelworks. Instead of an impregnable fort, a small brick house of only one storey, which was not entered into over a drawbridge, but through a simple door with the inscription 'Agricultural Department' on the sign outside. The feudal lord was a thickset, ordinary man with the title of *Kreislandwirtschafter*.

There were some small connecting rooms with unintelligible signs on the doors in Russian, men and women bent over large volumes of records, the characteristic smell of *muzhiks*, civilians coming and going, conversations in Russian and German, people weaving in and out between tables and from one room to another. The atmosphere was foul and oppressive, but above it all rang the piercing, imperious voice of the 'feudal lord', a lacerating noise that sounded as though Mr Dutz was probably scolding a humble son of conquered Russia. This atmosphere, with a local undertone and noises heard through the wooden doors, was my first impression of the 'court' of a powerful head *Sonderführer* and the treatment he bestowed upon his humble subjects.

Dutz reigned over those unfortunate souls in a language unknown to them, forcing them to put up with a string of insults and curses in ignorant silence. What was that tall fat man saying to them? Standing there in his grey uniform adorned with a silver eagle with outstretched wings and a cross clutched in its claws. This cross was different from the ones that they had always seen in the Orthodox churches of their own land, before the Bolsheviks had pulled them down. For this simple *muzhik*, born and bred amongst the wheat fields and the sunflowers, this emblem held as little meaning as the hammer and sickle. All he knew for sure was that the fat man owned the village, along with the powerful and violent warlords beyond the Niemen who had brought down the symbols of the proletariat revolution only to replace them with their own. That was all he was able to make out. Meanwhile, the interpreter, Mrs Kraft, a German-speaking Ukrainian, translated the harsh words of their boss to him, as the villager bowed his head, resigned to his situation, looking at that shining silver eagle that seemed poised to swoop down and suffocate any sign of rebellion.

Dutz did not make me wait, and he listened to me courteously. We had planted several thousand landmines in many parts of the district under his control and I had to show him their whereabouts. The meeting came to an end and he asked me to tell him as much as I could about the situation on the nearby front. As a simple *Sonderführer*, not a single German officer had deigned to give him the slightest piece of information.

When our Eighth Army was deployed along the Don in July of 1942, all the *Sonderführer* of the area and those of other regions further from the front reacted positively, as the war was moving towards the Volga and some were confident that victory was close at hand and the end of the war was near. From others there was a negative reaction, as they found themselves without any military protection. In any case, the battles were moving eastwards towards the Volga: the herds would graze in less danger than in the present minefields and the peasants would return to their work with enthusiasm, in the knowledge that they were far from the Bolshevik threat. Even Dutz and Schnitzler couldn't help but pore over the map of Russia, which was a gift from Mrs Kraft who had taken it from the Bolshevik school where she had been the German language teacher until the year before. But if Dutz and Schnitzler were so hopeful and satisfied, *Sonderführer* Kurt Hoffmann, former combatant and a realist, contemplated the new immense expanses that stretched from the Don and the Donets to the Volga with more than a little suspicion. They were vast and very fertile lands, but they were unprotected. How did Germany propose to defend them if troops were already scarce? Kurt Hoffmann was sceptical about the possibilities of victory and disagreed with his colleagues from Luganskoie who saw everything through rose-tinted spectacles. A personal motive also lay behind these private thoughts: now that the front had moved towards the east, if the partisans tried another attack, to whom would he run for protection? To the Ukrainian police?

A short while later, Kurt Hoffmann fell victim to an ambush by the partisans. A spray of gunfire took three lives at once: the Ukrainian chauffeur's, Annie the interpreter's and his own. The car overturned and the spilled petrol caught fire, reducing the three victims to a pile of ashes. A black column of smoke from the flames rose from the track and could be seen from miles around.

When Dutz and Schnitzler received the news in the Gorlovka office they went immediately to the scene of the crime. Dutz took off his hat and crossed himself, and Schnitzler, an atheist, just took off his hat, trying his hardest not to show how upset he was in front of the few Russians present. A local chief of the Ukrainian Militia, the impeccable Lopatnikov, under exclusive orders from Dutz, carried out a meticulous search amongst the smouldering remains of the car and found a small piece of grey-green cloth from Hoffmann's uniform. That was all that was left. He did not bother to search for the remains of Annie's red dress or the Russian chauffeur's coat. Then they left.

Afterwards, the family members of both Annie and the chauffeur searched with eyes bloodshot from their tears for some kind of keepsake from their beloved in that pile of ashes and twisted iron. First they had to wait for a few labourers to dig a ditch in which to bury a wooden box with the inscription: '*Sonderführer Kurt Hoffmann 1911–1942*'. On the burial mound they placed a notice with big letters reading: '*Kurt Hoffmann fell here in a partisan ambush*'.

In the little box, Dutz just placed the small piece of grey-green uniform, refusing a basket of human remains that Schnitzler offered him. This piece of cloth belonged to his compatriot without a doubt, but the ashes, who knows… Kurt Hoffmann had been a German soldier and he had died for his country. Dutz did not want him to share his eternal resting place in Russia with a native and an interpreter, however German she might be. Schnitzler understood this and he stood aside to throw the ashes to the wind.

Lastly, Dutz put a German helmet on the cross and ordered them to burn an inscription into the wooden cross reading '*Sonderführer*'. The word almost took up the whole of the cross, hardly leaving space for the initials of the deceased: H.K. The idea was to make sure that the soldiers and civilians driving along the Shevchenko trail could clearly read the word '*Sonderführer*' on the tomb as they passed, and the German helmet that crowned the cross was there to make them see that one of the privileged *Sonderführer* of the *Landwirtschaft* had died at his post while working in Russia, just like any soldier who died at his post while fighting.

GAMMA, KARL, DORA
AND THE
HAND GRENADES

To THROW A HAND GRENADE at exactly the right moment at an enemy can save your life, but to throw the device, not hear the explosion and to see it, rolling like a harmless ball, can mean your death. A grenade not exploding from time to time was just one of many risks to be expected. However, for a sporadic fault to become a habitual occurrence was a grave state of affairs, perhaps attributable to sabotage but not to a design fault. That model of grenade had been regulation weaponry of the Italian Army for years. It had been tried and tested thousands of times by soldiers in the battlefield.

The rumour spread that a high percentage of that model of our hand grenades were not exploding. The high command decided to carry out urgent testing in the presence of a commission of the various branches of our armed forces, in order to stop the rumour and to re-establish trust in the device. A remote place was chosen for the testing and a number of cases of the bombs in question were brought from different depots in order to carry out a demonstration.

As a precautionary measure because of the explosions, and under the watchful eye of the anti-aircraft batteries, we stood in a wide semicircular formation as the general reiterated his confidence in the efficiency of our hand grenades, saying:

'Gentlemen, this is the SRCM Model 35 grenade, manufactured with precision and with a record of many years of use. It is equipped, as you know, with two safety devices that allow its safe transportation in a knapsack without the risk of an accidental explosion. The detonator is neutralized by a metal pin that will not allow it to explode even if the grenade itself is flattened.'

The general gave a soldier the order to gather several grenades from different cases and he picked one of them at random. With an ostentatious gesture he took off the first safety device and, flourishing it and shaking it in his hand to show that the first device was just an 'extra' precautionary measure compared to the second one, he said in a loud voice, so that everyone could hear him:

'Now, when I throw this, the force exerted as it flies through the air will cause three little blades to open out, releasing the second safety device and allowing the grenade to explode as it hits its target.'

Having said this, he threw it with great force as far as he could. He did not notice that his big German Shepherd was standing next to him. Seeing his master throw an object, the dog shot out after it to retrieve it. The vision of that poor animal, running at top speed after the grenade, deaf to the shouts of his master, sent a tremor through the ranks. The bomb landed, but did not explode. It bounced on the ground and the dog grasped it in his jaws, biting it and shaking it furiously before proudly bringing it back to the general.

Now we were once again shocked and horrified: although the bomb had not yet exploded, without its two safety devices, it would do so at any moment, killing the general, his trusty dog and those who were standing, stupefied, at his side. It had happened in a matter of seconds. We did not know whether to laugh or cry and were sure that we were fated to a tragic end.

Then a courageous sergeant opened the dog's jaws, took out the grenade with some difficulty and, as others came swiftly to his aid, he held the dog with one hand and threw the grenade as far as possible with the other.

This time there was no explosion either. White as a sheet, traumatized by the direction that the demonstration had taken and humiliated by the risk that he had made us run, the general understood that even when subjected to such outrageous treatment, that grenade had failed to explode, and something very serious was going on. An investigation had to be launched immediately. The consignment of grenades was confiscated and an investigation was opened. A lot of people thought that it must have been political sabotage in the Italian factory by the Communists in solidarity with their Russian brothers.

A few days after this absurd and, thankfully, bloodless episode, I received an assignment to draw up a report on the least conventional and most unfamiliar weapons used by the *Wehrmacht*. The aim, I was told, was to give those in charge of our military weapons the incentive to supervise more closely their design and manufacture. (In all truth it was enough to compare the effects of the superior German hand grenades to our own...)

It was June 1942. Lieutenant Wolfgang Sänger, who had been assigned as my escort by the command of the Southern Group of Armies, advised me to witness some of the new weapons that were being used during the siege of Sebastopol – one of the most imposing and impregnable fortresses in the world. The Russians were defending it to the death against the German and Romanian onslaught, to avoid having to withdraw their fleet from that strategic natural port.

A few hours later – the heat was already intense – we covered the 300 miles that separated Stalino from Yalta in a 'Stork'. Flying low over the Crimea, which was occupied by the Germans, I could see an incredible number of tanks and vehicles of all kinds advancing on the besieged city.

We landed at an improvised airstrip situated about 30 miles from the coast. A military vehicle took us as far as the Germano-Romanian rearguard along a road that had been purpose-built against possible air raids, which were unpredictable because of the mountainous nature of the peninsular. During the journey the clamour of the artillery became more and more deafening. Apparently, there were hundreds of thousands of men fighting on the battlefield. I asked Lieutenant Sänger where we were headed. After providing me with a padded helmet and ear plugs, he answered:

'You are going to meet three very important characters: Gamma, Karl and Dora.'

Not knowing whether the names corresponded to a code for secret weapons or simply to three officers from espionage, I kept quiet. We left the vehicle and walked for a few minutes in a trench protected from snipers. We had to become part of that unimaginable siege and the lieutenant made me take all the necessary precautions. From the air I had been able to see that in order to defend the port the Soviets had surrounded it with colossal fortifications and had even gone as far as building an underground city. Forcing them to surrender seemed like an impossible job.

Suddenly we came across a vast industrial contraption with what looked like a smokestack sticking out of it at a 60 degree angle and pointing at the port. I understood what that monstrosity represented when its 'smokestack' every so often let off a huge outburst of fire accompanied by a terrific explosion – which almost burst our eardrums despite the earplugs. The lieutenant shouted the introductions to this first character: it was called Gamma and was of the same lineage as

'Great Bertha', the famous German cannon that had bombed Paris during the First World War from over 60 miles away.

Sänger gave me details on this piece of artillery that I would never have seen had I not been given the report to write. It had been built specifically to attack impregnable bastions, such as the Maginot line in France or the fort of Sebastopol in Russia. Gamma, with its short cannon, shot 427mm 2,030-pound missiles to distances of around 9 or 10 miles. It needed 235 men to work it.

Amidst the uproar of this first introduction, my impatience to meet Karl and Dora began to grow. We moved to another area on the front to meet Karl, also called Thor by the troops. It was another gigantic piece of artillery, conceived in order to demolish fortresses with 4,840-pound missiles. Each shot from its 16-foot cannon forced you to cover your ears with your hands, even when wearing earplugs.

Time was pressing and amid that incredible din, Sänger introduced me to the third character, which made Karl look like a midget: this was Dora, also called Big Gustav, the biggest piece of artillery in the world, with a calibre of 800mm. Transporting it in pieces required sixty wagons, its cannon was almost 100 feet long and it shot 10,560-pound high explosives missiles to a distance of 23 miles, although it could also launch 15,400-pound missiles. The missile and the propellant together measured almost 25 feet in length. It could fire no more than three missiles per hour.

Dora stood on four railway tracks and was protected by two battalions of anti-aircraft artillery equipped with the famous 88mm guns. The soldiers who manned and protected it came to 4,120 men and setting the direction of fire alone took 1,500 specialists. All this personnel was under orders from an army general, assisted by a colonel. With just one shot from its cannon, Dora destroyed the whole gunpowder magazine of Severnaya Bay, 90 feet below ground.

When my three days' visit to Sebastopol was over I was greatly relieved to get away from that death and destruction at the front. Lieutenant Sänger flew me to the training area of the *Wehrmacht*'s '*Aufmarsch*' groups, who were capable of capturing an enemy position defended by a contingent two to three times bigger than their own. I had already heard of them, but when I saw them I was more impressed than I had been on seeing those enormous pieces of artillery. The truth is that while those fantastic cannon were the fruit of true German military tradition and a technology capable of constructing such powerful weapons, the *Aufmarsch* commandos were a luxury within reach even of an army without an excessive military budget. Their basic structure was a squad of ten soldiers who got along well together – preferably recruited from the same region, city or ideally the same village – trained like a football team. The command was entrusted to the eldest or most audacious and the other nine formed two groups, one of five fusiliers and the other of four machine-gunners. This structure of ten always acted as a single unit. Its members knew their place at every single moment and only obeyed orders from the squad leader. This man was subordinate in turn to a non-commissioned officer or an officer, according to the number of squads.

Lieutenant Sänger told me that when 'Operation Barbarossa' was launched, the *Wehrmacht* had 45,000 *Aufmarsch* squads, which they used to inflict the first incredible defeats upon the Russians. They were equipped with the famous MG 34 machine-guns, whose fire was equivalent to about twenty fusiliers. Those squads were a war machine capable of winning against forces twice their size in number.

At the end of the inspection and without the need to fly anywhere else, my colleague decided to introduce me to the small tank they called Goliath, specifically designed to destroy barbed wire barriers and other obstacles without risking lives. Goliath had no driver and advanced with a cargo of 175 pounds of explosives that, with an electric charge, could be blown up from a distance through a very thin cable. Later I found out that in the battle of Kursk the Germans used a number of these Goliaths against the avalanche of dogs armed with explosives that the Russians had trained to jump under enemy tanks.

I thought that now I had more than enough information, but Lieutenant Sänger did not want me to leave without showing me how the *Nebelwerfer* fired, a replica of the famous Russian *katiusha*, named 'Stalin's organ' by the troops. The thirty-six missiles that a *Nebelwerfer* would launch simultaneously produced such heat that it caused the enemy to die from their blood vessels exploding.

Just over a week was enough for me to obtain first-hand information on the German technology of their superior weapons and on the far-sightedness of their Chiefs of Staff in staking their best efforts on the troops' combat capacity.

I drew up my report and handed it in to the staff officer who had given me the assignment. I only heard his comments on it later through a third party.

Our army was antiquated in its training methods and concepts of war – a war that had gone from being static to being a war of motion. Moreover, the Italian industry at the time lacked the necessary capacity. Perhaps we would have fought better if, instead of having to face the Soviet tanks and armoured vehicles, we had fought against the great cavalry regiments that the Russian Army kept in reserve on the so-called 'steppe front'. The Izbushenski charge, carried out by the Savoy Cavalry Regiment in the last great chapter of an already outmoded war, could be compared in some degree to the German *Aufmarsch* squads. Colonel Bettoni, commander of the regiment, received praise from a General of the *Wehrmacht* and admirer of the exploit, which read: 'We would no longer know how to carry out such a charge. It was an extraordinary feat.'

KATIUSHA'S WELL

A MAN AND A WOMAN lay face down next to Katiusha's well, both with rusty nails through the neck. One hand was still twitching on the bar of a little cart with its wheels sunk into the mud under a load that had since disappeared. Some chickens clucked and scratched around the ears of corn, and a large black raven croaked as it swooped down over its prey. To complete the scene, a little boy hopped around barefoot, beating his chest, crying out loud and wildly tearing out his hair. He then threw himself to the ground, dragged himself along like a snake up to the two corpses, whose blood soaked their clothes and the ground around them, and stared at them, lost. Then he resumed his dance around the dead.

The cries drew some civilians to the spot. Who could have tried to harm the old lady? Katiusha was 80 years old and the poor thing could not venture further than her vegetable garden. She was alone with no children, and not even the Bolsheviks had stopped her from cultivating that hectare of black earth, irrigated by the purest water from her well, allowing her just about to survive on what she grew.

'Rape her? I don't think they would have tried it, seeing how bald she is...' said old Pamilov, who had seen quite a lot in his day and was not about to become frightened over the cries of a child, nor drop his usual sarcasm.

'Perhaps it was the Germans who slept in Liudmila Barenkova's house last night? Then again, the choice between Liudmila and Katiusha isn't difficult!' added Simonov, carrying on the old man's joke and laughing like crazy.

Simonov was ugly and crippled. They called him 'sheepskin' because of his short curly hair.

'Well, there aren't any women left... If they've taken them all to Germany, they'll have had to make do with Katiusha!' said ageing Maria, keeping up the joke.

However, when they arrived at the well, the gruesome scene that met their eyes froze their laughter. They approached with respect and crossed themselves repeatedly. Old Pamilov was the first to pluck up the courage to bend down over the corpses. Maria went over to the child with affection. He had stopped his cries when he saw them arrive. Simonov stood at their side, staring at the little cart emptied of the load that had weighed it down, and shouted like a man possessed:

'Murderer! Robber! Thief!'

Maria, believing that Simonov had caught the murderer, turned around. Then, seeing that this was not so, and angered by her disappointment, she stood pensive in respectful silence.

'Katiusha! Katiusha!' cried Pamilov, walking around the bodies. Cautiously and reluctantly, he tried to lift their heads. 'Sheepskin' tried to help him, while the child, seeing what they were doing, resumed his desperate cries, this time even more heart-rending than before.

'In search of wheat,' murmured old Pamilov, cleaning the blood off his hands with earth as he stooped over them, crossing himself several times and muttering unintelligibly.

'Pamilov, Simonov, Pamilov, come here!' shouted Maria from Katiusha's house.

Had Katiusha been killed as well? They ran up the craggy path to the house in fits and starts. The fact that two unknown people in search of wheat had been killed was gruesome and contemptible, but these kinds of killings were a common occurrence along the road to Kantemirovka. Of the thousands of people arriving from all over Russia in search of wheat in the Ukraine, there were those who, instead of travelling for hundreds of miles on foot like the rest of them, lay in wait to steal the grain that was the fruit of such risks and effort. Had Katiusha been killed by thieves? The old lady was as poor as they were. Just like Pamilov and Simonov, Katiusha had her wheat well hidden. Katiusha had never harmed anyone... The three of them lived behind the hollow, only half a mile away, and if it was the wheat they were after, then they and their families were also at risk. Pamilov and Simonov now regretted their previous sarcastic comments. They felt solidarity in face of the mysterious murderous hand that was perhaps continuing with his ambush. Maria came running up to them.

'Quickly! Katiusha's dying! They've choked her! Can you imagine? Strangled!' she cried.

Inside the *hata*, on a wooden bed, amongst a pile of dog skins, lay

Katiusha, with her ancient eyes popping out from the effort of having tried to break loose from her aggressor. Her black headscarf had come off, uncovering her bald head. Viscous saliva seeped out of her toothless, livid mouth. She seemed to be dead. Fear and pity glimmered in the eyes of old Pamilov and his companion. Only one of her bare feet showed signs of life, an almost imperceptible tremble. Pulling himself together, Pamilov made her swallow a couple of sips of vodka and put a damp cloth to her forehead and neck. There were clear signs of the hands that had tried to strangle her. Katiusha started to recover little by little.

Meanwhile, Maria had prepared a miraculous concoction of herbs and Katiusha began to move her hands and her eyes, then slowly to move her head, until she had revived. Then, when old Pamilov had finished explaining what had happened, the old lady made an effort to respond. She was slowly recovering, and was trying to establish whether or not their suspicions were well founded· the hands that had tried to strangle her must have been the same that had taken the lives of the wayfarers by the well. She remembered that during the evening a man, woman and child had stopped off at her house to ask for water. Tired and thirsty, they were dragging a little cart that could scarcely support the weight of three big sacks of wheat it was loaded with. A stranger who had spent hours trying to convince Katiusha to give him some flour in exchange for a broken watch had offered to take them down to the well so that they could rest for the night away from the dirt track and the clamour of the military convoys. The other outsiders had accepted and in this way Katiusha was free from that pestering individual who was most likely quite dishonest.

A short while later, when she was already in bed, the stranger had appeared in her house and, without even giving her the time to cry out, he had tried to strangle her.

When they took Katiusha to the well in a handcart, a group of civilians had surrounded the corpses and were commenting on what had happened. They were organizing themselves into groups in order to try and prevent the same thing from happening to them. It was midday, the time when a mob in search of wheat would usually make use of this spot to rest and to drink the excellent water from the well. Some of them were lying on the ground, overcome by fatigue, acting as if nothing unusual were going on. Others were cooking rolls on two little improvised campfires and were eating, chatting or sleeping. Old Pamilov became enraged when he saw their indifference: unable to contain himself, he showed his indignation by raising his voice at them. Nobody took the slightest bit of notice. They were city folk from many different regions of Russia and they knew full well how the yokels of the Donets basin resented strangers. Old Pamilov's face gave away his rural origins, betraying him as an enemy of the city dwellers and of the wheat pilgrims. Katiusha saw that the child was the same one from the day before, but she could not see the corpses of his parents, as the villagers were already throwing the last spadefuls of earth over the improvised grave that they had dug. Nobody called the Ukrainian Militia who were 'always so busy'. Then again, the nearest police station was several miles away. Who knows where the assassin was now after so many hours; surely he would be pulling his cart loaded with the stolen wheat, alongside thousands of honest people who had obtained their loads through the sweat and toil of travelling hundreds of miles of dirt track over many weeks.

Simonov skilfully placed a cross made of acacia branches on top of the earth tomb. This cross was without a helmet, and it stayed thrust into the ground near Katiusha's well for several days. Then an unmerciful hand removed the fragile religious symbol and Katiusha's well regained its function as an oasis for tired travellers in search of wheat.

Some soldiers adopted the little orphan as their mascot.

Although the cross was no longer there, each time he passed the tomb old Pamilov would look apprehensively over his shoulder and cross himself. What he could not quite understand was why the murderer had wished to strangle Katiusha without taking the flour from her cupboard. Nor could he understand why he had not finished her off. Perhaps he thought he had done so. Pamilov was old, and he did not lack courage, but he was careful and he had seen quite a lot in his day. He decided that if one day a stranger asked him for flour or wheat in exchange for a broken watch, he would not say no.

STAROSTA KOVALIENKO

LEONID ALEXEIEVICH KOVALIENKO, *starosta* of Rikovo City, invited me to his office to explain how the civilian administration in the Ukraine was co-ordinated with the occupying army. In my position as liaison officer with the *Wehrmacht* I needed to know about the link between the local authorities and the allied forces, as there were a number of conflicts, and confidence had to be restored in all the areas involved, with German relations taking precedence of course.

Kovalienko was a cultured, open and intelligent man, so I was quickly and easily able to understand his duties as *starosta*, as well as those of his assistants. He showed me a map indicating the division of the vast Ukrainian territory into districts, or *raiony*, managed by the head of the *raion* upon whom the *starosta* also depended, and whose designation was the responsibility of the occupying army. Naturally, the anti-Bolsheviks who were sufficiently prepared for the job were elected by preference. The Ukrainian militia, trained by the *Wehrmacht*, carried out police duties. After my first visit, while the front was held near Rikovo, I had quite a lot of contact with *Starosta* Kovalienko. We managed to develop a relationship that went beyond our respective duties, based on my respect for his capabilities.

The commander of a section of the police, Lieutenant Seelke, wanted to prove his friendship and reciprocal camaraderie by inviting me to dinner in the ceremonial hall of the huge and horrible 'Bolshevik-style' palace, called the 'Force of the Proletariat', which had been the party headquarters. After introducing me to his closest staff members, he seated me at his table. The walls were adorned with enormous Nazi banners and Italian flags and portraits of Hitler and Mussolini.

Unfortunately, a few days later, Seelke and his section were destined to go elsewhere. I was sorry because, knowing the methods of the German military police, I doubted that their replacements would continue his moderate style of management. During the banquet, Seelke himself gave me some useful advice, warning me in particular about a certain Anatoli Lavarov. As head of the *raion*, Lavarov had plenty of power, and was to be feared. He had gained an almost absolute trust from the German authorities by falsely denouncing honest collaborators, and was perfectly capable of ousting anyone who was in his way and replacing them with people of his own choosing. Unfortunately, the investigations that Seelke was secretly carrying out on Lavarov were only in their beginnings and I supposed that, after his transfer, they would be buried.

A few days after he left, his replacement, Lieutenant Scheung, introduced himself at our headquarters. It was one of those unpleasant autumnal days in which snow and rain fell alternately. The lieutenant entered in his soaking wet cloak. In the flickering firelight of the stove his face unnerved me. Without taking off his coat or waiting for me to finish greeting him, he checked that nobody could hear us, and came straight to the point, rapping it out in an officious manner. He had received some very important and urgent instructions from the Stalino police. Many former Communists holding office in the city had to be arrested, and amongst them was *Starosta* Kovalienko.

Vexed by this unexpected order, I asked him what evidence the arrest was founded on, and added that Kovalienko, along with numerous other people on the list, had been chosen by our high command, and they had always been true to their responsibilities. However, Scheung would not have any of it and just read me some information on the most important of the culprits. Amongst these were the charges against Kovalienko, who at the age of 15 had been a militant with the Young Communists; he had then become qualified as an industrial engineer in Moscow in 1927 and had immediately been appointed as director of Rikovo's number 5 industrial school. According to the order from Stalino, the information revealed that he was a disguised Communist acting as a double agent. I refuted this strongly and expressed my convictions against these accusations, which reflected the opinion of the Italian command. I pointed out that for quite some time both Kovalienko and the others had carried out their duties faithfully, serving our interests and thus risking their lives, as well as those of their families, in the event that we would have to abandon the areas that we had conquered. The fact that the Bolsheviks had shot his father and deported his brother to Siberia constituted, in our view, a further reason that was more than sufficient to judge his allegiance as sincere, despite his erstwhile links with the party that had been forced upon him at the time. I inquired what fate awaited the accused and he answered that they would be subjected to an interrogation and trial. Those who were least guilty would go to a labour camp. The others would no doubt end up before the firing squad.

I remembered Seelke's warning and I told him that he should be wary if the 'tip-off' had come from Lavarov. My objections were in vain and Scheung defended himself by simply stating that 'orders are orders'. He added that he had devised a plan, and intended to call most of those on the list to his office in order to arrest them en masse. The arrest of those who did not live in the city had been entrusted to Nagarianski, head of the Ukrainian militia, who would then be arrested by Liesenko, who in turn would meet the same fate, and thus all possible traitors to Germany would be swept away.

An unusual spark lit up the icy, nervous eyes of this former police sergeant, who had finally reached the seniority of officer after long years of obscure service. He gloated over this plan that would be the pinnacle of his career. When would a modest and unknown civil servant in the police force of a small German town ever have been able to become an arbiter of the law, in the coveted territory of the Eastern front? Well, there he was: imposing his will, making people tremble with a simple gesture, and then capturing the authorities of Rikovo, cultured engineers, doctors and writers, and locking them up... With his little provincial acumen, the invasion of Russia had made a drastic change in his life that was hardly even comprehensible to Scheung himself and had been too fast to allow him to adapt to the responsibilities of his new rank.

First thing the next day, two trucks arrived, preceded by a police car. A German sergeant got out of the car and said to me, 'I have come to tell you that from now on my men will take charge here.'

A little after midday the trucks, with the police car at their head, took the same road back, transporting around fifty suspects to the old GPU prison in Gorlovka. However, the arrests had been carried out in a manner very different from that which Lieutenant Scheung had promised. In the *starosta*'s house, for example, two policemen turned up at dawn and, between insults, they handcuffed him and, without giving him time to throw on a coat over his pyjamas, marched him to the closest police station in his slippers. Meanwhile, other agents searched his house and confiscated furniture and household goods, without thinking twice about snatching a gold watch, a bracelet and two rings from his wife. At ten o'clock in the morning hardly anything was left but the four walls, with gaps where the requisitioned furniture had stood. Just the bare essentials such as the beds were left in this cosy house, where two engineers of the metallurgic factory had lived.

As soon as I was informed of this, I asked Lieutenant Scheung to order the immediate restitution of the household goods, emphasizing that only after the results of the trial would such actions be permitted. Scheung did not expect to stumble across such a hard nut to crack nor, just when he believed his disproportionate police operation had scored a point, did he expect to have to take a step back. However, he did not give in easily, and tried to put the blame on the sergeant, saying that he had been over-zealous in his initiatives. The furniture was returned, as were the *starosta*'s wife's watch, rings and bracelet. She begged our help for a safe conduct pass to visit her husband in Gorlovka prison in order to take him shoes and clothes.

When I bumped into Scheung a few days later and asked him if he knew the outcome of the trial, he answered me evasively, leading me to understand that his suspicions had been well founded and that Kovalienko and the others, together with thirty or so Jews, were to be shot. I did not believe him, but the only thing I could do was wait. Days later, the rumour spread that a verdict condemning the prisoners had been given, as the lieutenant had said, and all that remained was the official confirmation.

Although the news was unofficial, it angered us. During his detention, in order to confirm the honesty of the *starosta*, not a single anonymous accusation had come in. This was not for want of enemies.

The Kovalienko case, along with those of the municipal engineer, Parjomenko, of Liesenko and of many others, became part of the repertoire of ideological injustices committed by little men with too much power.

However, Rikovo could not remain without a *starosta*, and they proceeded to appoint a new mayor, falling upon a likeable lawyer, lucky survivor of the tsarist era.

He had not been at his post for long when, one sombre evening, the door of our counter-espionage office opened and there, standing in the doorway, enlarged by the darkness, was the 'spirit' of *Starosta* Kovalienko. He stepped forward a couple of paces into the room and the central light shone on his cold, sunken eyes that pierced through me. The spirit had a human texture, unkempt hair, a set mouth and an

impassive expression. Was this a ghost or a living being? They had executed Alexeievich Kovalienko. Had he risen from the dead and come to
take his revenge, convinced that I had betrayed him to the Germans?
The idea crossed my mind and I must confess that the blood froze in
my veins. I pulled myself together, got up and held out my hand, per-
plexed, and stuttered a greeting. He said, 'Good evening, Lieutenant;
here I am. I have come to speak with the colonel. Is that possible?' From
the physical contact with his hand and from the sound of his voice I
could tell he was not a ghost. 'I am so pleased to see you,' I said, still
somewhat under shock. 'I was sure they would acquit you.'

The colonel summoned the *starosta* and Dr Parjomenko, also acquit-
ted, to our command post along with a Russian interpreter. Lieutenant
Scheung had not yet turned up as, surprisingly enough, the German
police in Stalino had not informed him of the liberation of the prisoners. While we waited, Kovalienko told us of the developments of the
trial. He stressed the severity with which they had been interrogated by
the security services and said that when no guilt had been proven,
almost all of the accused had been freed and authorized to return to
their posts.

At that moment Scheung entered. Face to face with two of his victims
he felt he had fallen into a trap and he paled. We all stared at him in
eloquent silence.

'I have decided that from this day onwards the *starosta* and the others
who are innocent will return to their posts. This is why I summoned
you here. That is all,' said the colonel.

Scheung opened his mouth to say something, but faced with his
failure he decided instead to give a summary military salute and left
the office.

After the meeting, the *starosta* said to me under his breath, 'It wasn't
the lieutenant who informed on me. If it had been Scheung, a German
against a Russian, my fate would have been sealed. No, the one who
wanted me dead was that swine Lavarov, but he will pay for it; I am sure
that one of these days his Bolshevik friends will return and they won't
give him the time to say one word in his defence.'

In the following winter months of 1943, all the towns around the
region of Rikovo were falling into the hands of the Russians, but as fate
would have it the city itself stood at the apex of the wedge of land that
the Germans had managed to maintain against the Soviet onslaught.
The rumour then spread that each time the Russians recaptured a

town, they put on summary trial anyone who had collaborated in any way with the invaders. Almost totally without food, pounded by constant bombardment from both the air and the ground, with a typhoid epidemic and without medicines or supplies, the population of the Donets basin lived through weeks of an atrocious nightmare. Whoever feared Soviet reprisals fled towards the west in an attempt to reach the Dnieper, hoping to rebuild their lives elsewhere. All of the military headquarters were transferred and one fine day, Lieutenant Scheung's section also left in horse-drawn sledges and a truck. The column took to the road dejectedly, heading towards the Dnieper in the footsteps of thousands of civilian fugitives. Nobody even thought to ask to see any of the civilian's safe conduct passes or identity papers any longer.

'Lieutenant Scheung Chi Kai, Lieutenant Scheung has run away,' said a *muzhik* tersely, as, numb with cold, he concentrated on carting away a door. He had packed his little sledge with a window frame and some floorboards ripped up from the majestic Proletariat Force building.

I took a look inside. With rudimentary tools, other civilians were stripping the rooms like vandals. The enormous doors and the ostentatious woodwork of the party headquarters were a tempting source from which to gather wood. The floors were covered in drifts of paper and stripped of furniture and possessions. Only the metal frames of a few beds and a desk or two stained with ink remained there. They had even ripped out the electric wiring. A door lay there off its hinges, upon which, half peeled off, was an enormous poster from the commissariat, like a memento from the past.

The *starosta* did not want to abandon the city, so he entrusted his wife and children to the Italian officer in command of the last column leaving for the Dnieper.

'I am staying. If I leave chaos will reign. Who would replace me with the Russians on the verge of arriving and in the knowledge that many *starostas* have been hanged in the marketplace?'

One day in April 1943, when I came back to Rikovo, I bumped into Lieutenant Scheung. He had just come back, as if nothing had happened, ready to resume his duties, but he now had his section quartered in a very different way. During the retreat he had almost reached Leopoli in Poland, and during the long journey there and back he had lost more than half of his men, supplies and stores. Now he wore a tattered uniform, visible proof of the odyssey.

'If we have to withdraw again like this winter, I'll kill myself,' he confessed to me. 'We Germans have no other choice if we lose the war.'

An overwhelming foreboding of tragedy weighed upon the half-deserted streets of Rikovo, on its portentous metallurgical factory, the blast furnaces and the chimneys, void of their habitual plumes of smoke. The Germans had, for almost two years, put all their energy into partially reconstructing it and, just at the point of obtaining the first fruits of their titanic efforts, they were obliged to abandon it to another fate. The front was only a few miles away and, just behind it, new Soviet armies were regrouping.

As I passed in front of the town hall on leaving the city, I was about to enter to say hello to the *starosta*. I would have done so had I not remembered that, according to word of mouth, when the Russians had arrived in February some civilians had found Lavarov's corpse in a great pool of blood. Of course, nobody bothered to report it because the German police were already retreating towards the west. I associated that memory with the confidence displayed by Kovalienko when he said, 'If his Bolshevik friends come back one day, Lavarov won't even have time to say one word in his defence.' However, I did not wish to encourage an unfounded theory. 'Lavarov did not want for enemies,' I said, continuing on my way.

When the news of the German army's partial evacuation from Stalino was announced, there was no mention of Rikovo, which remained implicitly framed in the flexible defence operative plan, to achieve the reduction of the front line.

How much history was omitted in those concise military communiqués, that did not even report the death of Kovalienko, *starosta* of Rikovo, anonymous victim in that vast golden expanse of wheat and sunflowers, now free of snow, trampled beneath the galloping Soviet armies on their victorious road to Berlin.

THE MEN
FROM DIREKTION XII

T HE GERMANS FACED enormous difficulties
in trying to root out the great riches from the Ukrainian subsoil. They
set up a headquarters for the 'coal war' in the imposing Don Donec
Kohle building in Stalino's Axen Strasse.

Unterofizier Enz pointed out a wavy red demarcation line and under-
lined a Roman numeral with his pencil. 'Twelve,' I said in Italian.
'*Direktion zwölf,*' he replied sharply in German. The implacable eyes of
the Führer, dressed in the *Wehrmacht* uniform in a colour portrait
hanging to the right of the armchair where this stiff German officer sat,
seemed to be staring at the black-framed map on the wall. 'Are ten
tonnes enough?' the vexed sergeant asked me. 'I am afraid I cannot give
you more for the moment. The only mine that produces decent coal is
mine number 3. We have hardly even resumed production in the others
and can only extract coal dust, which is useless. Since it is not that far,'
he said, pointing at the blue spot that showed its location on the map,
'and the road is good, if you take the workers with you to load it, it
should be very easy. We cannot afford to use the few workers we have
there to do the job.'

His rough hand traced a few illegible words on some graph paper,
which he authenticated with a rectangular rubber stamp, reading
'Direktion XII'.

'The cost,' he added, 'at fourteen marks per tonne is… fourteen
times ten: 140 marks.'

A warm ray of July sunshine gently caressed that austere and imper-
sonal atmosphere, presided over by the firm grip of this stern sergeant.
I looked at the silver chevron on his grey-green epaulette, edged with
gold braiding. A German sergeant at the head of Direktion XII? I did
not want to miss the opportunity to check up on what they were doing
in the recently invaded fertile Ukrainian heartland. He explained that
there were people trained in mining recruited from the Ruhr basin

serving in Direktion XII. The assignment to re-establish the mining production in the Ukraine was both difficult and unrewarding, because the Soviet army and the workers had carried out the systematic destruction of the sites before retreating towards the Urals. In matters of destruction, the enemy triumphed. There were hardly any usable mines left and the extraction equipment had been sabotaged to prevent renovation in the short-term.

'We have gathered together the largest amount of *Arbeitskräfte*, workforce, as possible, with great effort,' added the sergeant. 'But we need thousands of able men in order to speed up reconstruction. My colleagues and I will no longer be here when the expected contingent of miners arrives. The *Sonderführer* are coming to replace us so that we can join the advance towards the east and organize reconstruction in the Caucasus, as we have done here, but in the petroleum industry of course.'

He continued to explain as he walked me to the car that was waiting opposite the Direktion XII building, the only building left standing at the immense Kuznetsovka mines.

Two gigantic black pyramid slag heaps rose above the enormous concrete structures and their corresponding machinery, which had all been demolished by dynamite. Amidst the rubble, caught off guard by the unexpected order to destroy everything, stood a derailed wagon, intact, and still with its load. Rusty steel cables trailed off into the dark half-collapsed tunnels that were precariously propped up by iron frames twisted by the blast. Rust was everywhere. The enormous valves of a steel heart that, when it was beating, gave life to an infinite number of mechanisms, was now destroyed and paralysed. This vast organism lay buried under the wheat and sunflowers of the Ukraine's fertile epidermis.

From the windows that rattled in the wind, still just about held in their frames, a sprinkling of fragments rained down with an almost cheerful pattering, the only sound in that world of disintegrated material. I walked through the galleries of broken concrete, the ravens calmly circling the skies above the black pyramids and the destruction, where Sergeant Enz had pitched his tents, like an archaeologist who anxiously excavates in order to resuscitate an era that has been buried for centuries.

Out of all of this destruction, the tapping of a typewriter could clearly be heard, coming from a window that framed the figure of a person bent over work, concentrating hard on who knows what problems.

Two opposing forces of equal power in a head-on collision: destructive inertia and reconstructive energy. Two wills confronting each other as the product of the terrifying shock of two revolutions, of two imperialisms. This was not something that Sergeant Enz thought about; he saw the ruins as something normal, as a logical consequence of war, and he did not understand why I was contemplating the rusty little wagon, the enormous cogged wheels and the remains of a gigantic disjointed capstan, with fascination. Now that they had defeated the Russians, with immense patience and much constancy, perhaps everything would return to normal within a few years. In his boundless pride as victor he was not worried about the complexity of the problem. As sergeant of a company of sappers, in command of the Ukrainian technicians and a few hundred workers, following in the wake of the retreating Russian Army, he could not see the insignificant triviality of his existence compared to the enormity of the task. In the principal eight demolished coal mines under his Direktion, the daily extraction hardly amounted to a few hundred tonnes, a meagre amount compared to the thousands of tonnes that were being produced before the conquest. The new, recently opened mines of carboniferous outcrops could be expected to yield a certain quantity of coal, despite its poor quality, since it was extracted by the antique means of pure brute force, due to lack of new machinery and electrical power. However, the sergeant did not become disheartened. His orders were to attain a production of a few thousand tonnes of coal. Since this was the Führer's command there was no quibbling over it. On the other hand, it was encouraging that the *Wehrmacht* had recommenced the advance; the rest would be taken care of marvellously by his successors, the *Sonderführer*.

The immense black pyramids were soon behind me. The stoutly built figure of the German sergeant, lost amongst those strange heaps that resembled giant sepulchres, gradually got smaller and smaller, until he became a dot on the landscape and disappeared, while deep down in my heart his task seemed increasingly unattainable and his illusory confidence more and more absurd. On the trail to Makeyevka we passed by other pyramid slag heaps, standing like sentinels above ruins identical to those at Kuznetsovka, many more piles of concrete rubble, iron and rust, with their corresponding Sergeant Enzes, tiny and insignificant, toiling amongst those funerary monuments in a suicidal civilization.

I did not know the *Sonderführer* Weinizzer personally when he telephoned me to inform me of his visit. He called from Kuznetsovka, where he had just arrived a few days before with another chief engineer

from Direktion XII. I knew that the two Germans lived completely isolated in that half-destroyed mining town that became almost completely
empty come nightfall. They only had one car, which kept breaking
down, forcing them to get around by horse and cart. I thought they
could consider themselves lucky though, despite the things they lacked,
compared to the millions who found themselves 'first in line' on the
Russian front, or in the German industries.

Now that others had replaced the iron fist of Sergeant Enz in
Kuznetsovka, things had changed. With the front only a few miles from
the ruins, there was a constant toing and froing of troops, giving moral
and material support to the reconstruction. When the front had been a
few hundred miles away a few months beforehand, the solitude of those
two *Sonderführer* amongst thousands of Russian workers was self-evi-
dent. They were the only two Germans who went down into the
recently opened tunnels, badly lit with oil lamps, alone, foreign and
ignored, despite being in charge of a small army of defeated enemies
with whom they were supposed to win the coal war for Germany.
Moreover, Weinizzer seemed to be a good man, in contrast to the military uniform that he wore. He was a technical expert in mining and he
had undergone an arduous apprenticeship during the First World War.
After the humiliating interval of the defeat, the resurgence of Nazi
imperialism and its policy of vital space had catapulted him from the
Ruhr to the Ukraine. He was given a specific and onerous objective
with great responsibilities: the intensive expansion of the inexhaustible
coal reserves of the Donets basin. This was in order not to depend upon
the Reich, and to reach a production of thousands of tonnes, allowing
the progressive recovery of the 'liberated' Russian industry, along with
helping Germany. The region's factories had to be rebuilt and devoted
to the production of railways, armour-plated sheet metal for tanks,
ammunition and steel, with the short-term objective of cannon manufacturing if necessary. With coal from the Ukraine, iron from Kierch
and Mariupol, oil from Maikop and Krasnodar and very soon from
Baku, Germany would thus take the definitive step towards victory.

I listened to this determined man in complete astonishment that
someone as mature as he, forced to live alone with a colleague amidst
the ruins of Kuznetsovka, was explaining these goals to me with such
conviction and certainty. There was no doubt that, all things considered, he had to have a faith in his work plan no less unbreakable than
that of the Germans who had taken on, practically alone, the definitive

conquest of the Eastern front, one of the richest territories of the Soviet Union. However, was there a relationship between his faith in victory and a realistic evaluation of this war potential? At the margins of his undeniable professional competency, Weinizzer thought that, failing protection from the *Wehrmacht*, which was concentrating its efforts on Stalingrad at the present, a few Italian soldiers could safeguard his dignity, which was under threat from the Ukrainian militia that had been assigned to him.

He reached his objective, increasing the production in the mines of Direktion XII over the last few months and supplying the steelworks' blast furnaces with his coal; in turn, the gas from this propelled three thermoelectric plants. In Ivanovka over 2,000 miners were working to extract top quality coal for the locomotive steam engines and the 2,000 tonnes that were produced daily from mines one and six constituted reserves that were not to be scoffed at.

Thanks to the reduced Italian garrison, Weinizzer did indeed receive armed protection and managed to obtain the recognition he expected for his large and risky task. The protection did not last long, though, because the Italian troops were transferred to the front, leaving only the Ukrainian militia. The partisans, who were lying in wait, took advantage of the situation and a few days later the *Sonderführer* suffered an attack on their residence. The news of this spread from mine to mine like wildfire, but the miners of Direktion XII continued to go down into the pits in an orderly fashion, as if nothing had happened. *Sonderführer* Rokumenke arrived immediately to replace the partisans' victims. Without being discouraged by the events, Rokumenke continued with the coal war in the Ukraine that had been conceived by the German technical staff and was manned by an army of Russian workers. The objectives were still Germany's victory and the annihilation of Soviet Russia. Even the coal war would not last long because, on the Stalingrad front, General Paulus' Sixth Army was about to be surrounded by the Russian counter-offensive, which immediately aimed at the Donets basin, recapturing the Kuznetsovka mines and Direktion XII.

The other *Sonderführer* did not survive the wounds from the attack. Weinizzer was convalescing and pleased at the prospect of returning to the *Heimat*, the homeland, to enjoy being with his family and to have a well-earned rest, when the Soviet armoured cavalry, in a daring manoeuvre, cut off the Stalino–Dniepropetrovsk train line about 125 miles from his base. This was the first time that the *Sonderführer* felt the lash of the counter-offensive at such close range. With this Russian manoeuvre, accompanied by tremendous breaks through the front and an infinite number of other surprises, he finally discovered the truth. With the Soviet army 125 miles to the rear, the road to Germany remained blocked by those 'barbarians'. In the hospital train in which he was waiting, there were hundreds of compatriots crowded together, in a worse state than he, also longing to return to the homeland to see their families. Of course Weinizzer, after the Führer's speech in November 1941, no longer really believed in victory. However, now he could see for himself that the enemy was neither defeated nor liqui- dated. How else could they manage to block the passage of so many hos- pital trains that, like his, were returning the courageous German soldiers to their homeland? Unrepentant, he racked his feverish brain with these questions and his only answer was the echo of the impetuous blizzard that mercilessly rattled the windows of the carriage, standing dead in its tracks. The ominous gusts of wind tearing and whistling around the signal posts of the great railway junction exacerbated the obsessive memory of his frustration, reminding him of that 'army' of machinists and miners in which he had once placed all his conviction of winning the illusory coal war.

When by pure coincidence Sergeant Enz's company came to Mariupol, I learned that he was retreating from the Caucasus with the last units of the First Army, and that he was going to the Donets basin. He no longer came in pursuit of mining utopias, but to contain the unstoppable Russian force heading in the direction of Germany. He asked me for news of Kuznetsovka and I told him what I knew. He was not surprised when I told him that the mining complex, where he had shovelled the first spade of reconstruction, was back in the hands of the Russians. Sergeant Enz had changed radically. Now he was a pessimist like the others, resigned to the fact that the war was going to be long and difficult, and that in order to win there would be need for fighting, and they would have to postpone the reconstruction of mining and industry.

That was my last meeting with the men of Direktion XII. In the lands of the Donets basin, so full of history, those black pyramids next to the Kuznetsovka and the Sofievka mines seemed like real hieratic tombs of a great civilization that had been extinguished; and the men of Direktion XII, the living and the dead, seemed to me like the spirits of kings, wandering tormentedly around those steaming mausoleums of their aspirations, which were buried now for ever.

THE BLACK
SILK DRESS

A SMALL CHILD loading and unloading a
little home-made toy wagon, a woman stripping corn off the cob, a man
with a magnifying glass mending watches, and a young girl devotedly
ironing a black silk dress.

These were my first impressions of the watchmaker Gorshkov and his
family in 14th Street in Ordzhonikidze, in July 1942. I had been told
that I would find lodgings in their house because, despite the shortages
imposed by the war, the Gorshkov family had managed to maintain a
certain standard of living. This was thanks to the father's profession,
which was particularly profitable in times when new watches were not
to be found and one had to be skilful to mend the big old mechanisms
from the times of the tsar.

The local guard who accompanied me told me what he knew of how
this family had become wretched during the war, but said that they
would without a doubt lodge me in a good room.

On my arrival, the woman stopped her task, readjusted the white
kerchief on her head and lavished greetings upon me with a friendly
and welcoming smile. The tireless fuss made by their puppy dog also
attracted the attention of the other family members, who greeted me
with a nod of the head. The child stopped playing and clung to his
little wagon jealously, looking me up and down with two big, frightened and curious eyes that were unable to hide a certain amount of
suspicion.

My escort exchanged a few words with the lady of the house and bid
us farewell, assuming that his mission had been accomplished. There
was in fact little need for great long explanations, because during the
eight months of occupation, the mother, Louisa Gorshovka, had seen
quite a number of soldiers seeking lodgings. She showed me to a small
room where there was a very clean little bed, crowned in Russian style
with three embroidered cushions, whose taste left a lot to be desired.

On the walls there were some photographs from different periods and in front of the bed stood an icon. In the meantime, I found I was unable to refrain from looking through the thin blue curtain to the adjoining room, where a pretty young girl was lovingly and meticulously ironing a black dress.

'Good morning,' I said to her in Italian, through the thin partition.

'Good morning,' she answered, also in Italian, raising her big brown eyes and almost immediately lowering them again modestly as they met with mine.

I asked permission to enter, so that I could see the object of her attentions more easily. 'What a beautiful black dress,' I said. 'Is it silk?'

Valentina shyly nodded and blushed from her neck up to her tiny little ears 'Yes, silk; very fine silk,' she answered, smoothing the slender fingers of her beautiful hands across the creases in the material so that I could look at and admire its translucency, before adding, 'Russian silk, Russian...'

That rhythmic repetition of the adjective revealed a patriotic pride that aroused sympathy in me. She then directed her gaze down her humble dress of printed flowers, whose repairs were darned like patchwork, and she said, 'You all think that the Russian people always poor. Russian people before the war not ragged like me now.'

I looked at her mended but immaculately clean dress, her sculpted legs and her tiny feet inserted into their white leather slippers, as was the Russian fashion at the time. Timidly, Valentina moved away from the table and towards a cupboard to take out an envelope from which she pulled out a photograph, telling me, 'This is Lieutenant Luigi. He gave it to me before going on leave to Italy. Very good man, the lieutenant; always very kind to our family.'

I recognized the man in the picture. It was the face of one of my countrymen who had fallen just a few days before. Poor Luigi! Before bidding farewell to the Gorshkov family, whose house he had lived in through much of the winter, he had wished to leave them with a souvenir of him.

Valentina tended to spend time with me during the following days and I whiled away my time listening to her stories. I was recuperating there from a frozen right leg, because in the field hospital there was only room for emergencies.

Valentina, who had been studying in her second year of medicine at Jarkov University, along with her brother Grigori, just as the German offensive 'Operation Barbarossa' had started, was forced to flee hurriedly from the city in danger. Unexpectedly, her brother immediately joined the armed forces and she undertook the 370-mile journey alone and on foot. She arrived at her home just in time to say goodbye to her eldest brother who was off to the front to serve as a pilot. Both brothers were ill-fated. Grigori fell in Kiev as soon as he reached the front and Alexander, after a month of fighting, disappeared with his plane on fire behind the German lines. What hope did she have left? Polina, her eldest sister and a qualified textile engineer, had been working for over a year in the factories in the Urals and certainly could not return. The Russians had retreated to the east of the Donets and her sister was behind that 'barricade'. To cap it all, Niusia, Polina's twin, who was extremely intelligent, but odd, had left for Germany as a volunteer in one of the first convoys of workers. Clouded by her ambition to see the world, she had forgotten that the West at war would not reveal the wonders that she had dreamed about to her, a creature of a regime that was universally detested. It was much more likely that they would welcome her into a wooden hut, fenced in with barbed wire, like a prison, in the shadow of an enormous grey building at some factory or another in a German industrial town.

Apart from two postcards with a brief description of how she was, nothing further was heard from Niusia. Then a friend of hers who had returned from Germany, crippled from an accident at work, told them of Niusia's transfer, and that it was likely that the post was very much delayed. However, she told Valentina that her sister's firm had been destroyed in a horrendous bombardment in which many workers had died. She had not been able to obtain any information from the German labour office.

The disasters increased when the voluntary workers started to become scarce and the Germans began forced recruitment. Valentina, taking advantage of the good relations that her family had with the *starosta*, had managed to avoid this by obtaining a job as a typist, prolonging her relative peace of mind by a few weeks. At the end of the day, however wretched the Gorshkov family was, they could not consider themselves as the most unfortunate victims of the war. There was some money coming in and they had some food on their table.

On the day that she had turned 17, continued Valentina, her father had given her this black silk dress as a present, along with some shoes. This present had no parallel in Russia, even before the war, because material was rare and expensive. Of course, her father was indeed a craftsman and earned money, but not for such expensive presents as this and for such a numerous family.

She had worn the black silk dress and the shoes for the first time on the day she had been invited by a few friends to a party, along with a touch of lipstick, painted nails and even a few drops of French cologne that she jealously guarded in a little bottle, given to her a year ago by an American engineer at the Kramatorsk machine-tools factory. She was splendid in that dress, and could have competed with the most beautiful of western girls.

'At that time,' she said, 'papa earned 1,000 to 1,500 hundred roubles per month and we were eight children. As a student, my allowance was only just enough to live on. But if I had finished my degree, as a doctor I would have earned enough to buy myself a pretty dress, long down to my feet, and golden and silver shoes like in the American films. I'm going to show you the model that I would have bought.'

Having said this, she pulled out a Russian fashion magazine from between some books, and to my astonishment she flicked through pages and pages of beautiful models, of men and women in casual attire, and in day and evening wear, until she came to her favourite, an elegant couple in formal dress.

The man was wearing a proletariat cap, but in compensation sported an impeccable tailcoat; and the lady wore a white satin dress with lamé trimming.

Valentina noticed my astonishment.

'You believe also before the war all Russians poor and in rags. It was not like this until the Germans brought us such misery.'

I said nothing, but the combination of the proletariat cap and the dress coat seemed incongruous to me.

One day, a German order arrived decreeing the immediate census of all Russian employees in official employment, with the objective of recruiting more young people into their workforce, replacing them with older people or those unfit to be sent to the West. Naturally, the decree would also affect poor Valentina.

Her parents begged me for help. I promised them that I would do what I could by speaking to the inspector. Valentina calmed down a little when, thanks to my negotiations, they granted her a two-month deferral. Then, an unexpected order arrived obliging me to leave for another destination and I had to say goodbye to the Gorshkov family, promising them that I would come to see them as soon as I returned to Ordzhonikidze.

Not even two months had passed, when one day, on a dirt track alongside the Don, a female figure came towards me from one of the many groups of civilians that were tirelessly making their way towards the east in pursuit of the mirage of bread. Her eyes were fixed on me, and when she spoke my name, I recognized her voice.

She looked coarse in that long, rustic, dusty dress and I hardly recognized her. Her bare feet sinking into the dusty track were swollen and deformed. The only things that animated her mud-stained face were those lively eyes and bright white smile. She did not dare to hold out her hand to me, as it was sweaty and swollen from holding the handles of the cart. When I held out mine, Valentina drew back. Embarrassed, she hid her hands under her apron.

'It's you, Valentina!' I exclaimed after a couple of seconds of uncertain stupor.

She did not answer me and just nodded her head, smiling. Then she tried to cover her face with the back of her hand, as if shielding herself from the sun, and hid her feet in the dust.

'You are going in search of wheat as well, Valentina? A few days ago I wanted to send you half a sack as soon as I had the opportunity.'

'You are not going back any more... and anyway, you would not find our house,' she answered, still smiling. 'You make war. How do you know if Valentina dies of hunger in the winter because of no flour? You don't know that in Russian winter we live like ants!'

The unending line of civilians continued to file past along the dirt track. Stooping, weak from the effort, almost dragging their own bodies along, pushing and pulling two-wheeled carts of all sizes. On top of the shapeless loads of domestic furniture lay babies in nappies, placed on mattresses and blankets like fragile objects.

Valentina turned her head back towards three other people, disfigured by fatigue, leaning their worn-out bodies against the cart.

'They are coming with me,' she said. 'They are good and courageous! We have agreed to share both the risks and the fruits of our efforts. You know this boy; this is Zais the violinist, and our two friends are Zoya and Anya, who studied in the Stalino Conservatory with my cousin.'

'And where are you hoping to reach?' I asked.

'They told me that between Kantemirovka and Boguchari there is still the possibility for good "exchanges". For women's shoes in good condition, eighty kilos of wheat, and for a dress, up to 120 or 130. I have brought the black silk dress and the shoes that you saw that day. Mama also gave me the sheets from Niusia's bed. Poor Niusia... she will not be back for sure!'

Valentina's face darkened and suddenly the light in her eyes went out.

'Your black dress?' I cried. 'Was there nothing else?'

Valentina shook her head. Two tears traced tracks down her dusty cheeks.

'I was at a party in the *starosta's* house that evening when a *russkii samolet*, a Russian plane, launched many firebombs... One fell on Mama's cobs of corn and burned all of the corn and the house as well. The same happened to Nadia Ekimenko and the house on the other side. Mama, Papa and Yakov managed to save themselves and get the little that we had out of the house. When I got back, nothing was left. Papa had no more watches... And now, nothing, nothing: *Nichivó!* They all sleep in Grandma's little house in Ionikommonard Street. *Takova voina*, that is the war.'

And as if those words comprised the whole world, including the tragic destiny of her family, her eyes regained their shine and began to smile again. I could not find any words of consolation. She intuitively felt that I was disturbed and broke the silence by bidding me farewell.

'I have to go,' she said. 'My friends are waiting for me. We still have a long way to go. Will I see you before the winter? Or are you going to Italy like Lieutenant Luigi?'

'No, I am staying, Valentina. Also for me, *Takova voina*.' I stopped an Italian truck that was driving slowly along; it was empty. The driver understood the situation, got out and opened the back hatchway to help Valentina, her friends and their cart into the back of the truck. Other civilians got in until it was full.

'I am going to Boguchari, Lieutenant. Where should I unload these civilians?', the driver asked me.

'We are going to Boguchari too!' interjected Valentina, as the spokesperson for all of them. 'That means less far to go!' she added, translating the good news into Russian.

The truck moved off down the dirt track, slowly disappearing into the distance.

Some time later, destined for Ordzhonikidze and the provisional command post of a German company, I wanted to fulfil my promise and visit the Gorshkov family. Perhaps Valentina had even got back. In

14th Street I found the old house burnt down. It took me a while to find the new house in Ionikommonard Street.

Just as on the first day, Yakov was playing at the door with his little wagon that he had had the good sense to save before anything else. He was fiddling with a black wooden puppet, smeared with tar. His father was working on his watches, but without his instruments he was not getting very far very fast. Valentina was not there. Her mother only knew a couple of words in Italian and I only a couple in Russian, so the conversation consisted mainly of gestures. She showed me a photograph that a soldier had brought them from the Turin division, bringing them news of their daughter. Valentina looked pretty, with her white nurse's uniform, in front of our field hospital.

'*Krasivi etot beili kostium! Muku privezli!*' (So pretty, this white dress. We received the flour!), she cried, lifting the lid off the only pan that was on the stove, boiling a white watery broth.

A simple sentence, with no emphasis or drama.

The father, who had not left his task until then, put his tiny cogs down on the table for a second and turned to me to ask, '*Kogda konchitsa voina?*' (When will the war end?)

I shrugged my shoulders and he scowled, muttering a few unintelligible words. He looked at the bubbling pan and repeated, '*Kogda konchitsa voina?*'

Whoever would have entered Gorshkov the watchmaker's house in March 1943 would have caught a mother at her domestic chores, a father mending watches and Yakov playing with his little wagon. On the smoky wall above the stove, adorned with a bunch of flowers, they would have noticed the photograph of a pretty 19-year-old girl in a nurse's uniform, flanked by icons of two saints, as if they were protecting her.

When the Turin division in Chejovo was surrounded, its field hospitals suffered the same fate. By not going to Germany, Valentina had decided to look after our wounded soldiers who had never done her any harm and had even helped her to the best of their means. She tried to find a way of escaping like everyone else. Her main fear was of falling into the hands of the Russians who would accuse her of being a spy because she had worked as a nurse in a field hospital, and would shoot her. They would reproach her, calling her 'woman of the Italians'.

She tried to flee in a sledge with three other companions. But where and how could they escape if the Russians were closing in on all sides?

Elena Kudina, who did indeed manage to return to Ordzhonikidze by escaping from the *Gosudarstvennoie Politicheskoie Upravlienie*, the state police, reported that Claudia and Valentina had fallen prisoner and had been subjected to a trial for treason, like herself. Her defence, that of having to 'go to Germany never to return, or work with the Italians' was of no use. Before the sentence was read, Elena had managed to escape, crossed the Russian and German lines and arrived home safely.

However, the Gorshkovs kept on hoping. Of their three children, God would surely save at least one.

INSPECTOR
FRANHART

L IEUTENANT WILLIE HILDEBRANDT, on transferring his management on to me, said, 'Don't put too much trust in Schwarz and be very careful with Inspector Hugo Franhart in particular. Above all, be very tactful with him because he is odious and very wilful. He is fearsome if he gets it into his head to be so. Never contradict him and if need be, outwit him.'

As his car sped off in a black cloud of summer dust, I thought about his words and decided that it would be best to be wary and try to get to know Inspector Franhart as soon as possible.

It was not long before the opportunity arose. I was walking in the centre of Rikovo, when I came across an unusually busy square that attracted my attention. I went over to take a look, but a German sergeant stopped me in my tracks, bellowing out what was written on a wooden sign nearby, in Italian and Romanian: *Access to the market by members of the armed forces is strictly forbidden today.* At chest height, hanging from a thick chain, the non-commissioned officer wore a metallic plaque, in the shape of an inverted half-moon, with an inscription in relief stating that he belonged to the *Feldgendarmerie*, the German military police. I decided to answer him in his own language. Hearing me speak in German radically changed his attitude and expression. Then he came closer and said in a lowered voice:

'As an Italian officer, you can take a quick look, but I warn you, it is not the best moment. Inspector Franhart is preparing a raid this morning.'

He emphasized the word 'raid' with a malign smile of complicity, but on noticing my indifference, and after repeating two or three times '*Razzia, Herr Leutnant*', he realized that I did not understand the word. Raising his eyebrows, and coming even closer, he added:

'*Herr Inspector Franhart zivil zabrali sevodnia,*' which in his linguistic cocktail of Ukrainian and German meant, 'Today Inspector Franhart arrests civilians.'

Despite not entirely understanding Russian, from the collocation of Inspector Franhart's name and the verb *zabral* (arrest), I understood that Franhart would be raiding this square where they were setting up market in order to collect civilians for deportation to work camps in Germany. I nodded, to the satisfaction of the policeman, who then returned to his post in order to block the passage of other soldiers who had arrived on the scene in the meantime.

I felt very curious, and thought that this would be the ideal opportunity to learn how the inspector operated to catch human beings and send them to work in German factories. I looked for a place where I could comfortably observe the toing and froing of people with their most unusual objects, such as window frames, antediluvian gramophones, broken windows and rusty nails, baskets of bright white chickens and sacks of potatoes, icons and unbound books of all sizes. I spent a few moments contemplating the spectacle, when as if by magic, some policemen from the Ukrainian militia appeared. They could only be distinguished from the civilians by their white armbands with the black inscription '*Miliz*' and the swastika with the German eagle. My attention was drawn to their showy display: in a matter of seconds, after the appearance of two other militiamen in khaki uniform and flat caps, who proceeded to shout the order to attack in Ukrainian, the militia pointed their long rifles threateningly at the crowd. The eruption in the square was fast and repressive, but I saw many civilians slip off down side streets. There were a few shots fired, although the crowd acted almost completely indifferent to them, understanding that they were shot into the air. I also told myself that although the Ukrainian militia were serving the Germans, it was not possible that they would shoot their own countrymen.

The non-commissioned officer of the *Feldgendarmerie*, flanked by two militiamen, had kept his ground until this moment. Now he marched directly towards a group of unfortunate individuals who had not had time to escape and were not offering resistance.

'Free me from the Germans, save me, *gospodin italianski Ofizier*,' I heard a female voice in the group say in Italian. 'They want to abduct me and take me to Germany.'

These vehement words spoken in my language intrigued me and enticed me to try to catch sight of her amongst those terrified civilians. I then saw two enormous imploring eyes, bathed in tears and fixed on me. I stepped through and ordered the girl to follow me and we managed to leave the square without a problem.

There was no longer a soul in the adjacent streets. The people knew that Inspector Franhart was carrying out a raid, and it was not a good idea to wander into the vicinity.

'My name is Lydia,' said the young girl, shaking my hand. 'I don't want to go to Germany; to Italy, yes. I thank all the Italians in poor Russia.'

Having said this, she walked away down the long *ulitsa* Mechevaia that led down into the valley where the lazy, almost immobile River Bulavin flowed.

Militiamen shouldering rifles were already escorting a column of 'captured' civilians out of the square. The sergeant of the militia police was leading them towards the command post, the realm of Inspector Franhart. Having seen his modus operandi, I wished all the more to meet the man himself.

I was finally able to satisfy my curiosity at a dinner that I was invited to by Captain Paul Mesen. When they introduced me, Hugo Franhart shook my hand vigorously, with a loud laugh of satisfaction. The reason for the party was the inauguration of Captain Mesen's new residency. Mesen was an elegant and refined man, and with privileges as commanding officer of a company of technicians, it had been easy for him to fix up his house without sparing on details. The electrical wiring was installed and there was a good swimming pool in the garden, with comfortable reclining chairs for leisure time, as if this were the Bavarian countryside and not Russia. It did not seem to worry him that the front was only a few miles away, since 'the plan is to continue with the attack towards the east as far as the Urals and perhaps further'.

Despite the presence of female company, Inspector Franhart kept me at his side throughout dinner and I felt obliged to put up with his repugnant odour of alcohol. Due to his drunkenness, he confided in me, telling me about his immediate objectives. Once the dinner was at an end, a Ukrainian orchestra livened up the party with music that instantly drew the couples onto the dance floor. Inspector Franhart did not follow his companions, who were eager to hold the women in their arms. Relationships with Russians repulsed him, as he considered them an inferior race, separated from the German culture and civilization by a vast abyss. While his companions had fun, his restless little eyes targeted possible victims for capture, perhaps with the intention of swiftly deporting them to the factories in Germany. He felt so smug and proud of having carte blanche from the Führer in the decision over thousands of people's destinies, that he could not keep it to himself.

Serving me my umpteenth vodka, he said in a serious tone, stammering through his tobacco breath and almost drooling:

'I bet you don't like these women either. If you only knew how crazy Captain Misen is over his Katia, Bender over his Zoya, Schwarz over his Annie, and Schnitzler over his Nina... So far as I'm concerned, they should let off steam while they can, but these are passions that lead to a loss of racial pride, of the German superiority, and they should avoid relationships as low as these... Well, if they lose their dignity, Inspector Franhart is here to prevent such indecent situations and to look after their good and the good of the Third Reich.'

He dried the sweat from his brow as it trickled down his ruddy cheeks in abundant droplets. He took hold of my arm in a decisive manner and whispered to me, 'A month from now, if they want another party like this one, my dear friends will have to find partners from Germany, which won't be very easy.'

His little piggy eyes, sunk into his cheeks, shining with perspiration, took on a light that was colder and even more sadistic, but I hid my disgust so that he would continue to confide in me.

'We have to win! We will get the workers that Germany needs. We will get them at whatever cost; the young, the very young and even the old, if we need them. Men and women, rich and poor, and great ladies such as these that are revelling here.'

With this, he showed me a photograph of his wife, a true *Frau*, eulogizing the incomparable qualities of the German woman and her genuine beauty, adding praises to the 'pretty Italian ladies with dark eyes and mother-of-pearl teeth', and to the Duce and fascism. In between, he added sarcastic comments about his companions, who continued to dance wildly, almost to the point of taking their shirts off. I had no choice but to give exaggerated compliments to the portrait of his wife and, as smug as ever, he put it back into his wallet, commenting:

'In the eleven months that I have spent here I have never had any dealings with Russian men or women. At least I can look any man in the face with my head held high. Anyone.'

He raised his glass, now filled with wine, and staring me straight in the eye, he compelled me to perform a ceremonious Teutonic toast.

When the first rays of dawn began to appear and we started to leave the party, one of the guests, an officer, called me aside and said to me,

'You must have a strong stomach to have put up with that fellow all night. Captain Mesen could not do otherwise than invite him, since all of the healthy women are being subjected to deportation to Germany and if he had not done so, Franhart would have taken his revenge. I must apologize to you on behalf of my friends.'

A surveillance patrol was marching past. The curfew was still on and there was not another soul to be seen in the street. Inspector Franhart, alone as alone as could be, staggered away whistling, towards a chauffeur-driven car on his way back to his world. The echo of sporadic gunfire from the artillery at the front could be heard loud and clear, as a reminder that the war went on.

A few weeks after the party, one thundery August afternoon, a colleague of mine, head of a battery of the Army Corps, came to see me to ask if I could help prevent the deportation of a girl named Liuba. She had been arrested at night in her parents' house in order to be sent off in a train heading for Germany. Her parents, in their desperation, turned to the officer whom they had housed in their home for a while, begging him for help. Liuba was their only daughter left, as the other two had already been sent to Germany and they had not had any news for months from their two sons, enlisted into the Red Army in June of 1941.

'I knew,' he said, 'that by not succumbing to the *Starosta* Alexeievich's desires, Liuba was making herself an enemy who would be prepared to make her pay for it. She is the prettiest girl in the village, driving everybody crazy with desire. This *starosta* is a pig who has gained absolute trust from the German authorities on the basis of vile acts. Despite this, I decided to go to the town hall. Thirty or so women of all ages, some of whom were almost naked and with tears in their eyes, were lined up in front of a door guarded by a sentry, waiting their turn for the medical examination. They escorted me to the *starosta*'s office. When I entered he hardly changed his expression, nor did he move his heavy weight off his armchair. I came straight out with it, demanding that he release Liuba because she worked as a cleaner in our command post. The hypocrite pretended to regret it, feigning dismay. He pleaded that it was now too late to do anything, and as an excuse, he turned cynically to the portrait of Hitler on the wall, and said very gravely in German: *Unser Führer hat das befehlt!* Our Führer has ordered it! I left his office determined not to let him get away with this, and not only to defend the dignity of the uniform that I am wearing.'

I immediately sent an orderly to Inspector Franhart with a note urging that Liuba be set free, and that she had been arrested erroneously by the Korsiun militia. His answer was courteous but negative, saying that as proof of her guilt citizen Liuba X had avoided the police on several occasions, using many cunning methods. This deserved a punishment that would aid the interests of the supreme goal: 'victory for the great people of the Axis alliance', and concluded by suggesting that the only solution would be to name an older woman to replace Liuba.

Aware of the friendship between the inspector and the *starosta* of Korsiun, I was convinced that such unyielding men were capable of anything. I remembered Lieutenant Hildebrandt's warning before he left: 'if necessary, outwit him', and a trick did indeed occur to me.

The following day I sent a sergeant and two soldiers, with helmets and bayonets fixed, to Inspector Franhart's office, with an official letter demanding the surrender of citizen Liuba X, a conscript born in 1925, accused of irregularities in the Italian headquarters where she worked, and that she be liberated in order to proceed with the relevant investigations and punishments that would take place exclusively under our authorities. Franhart could not refuse such an official request as this and Liuba, escorted by our non-commissioned officer, left Saint Nicholas's church, the sad antechamber of the livestock wagon headed for Germany. She was free. The trick had worked, but it was not safe for the girl to go back home, so we transferred her to Poltava, where some relations of hers lived, giving her two months' leave. When her time was up she did not return, and we heard nothing more of her.

Due to the aerial drop of Russian paratroopers we had spent hours combing miles and miles of forest at Krestovka, but to no avail. Our legs were suffering from this fruitless fatigue. I had just returned to the provisional command post when a sergeant announced the arrival of Inspector Franhart. The inspector came with Zoya, his secretary, a pretty Russian girl I had already caught sight of a couple of times in his office. Their sudden arrival surprised me. We began by chatting about trivialities. The German's attitude and expression suggested something. He seemed perturbed, anxious and was charming towards his secretary. As she stood at his side, Zoya's sidelong glances in her boss's direction suggested she had feelings for him. The subject of the conversation turned towards peace and a better world where there was no violence, the imperative being freedom for all, especially for the oppressed. Inspector Franhart was defending such noble ideals... None other than Inspector Franhart!

When they left, believing that they were hidden by darkness, I caught a glimpse of their bodies moving closer together. I understood that my suspicions about the Inspector's internal conflict had been well founded.

Great big flakes of snow fell from the sky on that January afternoon. It seemed as if Russia and the world were going to sleep under a big white blanket. The sentries, protected by their big fur coats, were unable to shake off all the snow that kept accumulating. With such bad visibility neither side could spring an attack. The troops of the bastion could almost relax.

Walking sluggishly through the snow and protected by a grey-green cloak and hood, I saw Inspector Franhart arriving. He came in, brushing the snow off his cheeks and the ice off his lashes with the back of his hand. Panting, and wearing an unusual expression of embarrassment and shyness at the same time, he told me he wished to speak to me alone. He checked that the door was closed so that nobody could listen. Then he asked me if, given the fact that we were 'proven friends', it would not be more pleasant to address each other on familiar terms. Next, he shook my hand firmly, visibly moved and with moist eyes. At first I thought that it was snow, but they were definitely tears.

Franhart, crying? I could not believe it. The inspector, that man of iron, with a heart that could not be touched by the cries of so many ill-fated individuals, was capable of crying? He blushed on noticing my perplexity. He realized that he had let his guard down. I was no longer up against the imperturbable inspector, the inflexible and strict fulfiller of his duties, but stood face to face with Franhart the human being.

Here is his tale:

'Zoya had been working in my office for six months and I decided to appoint her as my secretary. Under my orders was this young, graceful, intelligent and hard-working girl, who had learned some German, which helped me a lot. Through our constant contact, I came to realize that she was not a Russian girl like the rest; she was full of natural kindness and her soft voice... her beauty perturbed me. Day by day there was an obsessive desire growing within me. I did not have the will to resist it, as duty dictated. I let myself be won over without realizing it, and on one occasion, when her lips were close to mine, I kissed her.'

Franhart spoke like a timid adolescent confessing his first sentimental adventure to a friend. I listened to him, interested, wondering if this man really was Franhart or whether his infernal soul had come to play a trick on me. He took a brief pause and continued:

'For four months now we have not been apart for a moment. Only the night divides us, when I take her to her mother's house, behind the station. The German or Italian guards no longer give us the order to halt. They know who this couple is: Inspector Franhart taking his *baryshnia* to her home. Everybody knows that the inspector loves a Russian, that he is a man just like all the others.'

Tears began to flow from his little, round, sunken eyes, over his prominent cheeks, wetting his tunic and the silver eagle and swastika. He covered his face with his big chubby hands, sobbing, and went on, not daring to look me in the face:

'Tomorrow I am leaving for good. They are sending me to set up a new office in Kupiansk. The order arrived yesterday. It is irrevocable,' he cried, distressed, holding my hand warmly. 'Now you know that in Russia, Inspector Franhart is a man like any other. Protect her when I am no longer here. My successor knows everything and, if he fulfils his duty, he will have to send her to Germany, since Zoya, by being loved by a German official, has committed the crime of corrupting his inflexible sense of duty and he will have to purge it. Poor little Zoya. But you won't let it happen, will you?'

I calmed him down and told him that I would do my best to save her. He broke into laughter like a little boy, and kept slapping me on the back with his big coarse hands, showing his great friendship and happiness. His heart was free of the heaviest weight it had suffered in his life; he was finally a human being, one man facing another.

Franhart left at dawn one morning in January. I bumped into him near Zoya's house on his way to the station's transport control post to see if there was a convoy leaving for Stalino. Behind him were a man and two young boys dragging sledges of bulky equipment. This is how Franhart, the man who had been an inflexible inspector until the day before, disappeared for ever. There was not even a car prepared to take him. He had to make do with a modest place in some Italian truck or another, shared with Russian civilians. Later, I was told that he lost his post because one of his colleagues, whose girlfriend he had sent to Germany, had informed on him. Due to this the rumour got out in Stalino that Inspector Franhart had lived with his secretary, failing to fulfil his duty as a German. Zoya came to see me. She had no news from Franhart apart from two letters that she had received at the beginning. Kupiansk, the place where he had been sent, had fallen into the hands of the Russians when they won back Jarkov. The poor thing would not give up hope of receiving news of him; she could not believe that her Hugo would have forgotten her or fallen victim to misfortune. I told her that it would take some time to get word of him. She understood, and left in a very unhappy state.

But Franhart did not write back.

Those who claimed to be well informed said that he had been killed when some partisans attacked and set light to the German labour office, just before the Russians occupied Kupiansk. Sure enough, the fugitives from there also confirmed that the building had been set on fire. But there was nothing to confirm the fate of the inspector. At his new post he had gained everybody's esteem by helping people find work in Russia so that they could avoid deportation to Germany. Someone who professed to know better said that partisans had stripped him of his uniform and his jacket, shouting, 'Go to the devil, you and all the Germans!'

That was the last I heard of Franhart. Zoya did not come back to ask for any more news of him. I met her one Sunday coming out of church. She was wearing black. The mourning clothes gave a strange and grace-ful light to her clear porcelain skin and her platinum blonde hair. She was as beautiful as ever, but very weak. She saw me first and came over to say:

'Tomorrow I am going to look for him.'

She did not say where or when. She was not afraid to cross the whole of Russia in her search. If her love for her Hugo was so sincere and so strong, I would have liked to have believed the version given by the fugitive from Kupiansk that the partisans had stripped Franhart of his uniform and left him to fend for himself in the steppe, applying their own form of justice : killing the inspector, but the letting man inside live. If someone should find this half-nude vagrant wandering there and ask him where he was going, he would answer in the same way as his Russian lover: 'I am going to look for her.' But in that vast expanse, Inspector Franhart would have foundered.

THE MEN
IN CHARGE

A HEAVILY ESCORTED COLUMN of provisions was leaving from Kalach to Stalingrad as if it were a shipping convoy. The *Wehrmacht*'s enormous L.K.W. (Last Kraft Wagen) diesel trucks awaited the departure signal, belching out clouds of asphyxiating diesel fumes from their exhaust pipes. Two 'Storks', Fieseler FI-156 Storchs, appeared overhead, flying very low, then dipped their wings, and disappeared just as unexpectedly. The trucks revved their engines and the smoke became even more unbearable, before suddenly starting off on their way. We were left to contemplate the ostentatious display of power that gradually disappeared in a cloud of smoke. Another convoy of provisions was on its way to the besiegers of Stalingrad, where Paulus was fighting 'by fire and sword' against Rokossovski. Meanwhile, not far from this platform, the partisan named Sanchiukov was meeting his end in front of the firing squad, without so much as batting an eyelid.

'Long live Stalin!' he shouted as they shot him. He even found the strength and courage to spit out a derogatory 'Long live Russia!' at the officer who went to give him the final mercy shot to end it all. He had refused a blindfold. His last request was for a cigarette, as he stood with both hands and feet tied up with leather straps. They put a notice on the half-demolished wall used by the firing squad, both in Russian and Ukrainian, listing the crimes he was accused of and giving a summary of the trial.

A few yards away stood Nadia and Lydia, leaning against the bonnet of the police car. One was dressed in black, and the other in white. This was all they had been able to find in the way of mourning clothes in their impoverished wardrobe. Both of them were very young. When Sanchiukov had breathed his last, they sat down, relieved. Serene smiles almost imperceptibly touched the corners of their mouths. They stayed by the car until the last shovel of earth covered the anonymous grave, wiping out the last traces of the murderous partisan for ever. He was not a murderer in their eyes only. All the other civilians who rose at dawn to attend his execution in Ionikommonard Street considered him a vulgar criminal and an assassin rather than a partisan. Nobody was sorry to see him fall down dead before the firing squad and afterwards, satisfied, they left to get on with their own affairs. Stragglers took the opportunity to have a chat before dispersing and greeting this new day that had violently sealed the young partisan's fate. Sanchiukov had killed Lydia's father and Nadia's brother, shooting them both at point-blank range on their doorsteps. Nadia had recognized him and reported him to the police, and he was caught before he could make himself scarce.

I wondered: murderer or partisan?

For Lydia and for Nadia, and for all those who had attended his execution, he was a murderer with over thirty victims under his belt, all within a large area where he had terrorized hundreds of families.

Sanchiukov managed to recruit quite a few of those who did not have the integrity to decide for themselves what to do about the occupying forces. He led an armed group, obtaining explosives and weapons from Russian paratroopers or traitors from the Ukrainian Militia, posing a threat for the Germans, who were obliged to reinforce the guard in all strategic areas, since they neither had the time nor the resources to organize a search in the woods. Sanchiukov's followers were unidentifiable, just as anyone who returns to their home with their papers in order would be. The German command saw the problem in real terms: choosing to be a partisan is something that attracts resolute and courageous men. Opportunities to operate were not lacking. The risks were relatively limited, since the garrisons were isolated, and law and order in the area was almost exclusively in the hands of the Ukrainian Militia and their friends, who were as corrupt as they could get. And Sanchiukov's group had plenty of roubles to bribe them with.

Thank goodness Nikolai Igorevich, head of Voroshilovgrad's 180 militiamen, had both nerves of steel and honesty that would stand up to any test. There was no doubt about it, and the first to say so was *Sonderführer* Von Piritz, who often invited him to his table at the collective farm. He entertained him with hearty banquets in this former aristocratic villa that by some miracle had stayed intact. Von Piritz had emptied the halls that had been transformed into warehouses, and had furnished them with the best chairs and tables he could get hold of.

Von Piritz presided over a great oblong table to which he had invited all his trustworthy men. The room had a very high ceiling. A beautiful silver serving dish was reflected in a mirror that almost completely covered one wall. In the adjacent room there were red leather armchairs and on the coffee tables were magazines and exquisitely bound books. All was lit by the soft light of wall lamps. Von Piritz was a gentleman of the old Bavarian nobility, tall and elegant. He wore a monocle and smoked a pipe, and although he sported the same *Sonderführer* uniform as his colleagues he was different from them, displaying such ease and elegance.

Two silent Russian women dressed in black with little white aprons served dinner just like faultless professionals. Two more women worked in the kitchen, labouring over the preparation of succulent dishes under the supervision of a *Volksdeutsche* from Voroshilovgrad. The meal was sumptuous, the conversation pleasant. I asked Von Piritz some questions about the Soviet organization of their agriculture, to hear his point of view. Nikolai Igorevich did not agree with the German, and I could see that for this Russian the past had to be forgotten; for him anything from Bolshevism was not worth talking about let alone analysing. Von Piritz, a German and an aristocrat, was more objective and admitted that there were good sides to the Russian collectivist organization and while the war lasted they were not going to change it.

I was just about to leave when Von Piritz asked if he could speak to me alone. He wanted to know what I thought about Sanchiukov's group. He had received death threats demanding he agree to certain requests from the shameless bandit. He reiterated his complete confidence in Nikolai Igorevich, pointing out, however, that he had few policemen to monitor the area, but that his subordinates obeyed him without question. Von Piritz had to visit the different *Sonderführer* within his area on a daily basis. This meant that he had to travel across miles and miles of almost deserted steppe, accompanied by an interpreter, an escort and his Russian chauffeur. It would be easy for Sanchiukov's men to kill him. Not that he was afraid of losing his life; he had already risked it on a number of occasions on the western front during the First World War. Of course, the concept of *Sonderführer* had not been invented at the time, and they were all just soldiers without agricultural or industrial responsibilities. He emphasized the fact that he was not prepared to die in an ambush and, like any other soldier, he aspired to dying an honourable death, facing the enemy with a weapon in his hand. He told me about a plan that he hoped to put into action as soon as possible, as long as the relevant executive body would approve it. The plan was to round up all of the suspected members of the group, and transfer them to another region, which would of course be very difficult, as it meant separating many individuals from their families and moving them away. The operation would no doubt raise strong opposition. Voroshilovgrad's steelworks and mines, which were beginning to recommence production, needed a workforce, and they would naturally oppose giving up their workers in exchange for others from other regions. Surely, the plan would not work. Would Sanchiukov and company continue with their villainy in the meantime? After all, there were other issues of much greater concern at hand than the partisans. A few hundred miles away stood Stalingrad, a dreadful incinerator that swallowed up men and arms.

I then took my leave, but before I went, Von Piritz wanted to speak to the head of the Militia, Nikolai Igorevich, in my presence. He arrived almost immediately, stood to attention and turned down the offer of a seat, however many times he was urged to make himself comfortable. I observed him carefully. There was no doubt about it: he knew how to play his role. He listened with great interest to what the 'boss' had to say, frowning, concentrating on his thoughts and outwardly showing agreement.

I looked at his physical appearance. My attention was drawn to certain details: he stooped slightly, irradiating servility; he was carefully dressed and his boots were made of beautiful natural calfskin leather that I almost envied. His fine hands were manicured and his eyes very sunken and shifty. At Nikolai Igorievich's suggestion, Von Piritz asked me to help him find a man named Misha Butenko, a mechanic who worked in a farm tractor repair shop located in our Eighth Army's zone. He was a valuable individual who had already helped the police on other occasions. This time he would have to be a double agent: the plan was to pretend to supply arms and munitions to Sanchiukov's group in order to locate them. A mock transport convoy would have to be organized between the Don and the Donets with the weapons hidden under sacks of wheat. Then, once these Russian weapons were in a secret hiding place, the partisans would be brought there.

With the help of our *carabinieri* we found Misha in a tractor repair shop. He was a very tall man, and as thin as a broomstick. He seemed to be a really pleasant fellow. He reassured me that he would contact Nikolai Igorevich as soon as possible to receive his orders.

A few weeks went by during which I did not return to Von Piritz's cosy villa, but every now and then I heard people speaking about the partisan Sanchiukov and his executions of collaborators. Apparently, now the group had moved towards Izium and Jarkov, where the terrain was rugged and the circumstances advantageous for their villainy. One day I returned to the collective farm and Von Piritz told me that Nikolai Igorevich was still persistently searching in the woods, hoping to carry out a successful raid. The German had complete confidence in his plan, even more so now that Misha was coming and going from the Don to the Donets pretending to be a Russian spy and, according to Nikolai, was a valuable informer. Good old Von Piritz never suspected that Misha had been buried for some time. A Romanian police patrol had shot him down on the Don's great trail after catching him with a sleigh full of arms and munitions hidden under sacks of wheat. He had shown the authorization from the German police, but the Romanians did not even bother to check it. The truth of the matter is that I could not see how he could explain such a permit. It was all the worse for him for having agreed to play such a dangerous game. Von Piritz was profoundly affected on hearing this, but what really infuriated him was that the Romanians had ignored the German authorization and had not checked its authenticity. Why was he still sending arms to the Don? Was it essential to continue running such a risk in order to protect himself? For the first time Von Piritz became suspicious of Nikolai Igorevich's mediation, and a seed of doubt was sown in the mind of the old Bavarian.

This suspicion was soon to take shape due to his right-hand man, a civilian called Volodia who worked as foreman in the area under his jurisdiction. Volodia had a hand in everything, as he was an arbiter of disputes, laying down the law. He was a veteran of the collective farming organization with eighteen years' experience, pulling all the strings and gaining confidence from the Germans, as he was an expert in the profession. He swore he had met Trotsky, whose ideas he disagreed with, naturally. However, he did not explain how, as an opponent of the Bolshevik regime, he had managed to arrive at a position with such a good salary that he was able to afford a car. With it he drove from *kolkhoz* to *kolkhoz*. He did not skimp on anything: he ostentatiously smoked German cigarettes, wore *Wehrmacht* boots with absolute impunity and without anyone commenting upon it. He dressed with elegance and knew how to hold a conversation, mixing up what he knew of German and French. It must be said that this extraordinary man was quite likeable, able as he was to adapt to whoever he was speaking with. He knew how to be discreet with his superiors, modest with his equals and firm and persuasive with his subordinates. It was rumoured that he was a hardened Communist in disguise, but no one volunteered the details. To sum up, he was a man who had climbed the professional ladder until he had reached the position of *starosta* and provincial governor, accumulating more and more responsibilities and prestige and almost unlimited power in his field – although he would say that he had always kept his distance from politics and Bolshevism. On the few occasions that I spoke to him he had always been extremely concerned about my affairs and had done all in his power to help me. His department was a genuine ministry with several offices, typists and interpreters, which dealt with farmers, workers, heads of *kolkhozes*, storekeepers and so on. Half of the Ukraine went there to receive orders, obtain permits, pay or receive money or find out about the guidelines of the German command.

I observed all of this each time I saw him, and asked myself what was genuine about him, how much sincerity and conviction lay in his actions when he obeyed and carried out the orders from his superiors. Nobody around me could answer this for me.

This was not resolved in my mind until a while later. This Volodia fellow and Nikolai Igorevich were the two principal actors in Von Piritz's 'theatre', but he did not know what kind of people he was dealing with. There is no doubt about the fact that this was a very complex affair. Not even an expert psychologist would have been able to fathom it out, let alone this honest man who was a slave to his duty. It was not his fault that fate put him up against these two extraordinary individuals.

When I bumped into him in the corridor of the 2nd Italian Military Corps headquarters at the end of December 1942, it took me a moment to recognize him: he had changed so much. He had aged. As always, he was neatly dressed in his uniform, but with the addition of a Russian goatskin coat. He was terribly thin, his face was very wrinkled and he wore a gloomy expression. The little convoy of cars with Voroshilovgrad number plates parked outside the building of the high command for the past few hours with their gas tanks empty was his. The two front vehicles loaded with equipment were pitted with machine gun fire.

I did not want to say hello so as to avoid any new problems, because there was no doubt that Von Piritz would ask me a favour. However, he was alone, amongst so many Italians, and must have felt very ill at ease.

So I went over to him. His face lit up when he saw me, as if he could not believe his eyes. The Russians were attacking Debaltsevo, which seriously threatened our left flank. There was no time for idle chat. His hardship was in fact the same as everyone else's: fuel. He understood that it was not because I wished him further difficulty that I could not help him, as he could see for himself the interminable columns of immobilized vehicles standing in the snow with empty gas tanks. The Russians had gained a real advantage with this shortage of fuel that had caught us unprepared.

The corridors were full of people continually coming and going. Nobody could hide their nerves. The constant opening and closing of doors, groups of crestfallen soldiers coming together and then dispersing yet again, exhausted liaison and dispatch officers passing each other with typed orders in official envelopes.

Von Piritz was shattered. He felt humiliated and did not want to confess that not a single inch of his farming district remained in the hands of the *Wehrmacht* any more. The Russians had won back their land and more besides. The day before, the battles had reached the *kolkhoz* and they had even fought in the large mirrored dining room. If Von Mackensen, the general in command of the *Wehrmacht*'s First Armoured Army, managed to close the breach, the following day a tough battle would break out in the most fertile area of crops, from which they had expected to obtain the best harvest. Never mind. That was the consequence of war. He had not heard anything from his subordinates of the *Kreislandwirt*. They would all just have to put themselves into God's hands, he said, and wait for His will to be done.

He asked me where he might get hold of a hot meal. He needed it badly, because in these circumstances, he was not getting any younger, and he felt he was on the verge of collapse. I suggested the headquarters of the farming district, the Kreis, as it was not really the best time to be sitting him down at a table full of Italians: I could envisage a very unpleasant scene taking place. He agreed and arrived just in time to see the director of the farming complex who was starting up his car on his way to Stalino to receive orders since the telephone lines were down.

The following day I went to the Kreis to get a chit for some honey and butter. The administrators tended to be quite stingy, but given the current situation I did not imagine they would refuse. The atmosphere there lacked the usual hustle and bustle, as if everyone had died and gone to heaven: the corridors were empty, the offices deserted and the shelves were bare. The only man I found was *Sonderführer* Bitt, sitting, as usual, in his office, speaking in a quiet voice with two female interpreters. He was there at his post, but they had not left a single file in the building. I asked for the chit for honey and butter, and without the slightest objection, he allocated 200 pounds of each. What did he care any more? I believe he would have given me all that I could ask for. It was the end. He did not have to tell me, I could read it in his thoughts. Bitt was not a soldier but a simple farmer, devoted to the land as if it belonged to him. Now that he had to leave he could not comprehend that these were simply the consequences of the war, subsequent to the chain of events of the last few days. He was very different from military men, for whom earth is just a cursed brown stuff upon which to fight. He was even more crestfallen and dejected than the grenadiers of Berlin's 3rd Division, who were forced to retreat in great haste from the Caucasus in order to close the breaches in the Donets.

Von Piritz and Bitt would also soon leave for the Dnieper, leaving behind almost two years devoted to the intense daily restoration of the farming economy in service of the war and the survival of the population. Meanwhile, Nikolai Igorevich would meet his end before the firing squad under the pseudonym of Sanchiukov, playing his role of double agent to perfection, down to the purging of his guilt. I was sorry not to have been in contact with Von Piritz in order to give him the sensational news, although perhaps he would have been disappointed and taken it as a personal failure on his part.

Von Piritz did not find out either that, when the ill wind blew, Volodia, instead of fleeing with all of the other personnel in fear of reprisal from the Russians, simply disappeared. He had left everything in order so that the Russians could easily make use of the administration of his province. This was emphatically stated by the storekeepers and civil engineers who left the area just in time to avoid falling into the hands of the Bolsheviks.

Volodia was a former Bolshevik civil servant, and had been friendly with Von Piritz in order to pass on information unscrupulously to his former bosses, prepared to change camp as soon as the wind changed. Who knows if one day, returning to these lands, I might bump into this man, perhaps now an honourable governor in a province of the USSR, without an ounce of shame for his past. It would not surprise me: the men in charge are always the same ones and however much politics might change they always come out on top.

Lydia and Nadia assured me that Sanchiukov was a bandit and, from their point of view, they would always be right about that. However, I asked myself how Sanchiukov would be regarded within the historical setting that he had lived through. He had not got rich, despite all the rumours. He had risked his skin and had killed those who did not share his anti-collaborationist views. He showed courage in the face of death and he had known how to keep up that risky act with such aptitude that his bosses had not even guessed at what was happening under their own noses. But that was just it: however justified the motive may be, shady dealings are not worthy of exaltation.

Due to the cold and to the precarious situation my notes here are sparse, but from reading over them I can relive those anxious moments. To do this it is enough to evoke two names: Von Piritz, with his world of pipe dreams and his frustrated enthusiasm, and Nikolai Igorevich, his trusty helper, a captain partisan, a hero for Russia and a murderer for Lydia and Nadia.

MADAME ANTONINA'S 'HEADQUARTERS'

I T WAS A SPLENDID EVENING in July of 1942. A mysterious luminosity made it seem as if, in addition to being fertile, this Ukrainian terrain was phosphorescent. The moon was not in sight; it must have been hiding behind a ridge in the steppe and, comfortably lying in a field of sunflowers or rye, was taking a while to come out. The air carried an intense aroma that was not from the wisteria; it seeped into your mind and heightened your senses with an irresistible strength that impelled you to satisfy them. The only things missing were the fireflies to add the finishing touches to the night, with their little sporadic magical flashes of light. Was this a dream or was it real? Was I *really* only a few thousand yards from the front or on summer holiday? I could hear people singing in Italian everywhere that night in Gorlovka. In the streets of the east district of town, from a few rearguard divisions of our Eighth Army, songs and voices were striking up in harmony. Galina was sitting at my side, listening and hardly breathing. She was wearing a simple white dress that showed off her graceful 17-year-old body. Her thick, dark hair flowed down over her shoulders, and lightly brushed against my cheek. We were at the door of her little house, surrounded by her simple garden with its few sunflowers standing in their beds. Beneath the stars, their heads were hanging. Only the flares, fleeting across the sky in flashes, reminded us that a few miles away, behind Chazepietovka, the war burned like embers under the ashes.

A few feet away, Victoria and Yura were whispering to each other. She was leaning against the door and he was sitting on the doorstep. I could not hear what they were saying to each other, but I imagined they were words of love. Yura carried a violin case. He was a violinist in the Coliseum's orchestra and he enjoyed the coveted privilege of being out during the curfew. He kissed Victoria and left. Little by little the voices switched off; guitars, balalaikas and harmonicas became drowsy and fell silent, the odd note playing somewhere close by before dying out. Then

I was alone with Galina's breathing; more pronounced now that she had fallen asleep with her head resting on the back of the rustic bench where she was sitting. From somewhere not too far off, the notes of a piano reached me. Where could this music be coming from? I strained to hear, holding my breath. Yes, I could see a glow in the distance, and then I could even hear voices. I stood up and crept closer to see better: a little dog heard my footsteps and started barking crazily. There was no way to calm it down. Galina awoke, stood up and looked around for me, calling in a soft voice, not wanting to be heard at such a late hour for fear of being shamed before her parents and the neighbours. She came over to the back gate where the little beast had me cornered. I did not know what to tell her. I explained my curiosity and asked if she knew who lived in the house where the lively piano music was coming from. She hung her head, not wanting to answer. I insisted she tell me, and she answered in a few words:

'Many officers, many soldiers, all night, and *zhenschini nehoroshie*, no-good women. Madame Antonina's house. Her headquarters,' she said to me in a mixture of Ukrainian and Italian.

The following morning there was a crowd of civilians at the market-place. One of my colleagues, who had also been in Russia for a few months, told me that word was out in the city that our divisions were resuming their advance towards the Don. Those who could were buying essential items before the units left and these things became scarce. While we chatted, a 'lady', so completely different from everyone else in sight, emerged from the crowd, halting the conversation with her flamboyant appearance.

She wore a hat full of feathers and was dressed in a tight-fitting jacket, which made her breasts protrude from the skimpy black bodice showing under her transparent lace top; her skirt only just covered her knees, revealing a pair of rather nice legs. She gave me a long and ambiguous look, bowing slightly, but purposefully, to one side. As my interpreter introduced us I could observe her more carefully.

Her eyebrows were two thin lines; her lips red, nails painted and face overly powdered. Her perfume was overpowering. The interpreter spoke to her in Ukrainian. I amused myself by trying to guess what they were saying from the expression on her face.

'*Madame Antonina, notre magnifique maîtresse,*' said the interpreter with a hint of irony. The 'lady', on hearing her name, gave me a slight smile. That said it all. Madame Antonina offered me an impeccably

pronounced *ciao* and continued on her way, disappearing into the
crowd. The interpreter hurriedly explained things to me. The lady in
question was the founder and manager of the city's two brothels used
by the armed forces. As it was rumoured that the front was moving
towards the east, many of Madame Antonina's *demoiselles* wanted to
follow the troops and leave the brothels. They had had to set up police
surveillance and the *starosta* himself had resolved the problem.

'Madame Antonina is a *real* character,' my interpreter continued.
'They say that before the occupation, she would indulge anyone for a
few roubles. Now, thanks to the war, she is the owner of two houses,
pompously called "tea rooms". She has recruited a group of pretty girls
to work for her and has become a wealthy woman with a tidy little fortune in German marks. Before the war there were no brothels in Russia.
Nobody knows how this woman managed to set up not just one but two
of them for the troops. Her girls earn quite a lot and they eat well. Since
they cannot be deported to labour camps in Germany, they have a further incentive to stay in this profession.'

While he explained all of this, I tried in vain to follow the feather hat
as it made its way through the market crowded with people so taken up
with their own business that they hardly seemed to notice this unusual
and eccentric figure.

The counter-espionage unit had the 'headquarters' of Madame
Antonina down as a possible centre of information for the enemy. One
of the two brothels was reserved for the officers and the other for the
troops. It was to be expected that the Russians had infiltrated spies as
prostitutes who could obtain valuable information from the clientele.

With the pretext of my fortuitous encounter in the marketplace I paid a
visit to the lady's 'headquarters'. The house that Galina had spoken about
to me might have been the residence of a wealthy businessman before the
revolution. In spite of the bombings it was miraculously intact. The first
floor was full of bedrooms, and it was reached by crossing a spacious
vestibule and a large hall that she called the 'ballroom'. It was in this
room that an elderly teacher from the Conservatory played the piano in
order to survive. She had been obliged to learn Italian music and even
some German folk songs for the single day reserved to the *Wehrmacht*.

After greeting Madame and having a brief chat with her with the help
of an interpreter, I asked her to introduce me to her girls, and I had the
opportunity to speak to almost all of them. They told me, amongst
other things, that Madame renewed their contracts every month and

that two thirds of their earnings went to the *maîtresse* for maintenance costs. As well as the good food, the free housing and the exemption from compulsory labour in Russia or Germany, they could save most of the good money that they earned.

I did not discover anything particularly interesting, although two of the girls took the opportunity to ask me to supply them with a permit so they could leave before the end of the month. They wanted to follow our armed forces at any cost, and some of their clients had told them that they were about to leave. They said they feared that their work would diminish if there were no troops. Apart from one very made-up girl who looked the part, the others were not only very young but seemed to be 'wet behind the ears'. They had no make-up on, and the only way they differed from their non-prostitute contemporaries was by their affected and luxurious way of dressing. They could afford to buy these expensive clothes with the tips they received on top of their fee since they did not have to share these with their *maîtresse*.

Summer in the Ukraine is brief. To prepare for another harsh winter, Galina decided to leave in search of wheat. Arming herself with courage, she took to the trail headed for the Kuban and the Volga.

I was given orders to co-ordinate some missions with the *Wehrmacht* along the tracks that led to the Don, which had been chosen as the deployment line in preparation for the battle of Stalingrad. Nadia and Zoya, the two enterprising young girls I had met in Madame Antonina's 'headquarters', followed the troops to the front, having managed on their own to obtain the safe conduct pass that I had not got for them. The astute Madame Antonina was furious about these first defections and did not wish to resign herself to it, so she paid two Ukrainian militiamen to find the deserters, arrest them and bring them back to the 'headquarters' as an example to dissuade the other girls.

Zoya and Nadia, unusually beautiful and richly dressed, could hardly pass unnoticed, so they were caught and sent back to the 'headquarters' in a truck. However, along the trail to Gorlovka that night, a group of partisans opened heavy fire on the truck with automatic pistols and they perished, along with other civilians and *Madame* Antonina's hired militiamen. The incident was talked about a lot, both because it was the first attack carried out by the resistance in the rearguard of the moving divisions and because the girls were well known.

The big clouds of black dust kicked up by the units that pushed the enemy back into retreat surrounded and isolated the partisans' attack that, with those burnt scraps of metal in the dirt track's ditches, left a message of death. The civilians threw a passing glance at them, almost indifferently, as they just continued to push and pull their little wagons along the road on their risky journey in search of wheat.

Faced with the foreseeable decrease in clientele, Madame Antonina kept only one of the houses working and gained the authorization from the German command to organise a small company for the transport of civilians within the 'liberated' territory. Madame Antonina was also able to obtain some fuel from the German counter-espionage, who were interested in infiltrating agents in order to find out as much as possible. Independently of the new business, called *Somsa*, or 'Sun', *Madame* Antonina continued secretly to manage another separate establishment for her faithful clientele, from whom she earned more, since she incurred fewer expenses.

For a while, *Somsa* worked very well indeed. In addition to passengers, it transported wheat and flour, almost all of it stolen from the silos in the Don, destroyed by the Timoshenko forces in their retreat towards the Urals.

The *Somsa* trucks loaded civilians, spies and deserters from the Russian Army, but the outcome of the war after the battle of Stalingrad forced many collaborators to move elsewhere. Finally Madame Antonina also decided to leave Gorlovka and head towards the west, taking with her truckloads of families, and instead of wheat, roubles gold and silver.

The Germans were about to evacuate Gorlovka and I wanted to know if there was any news of Galina. All her parents told me, resignedly, was:

'*Galina kaput, nie znaiem gdie, na fronte s italiantsami!*' (Galina is dead, we don't know where, on the front with the Italians.)

The little dog barked, as usual. I asked no more questions. They had already told me what they knew about their daughter.

When the Russian Army took the city, the old pianist who used to liven up the soirées in the brothel had not been able to buy a ticket to escape by truck. She was condemned as a collaborator by the Soviet commissar and was hanged.

The only one who came out unharmed at the end of this immense tragedy was Madame Antonina. Unrecognizable, discreetly dressed in black, without make-up, she opened a shop in Dniepropetrovsk selling icons and expensive souvenirs to the repatriating soldiers. She had become an expert antique dealer and during all the ups and downs was the only one who had survived and continued to make money.

THE FALLING
OF THE
AUTUMN LEAVES

I N STALINO, on the main road renamed
Axenstrasse, in a modern and imposing Soviet style building next to the
Great Opera House, command post A, or *Befehlstelle A*, was set up. At
the time I did not understand the meaning of the enormous sign written above the sentry box where an impeccable German sentry was
mounting guard.

All sorts of cars, buses, trucks and armoured cars were parked in the
esplanade in front of the main entrance, and the couriers on their
motorbikes, dusty from the Ukrainian dirt tracks, were skilfully swerv-
ing around the vehicles in order to deliver the dispatches without delay.
Vehicles with chains or caterpillar wheels could not park there, so they
parked next to the nearby *hatas*, little Ukrainian houses. There were
signs posted at intervals reading: *In der ersten Linie mit Raupenketten
fahren und parken streng verboten!* (It is strictly forbidden to drive and
park vehicles with chains in the main road.) It seemed absurd. The
civilian traffic was non-existent and the wide avenue had more than
enough capacity for the circulation of all kinds of vehicles, but perhaps
the Germans wanted to protect the asphalt of the grand avenue. As a
matter of fact, the military operations were going so well during those
days that nobody would have imagined the Russians were about to
regain Stalino. In Africa the Germans had just reconquered Tobruk,
and on the southern front two powerful armies of the Reich had broken
through to the Caucasus and taken possession of the first oil refineries.

A large notice in the entrance hall of the command post directed the
visitors to the various offices on the different floors of the building. I
had been ordered to co-ordinate my mission with the *Wehrmacht* in the
strictest secrecy. Edda Mussolini, the Duce's enterprising daughter,
had decided to come to Russia in Red Cross uniform. As she was
Mussolini's favourite child, and wife to the Italian Foreign Minister,
Galeazzo Ciano, the Italian supreme command wished to prepare for a

visit worthy of her position. It was my job to organize this, in close co-ordination with the various services. We had to furnish a small apart-ment in the Italian hospital in Stalino and assure maximum security without word getting out that it was for her. Since it was for the Duce's daughter, the German command co-operated fully and supplied a mili-tary aeroplane for me to fly to Budapest, not yet blacked out and still free from allied attacks, in order to buy whatever was needed.

Stalino had been transformed into a metropolis. There were traffic police with white gloves directing the traffic at the crossroads; the build-ings were fully occupied with war offices for the economy, the mining industry, farming and health; there were car parks for trucks, which were always full to capacity; depots for this, that and the other all over the place; cinemas for the armed forces with enormous posters and a show every night at the opera. There was the 'Coal Building', *Don-Donec Kohle,* advertised on a large placard of the *Wirtschaft Kommando,* which took care of economic affairs. It occupied several buildings and was con-tinuing to expand. Then there was the imposing Ukraine House, quar-ters for the rest and lodging of officers in transit ; and the *Soldatenheim,* the Soldier's House for the troops, which was a hive of activity. Not to mention the multiple Italian command posts, as well as that of the navy, which operated in the Black Sea, the headquarters of the Romanian command and the offices of the various air forces amongst others.

A special atmosphere of triumph spread through the city from the general idea that the operations were working marvellously, and that perhaps before the end of the year (it was the summer of 1942) Eastern Europe at the least would see the end of the war and the defeat of the Russians. Nobody seemed to be worried about the Soviet air force. Hardly any of the windows or lights were blacked out and the Russians did not venture into the skies given the supremacy of the German air force and the renowned 88mm anti-aircraft guns.

A few months later, when I returned to speak to an officer of the German command, the atmosphere had radically changed. I became alarmed as soon as I saw that the notice that directed visitors was no longer in its place in the entrance hall. I also saw an unusual movement of workers, removal men and soldiers coming and going all over the place, up and down the wide staircases, moving all sorts of furniture, archives and office signs. I asked a sergeant, who seemed to be in charge of the activities, for an explanation and he told me that the *Aussenstelle-Sud* offices were being transferred to Krivoi Rog. The *Befehlstelle A* was leaving for Ordzhonikidze in the Caucasus, and a 'command' was to substitute it in order to take care of the economy. I realized that those I had taken for workers and porters were in fact Russian prisoners, but I could not fathom why they were walking around so freely.

'We cannot waste men,' was the terse reply given by the sergeant. The two sentries, with their rifles in their bandoliers, one on either corner of the building, showed that they clearly did not fear that the prisoners would escape.

Millions of men were fighting in Europe; the Germans had taken the Caucasus massif and were now almost as far as the Ebrus hills. There were soldiers everywhere, and in Stalino, that great hub of activity, the only traffic was that of grey-green or light and dark brown camouflaged military vehicles, as if the war were being fought in the colonies instead of Russia. That day, for the first time, I saw the new units with their khaki uniforms, pith helmets and leather and canvas boots laced in the front, in armoured vehicles of the same colour along with matching cannon. The soldiers and the armament appeared to be fresh out of the factory. Some of the German officers, bragging that they knew it all, told me that nothing in particular was going on: these were just troops prepared by the Führer to invade the Middle East and link up with the Italo-German armies of General Bastico and Major General Rommel over in Egypt.

In mid-September, after a stifling summer, the first storms cleared the air as a prelude to winter. However, the autumn was mild and, above all, dry. The falling of the autumn leaves transformed the Donets basin into a revelation of fiery reds. Just like the seasons, the war had its stages and cycles. Stalingrad, still on the point of defeat, became a spider's web: an unknown factor. The Germans suffered grave setbacks with the Sixth Army in Stalingrad, as did the Romanians with their Third and we with our Eighth on the Don. These were the first blows on the southern front before its final collapse. Suddenly all appeared to be lost. The Siberian divisions spread throughout the area and recaptured hundreds of villages all over the place along with great amounts of matériel. The Donets had to be made into a bastion and there were no reinforcements available for its defence apart from the troops from the Don, men who had been terrified and overwhelmed by the power and superior numbers of the enemy. In the most critical stages of that deluge, I was given orders to obtain the largest amount of fuel possible for the transportation of wounded men, munitions and troops.

The fuel supply office was in the Smolianka headquarters. The blizzard was getting worse as I arrived and snow covered everything, causing the contours of the landscape to vanish. There was just one sentry mounting guard in front of the little *Wehrmacht* office, wearing felt boots packed full of straw to keep out the cold. Smolianka was a mining suburb of Stalino, planned geometrically with an industrial zone separate from the residential area. In the east the bungalows were equally spaced according to their size. The Germans had given the buildings women's names and there was a sheltered wooden notice board that showed the codified addresses of the various offices of the general headquarters.

In no time I had found the commander's house. He was about to have dinner, and he invited me to join him. He had been assigned the largest house in the centre of the housing scheme, furnished with comfortable armchairs, tables and a library. It was a little oasis of Europe that stood out in contrast to the poverty of Russia. Many of the orderlies had trousers with a red stripe and oak leaves on their lapels denoting staff officers of various ranks, and classifying this as a command post of great importance. The calm atmosphere of conviviality almost distracted me from my difficult mission: to obtain a large amount of fuel from my host. Fortunately, perhaps thanks to the good dinner and excellent French wine, I obtained much more than the minimum requested by my headquarters. The captain kept repeating that they had very little fuel, that it was very scarce, very *knapp*, and what he allocated would have to last us as long as possible, because from then on it would be useless to return for more. This prospect led me to make one last bid for fuel.

'The end justifies the means,' I thought. Going over this in my mind, I decided to raid the *kolkhoz* of Korsiun, which had received a consignment of hundreds of barrels from the *Wirtschaft Kommando*. Its astute director, Schwarz, whom I knew very well, had cautiously anticipated the situation and had obtained a good stock of fuel for his tractors and motor engine depot. I would take all I could. To ask him for a part of his precious reserve would have been useless, even if I swore that the outcome of a battle depended upon it.

I took precautions and ordered everybody to keep quiet. Dressed in white uniforms, like the Germans, nobody could identify us. Once the Ukrainian sentries were immobilized and disarmed, we loaded as many barrels as we could into the trucks and before leaving I left a note in

German so that the sentry was not implicated, and so that Schwarz would believe the plundering had been his countrymen's work.

We were already on our way down a dirt track along the Don when the Ukrainian militiaman informed his superior of our nocturnal raid. I later learned that Schwarz was furious about the theft, but never discovered who the perpetrator was. Poor Schwarz, a real Bavarian farmer to the last, so removed from reality that he believed the High Command Group of Armies would take care of his request for a replacement of the stolen fuel, even when the Germans had so many more important affairs at stake.

Von Mackensen's army occupied the city of Gorlovka, which was seen as the capital of the Donets basin with about 20,000 inhabitants during the period of maximum activity in its very rich coal mines. Von Mackensen's troops were under the Southern Group of Armies commanded by Von Manstein, which the remaining units of our Eighth Army were supposed to join in order to rebuild units capable of supporting the counter-offensive. We tried in vain to obtain orders and instructions by radio. When we finally managed to establish contact, the only thing we heard clearly was: 'Jarkov, Jarkov! We're getting out of here! The Russian tanks are in the suburbs!'

The situation in Russia between December 1942 and March 1943 was absurd and devilish. The only thing that could be relied upon for survival was the individual capacity or autonomy of each unit to get by as well as humanly possible. The regiments arrived at the front line just in time to close the breach, before being obliged to remove the garrison from it once again in order to rescue others. Between Panteleimonovka and Gorlovka we came across an imposing concentration of German armoured vehicles. The road was bursting with cannon, anti-aircraft machine guns and mobile batteries, armoured cars and trucks full of troops. Through this enormous traffic jam came troops of Mongols – Cossacks from the Caucasus – who were just as well equipped as the Germans, trying to make their way through with sleighs full of impedimenta. They drove their horses on, making use of any spaces that opened in order to advance just a few yards further. Suddenly the traffic jam narrowed like pincers and the animals went crazy, getting nervous and out of hand, and their muscles tensed as they were brutally forced back. The sleigh's shafts hindered them, they overturned their loads and their drivers, bewilderedly knocking against the armoured vehicles... which meanwhile advanced relentlessly, inch by inch, grinding up the ice, deafeningly, amidst the clouds of smoke from their exhaust pipes. The cries, the curses and the insults grew above the mechanical roar, without reducing the bottleneck, while overhead flew some 'Storks', far from the cries of our torment.

This is how the German First Armoured Army proceeded in their retreat from the Caucasus, while Rostov, having been evacuated, burned to the ground. Between Gorlovka and Panteleimonovka, from Iasinovatoe to Malaievo and Shanchekovo, in the streets of Stalino and the roads that met from the Caucasus, the situation was just as tragic and apocalyptic.

This was the Stalino that in July of 1942 had been like a metropolis, with its great big posters advertising shows at the opera and the passing of chain-tracked vehicles with chains prohibited in the main street, flanked with the imposing buildings of the *Befehlstelle A*, of the *Wirtschaft Kommando*, of the *Don-Donec Kohle*, of Italy's and of Romania's air force and navy. Now it was off-white and grey, like the armoured cars and the caterpillar vehicles that drove up and down this same main street, now frozen over with ice. The signposts at intervals that prohibited these vehicles no longer made any sense. The offices of the grandiose Economy Building had been transferred to Dniepropetrovsk, many miles to the rear. The soldiers in colonial uniforms of months ago could no longer be seen and their brand new vehicles would probably be in full retreat from the Caucasus, marked by the impact of war, with their drivers and troops, no longer in pith helmets, but in steel helmets.

GEORGI'S
BLOOD-CURDLING
SCREAM

ASLIM, ALMOST TRANSPARENT, shy little lady, dressed in black and wearing a black headscarf, had been waiting for hours before stepping out in front of me, wielding a letter and begging me to read it.

The letter was from an Italian navy officer based in the Crimea who was a friend of mine. He wrote to ask me if I could possibly take care of this lady he had sent, because as a *Volksdeutsche* she had been persecuted during the Soviet regime.

I patiently listened to her story. The Bolsheviks had shot her husband and she had been driven out of their home with their only son. She had raised him on her own with great hardship and despite her efforts to bring him up well, he ran away from home to enlist in the *Wehrmacht* the moment the Germans invaded Russia. He wanted to fight against 'his father's assassins and the oppressors of his people'. From that day, Georgi's mother had lost all trace of her son and desperately hoped I could help her to find him.

I explained to her that with millions of soldiers on the Ukrainian front, finding him would be extremely difficult. However, I could sympathize with her distress, and assured her that we would try to help her. If her son had enlisted in the army deployed along the southern front, where Italian troops were also engaged, our chances of finding him would be higher.

One night, two *carabinieri* entered the hut that served as our temporary counter-espionage office, dragging a drunken, handcuffed Russian with them. The man they had arrested was *Starosta* Pashkov. Moments before he had been caught firing bullets at an Italian officer, although none of them had hit their mark.

If Pashkov had shot at the officer with his heavy *nagan*, he had certainly not intended to kill him. Nevertheless, dangerous drunks were of course a common problem, and the Russian drunks in particular. In any case, the affair was the responsibility of the *Schutzpolizei*, the German security police, so we took Pashkov to the Ukrainian Command of the Gendarmerie, a few yards down the road.

The sentinel on guard knocked on the door three or four times with his rifle butt and Pashkov started to sober up the minute he recognized the grey concrete walls of the Gendarmerie. Breaking off his drunken song, he started to writhe around like a man possessed, struggling to escape from his captors. Seeing that this was to no avail, he changed tactics and began to plead for forgiveness from the *carabiniere* who had brought him there. He was terrified of letting the German commander see him in this state. When his pleas got no results, he unleashed another desperate attempt at escape. Gathering all his strength, he rushed at one of the Ukrainian guards, sending him sprawling into the snow, only to be brought down himself with a sharp blow to the back of the neck from the other guard's rifle butt.

Meanwhile, the door had opened and another gendarme leaned out in his slippers and vest, to inform us that Lieutenant Scheung had gone to bed and we should wait inside for him.

Accompanied by a non-commissioned officer, Scheung's interpreter entered, introducing himself as Georgi. He was a pale, blonde teenager who cannot have been more than 16 or 17 years old. He wore the *Wehrmacht*'s uniform with obvious pride and the enormous pistol that hung from his belt stuck out like a sore thumb. He was the youngest policeman I had ever seen.

He asked us what Pashkov was accused of before proceeding with the interrogation, but the *starosta*, instead of answering, began humming to himself. Georgi, who was obviously not accustomed to being ridiculed, punched him in the chin and knocked him over. Pashkov crawled behind a table where a typewriter stood. The moment he tried to get up, the interpreter gave him such a brutal kick in the behind that he sent him like a battering ram against the door that led to the prison cells.

For Pashkov, this second blow of humiliation must have been insufferable. He turned over like a wounded beast and got up with the clear determination not to be kicked about any more... Seeing his intentions, Georgi swiftly retaliated, unsheathing his pistol and, clutching it by the barrel, he gave Pashkov another savage blow to the neck. On no account was the captive going down though... Finally, thanks to the intervention of the non-commissioned officer, they managed to subdue the drunk and sling him into a cell to sleep it off.

Just then, Lieutenant Scheung entered the office. The hallway door opened and out came Georgi and the non-commissioned officer, pleased to have taken care of the last duty in the day.

We looked at each other in astonishment, hardly believing what had passed. Where had that 17-year-old policeman managed to find such brute force? Georgi smoothed his blonde hair, adjusted his uniform and stood in a corner to await his orders, while Lieutenant Scheung apologized to us for having made us wait. Since the non-commissioned officer and the interpreter had sorted the matter out, he hoped that we were satisfied.

The lieutenant of the *carabinieri* went over the details of the incident, playing it down somewhat and pointing out that Pashkov was under the influence of alcohol, which should be taken into account when judging him. Lieutenant Scheung retorted that procedure dictated he be sent to court before the German police in Stalino. It could not be tolerated for a *starosta* and head of a district to fall into such an unseemly state of inebriation. A lesson must be taught in order to prevent such incidents from recurring. With Pashkov arrested it would of course mean one less head of district, but it would be a significant example for all. This is what counted. This was the iron law of the *Schutzpolizei*, and woe betide the man who contradicted it.

I could not get that incredible scene or the brutal acts of the interpreter out of my head. This young boy was none other than the missing son of the *Volksdeutsche* woman my friend in the Crimea had entrusted to me. From this moment onwards I would try to scrutinize the soul of that 'righteous' adolescent, in the attempt to justify, condemn or absolve him. Like so many others, he too was the victim of an era marked by violence.

Shortly after the episode it was Lieutenant Scheung himself who told me the whole story. He had picked up a wounded boy in the battlefield at Jarkov, saving his life by some miracle. As a member of an ethnic minority, Georgi had suffered such humiliation all his life that he was astonished to find people respected him merely because he wore that grey-green uniform of the *Wehrmacht* and spoke the language that had aroused such contempt in more than one Soviet commissar in the past.

He had enlisted as a volunteer and had been in several battles. He was completely bilingual in Russian and German, courageous, tough and motivated. In fact, he had all the right qualifications for a position that the lieutenant needed to fill, so Scheung took the opportunity to employ him as an interpreter in his section.

As a quirk of fate would have it, one day the lieutenant and his men were bound for exactly the same area in which Georgi and his mother had suffered the worst persecution, a chance that opened up a horizon of possibilities for revenge for the precocious young man. He was granted the role of jack-of-all-trades in the *Schutzpolizei*, and tirelessly schemed against the partisans.

Since he could speak both languages, documents of all kinds passed through his hands first, and whoever wished to speak to the *Kommandant* could only do so after having explained themselves to Georgi. If there were arrests or searches to be made, dangerous people to eliminate or put out of action, Georgi was always the first to know about it. The young lad spoke with the tone of voice of someone who was used to giving sharp orders, orders that must be carried out without fail.

This was how Lieutenant Scheung described him to me, and as time passed I began to see this for myself. The area under his commissariat's jurisdiction included a large strip of land where our Eighth Army was located, immediately behind the front line. Therefore, during that summer of 1942 I had plenty of occasions to see him in action.

One day I came upon him with some Ukrainian policemen near the ruins of a factory, carrying out a macabre operation, and on seeing me he called me over to watch. His militiamen had dug a big ditch for the burial of a dozen or so civilian corpses that were lying there in a sprawling mess. They had only just been shot, and it was not difficult to guess who was responsible.

I made an instinctive gesture of disgust, and as I stared at him inquisitively he became nervous. How, I asked myself, could that 16-year-old boy have the authority – or the guts – to cut short the lives of so many human beings?

The Ukrainian Militia continued their grave-digging activity with alacrity, throwing spadeful after spadeful of earth into the ditch. Georgi, who expected my approval, felt instead the condemnation of my silence. To get out of his embarrassment, he exclaimed defensively:

'They were Communists and Jews, Lieutenant. They don't even deserve respect in death. They did so much damage when alive that it is even too good for them to die like this, don't you think?'

Georgi's eyes, those bright blue eyes, shone with a ferocious childish delight. They were asking for my approval like those of a child who is being scolded for an innocent prank.

Yes, he *had* just thrown his 'toys', terribly new and alive, into the rubbish bin, after having pulled them apart to find out how they worked, letting the springs pop out. Those toys were not good enough for him. From dusk until dawn he spent the day playing around with the young and the old, with adults and people of his own age, moving them around like puppets on strings, making them cry, laugh, rejoice and die. Who was going to curb this cruel behaviour? Certainly not his mother, thrilled as she was with her son's new influential position in the very same town where the Communists had scorned them. For her it was natural and more than justifiable that her son should take all the revenge he could: the essential nemesis with no exceptions made. Now, when fate had given her back her Georgi, the fact that her son should also be given the chance to take his revenge in the same place that his father had been executed was like a sign from God. She was too proud to notice that her son was digging his own grave. One day, just as in tales of old, the time came when poisonous fire rained down from heaven onto his roof.

Not long afterwards, a band of partisan commandos occupied Schebionka station. No time could be wasted in regrouping all available men to liberate it. Lieutenant Scheung called me. He wanted us to help him with soldiers and weapons if possible, as he did not entirely trust his own militiamen.

Soon the trucks were loading the troops on board and the detachment headed off towards Schebionka with the interpreter Georgi acting as guide to the expedition. The boy knew the area well and he offered to lead us in order to lower the risk of our being discovered. We advanced stealthily along incredibly rough tracks for almost two hours. Then we left our trucks hidden in a hollow, where we split up into small groups in order to surprise the enemy.

Schebionka was a small station like so many others in Russia. Its street lamps were now coming into view, but we heard no suspicious noises and saw no sign of anything strange to trouble the still of night. Dawn was about to break, and our approach would be more dangerous in the daylight.

We managed to reach the station in dead silence, without arousing any reaction. This was strange. Surely the partisans were not sound asleep. They would have been expecting our arrival and would have taken the necessary precautions. Were they laying a trap for us? Or had they already left? In the locomotive depot, the 'taff-poom' of a steam engine's piston could be clearly heard. This was the only sign of 'life' apart from our own breathing and the dim signal lights over the tracks. We advanced cautiously under the frozen star-lit sky, immersed in a still calm, an atmosphere which gave us the sinking feeling that something sinister was in the making.

This is how it came to pass. As soon as we entered the building, we ran headlong into four dead German railwaymen who had been shot at their posts. The partisans must have attacked so suddenly that the poor devils did not even have the chance to react. A few bursts of machine gun fire at point-blank range had nailed them to the spot. The only other traces of the incursion were a few hammer blows they had paid to the telegraph and telephone equipment, smashing it to smithereens. The wide open doors let the relentless cold night air flood in. The bodies of the four victims sat petrified at their posts in the positions they had been in when they were surprised by death.

In the light of our hand-held lamps the decor took on sinister and unforgettable forms, just as unforgettable as the sudden, blood-curdling scream that Georgi let out as he was stabbed through the heart while inspecting the adjacent rooms.

He was the only victim of our expedition that night, and he died without uttering a single word. Life abandoned his body as if in all haste to depart. He mysteriously fell down dead in the darkness, and the hand that had driven that dagger through his back and into his heart had abandoned its grip even before the death cry issued from the boy's mouth. It happened as quick as lightning. Were the bandits playing a dirty trick on us, drawing us all into a trap with his scream in order to kill us all at once?

This was not the case. Dawn broke, the shadows dissipated and Schebionka stood for a moment enveloped in silence. Then the town slowly began to wake up, unaware of the events that had passed that night in the station. A pale ray of sunshine broke through the whitish-grey cloud cover and lit up Georgi's face as he lay on the improvised stretcher that we had made for him out of rifles. Now that he was dead, he no longer had that scowling, ferocious temper, that icy stare, that cruel sneer on his lips. Now his face was as nature had made it - a young lad still in his adolescence.

As we put him into the back of one of the trucks, nobody shed a tear.

This led me to suspect that the perpetrator had not been a partisan after all, but one of his own militiamen. We left Schebionka as soon as some soldiers had arrived to man the station and search the area, and the technicians had begun to repair the damage and re-establish communications.

Since there was no military cemetery, we buried Georgi under an enormous acacia tree. His mother had to make do with a cross and a German helmet placed on the mound of black earth, with the following inscription above it: *Georgi, born 1926, died 1942 for his German Fatherland.* Her son was dead and she was alone in the world, but she wanted a tomb for him in the Italian military cemetery, a few miles from the city... Too many people sat in the shade of that acacia tree in summer, and the bones of her son would never rest in peace with so many Russians around. Her request was respected and Georgi came to rest amongst our own soldiers' crosses.

With the advance towards the Don, Lieutenant Scheung and his men were transferred in the direction of Stalingrad. Two winters and two springs had already passed. A long troop train was taking the survivors of the great battle back to Italy. With us came two Ukrainian boys who had lived with the troops for many months. They were alert, helpful and as affectionate as puppies. They had nobody left in Russia and wanted to start a new life in Italy.

We did not have far to go when a violent allied air raid on the Messerschmitt aeroplane factory in Wienerncustadt caused us to lose one of them. He had wandered away from the train during a stop and had not managed to get back to us in time. He ran with all his might, desperate to reach the train, but the locomotive was picking up speed and we were powerless to stop it, as he struggled to reach us before coming to a halt and waving goodbye. It was like an imploring gesture of appeal, a melancholy farewell to a new life so foolishly thwarted at the beginning of a great adventure. We wanted to pull some kind of alarm to stop the convoy, but we were seated on a flatcar and it was impossible.

His friend in the train was sobbing because now he was more alone than ever.

The train let out a long high-pitched whistle that was quickly muffled as it entered a tunnel. It was like hearing that last scream let out by Georgi upon his death in Schebionka station.

In a melancholy association of ideas I hoped that the young lad lost in

Wienerneustadt would find the strength to hook up with a transit heading in the opposite direction, to return him to Russia where, although just as alone and defenceless, he would have a future in the immense spiritual heritage of the land that had given him life.

If Georgi had also stayed in his father's homeland, perhaps he would not have regained his childish features only when a dagger had cut off his life, restoring the purity of his youth. That last desperate scream would have had a different echo and his life would not have been in such haste to abandon his body.

WHO IS THIS
MOTORWAY FOR?

T HE AMOUNT OF HEAVY military traffic we
came across told us that we were approaching Dniepropetrovsk. The
road was wide but jam-packed with vehicles. Numerous tanks heading
in the opposite direction further complicated matters. Since the battle
of the winter of 1942, the Führer's headquarters had been in
Zaporozhie, at the entrance to Dniepropetrovsk, and Field Marshal
Von Manstein had set up his command post there. The impressive
organization of rearguard operations, almost all of which were situated
on the banks of the Dnieper, showed the strategic importance of the
southern sector of the front. At the entrance to Pavlograd there was an
amazing number of machine workshops for the vehicles of the
Wehrmacht and its allies. Big white signs meticulously listed the different specialities of the repair workshops so that there was no confusion
as to where to go for such and such a vehicle. The initials H.K.F. of the
Heereskraftfahrzeugen, or the Army vehicle depot, were predominant.
The foresight with which this enormous complex was organized really
was admirable. The parking lots were paved with cement, the barriers
painted black and white and the prefabricated houses made of wood
for the personnel in transit all betrayed the supervision of a planner
with the conviction that he had to create something solid, built to last.

On this sunny morning in April, we had the feeling that we were not
in a conquered land, but in a country where we could settle down for
good. Amongst the many German and allied soldiers that populated the
numerous roads, the few civilians and uniformed locals that crossed the
main road were hardly discernible.

There stood Pavlograd, punished by so many battles, but with its
enormous church and gold dome still miraculously intact. Our column
managed to make its way through the traffic jam and finally head
towards the great river. In contrast to the plethora of workshops that we
had left behind, here the *hatas* were so clean and newly whitewashed

that they looked as though they had just popped out of the oven. Whole families were busy doing up the houses, as they always did each spring according to an old Russian tradition, as if the war were not in progress.

All over the place, dominating everything, were the gigantic road-works for the Berlin–Stalino motorway which cut across the steppe on an elevated embankment. Thousands of people, mostly women and teenagers, worked non-stop on the grandiose construction that would soon allow rapid and smooth travel between the opulent lands of the Donets basin and the main centres in Germany.

With the great winter battle fresh in our memories, a battle that had seriously jeopardized the summer operations, what meaning could this mammoth construction have, a seemingly impossible undertaking, stretching from the Dnieper to the Donets and hoping to go as far as the Rhine? What were those established directors of the Todt organization thinking, lost amongst so many Russian workers apparently at the service of the supreme interests of 'Great Germany'? Perhaps an unbreakable faith prevented them from seeing that in the near future the construction would be advantageous only for the Russians. This unending 'bridge' over the steppe was like a surreal vision, a mirage. The grizzled and weather-beaten faces of the men from the Todt organization, having suffered the rigours of the Russian winter, seemed completely out of touch with reality.

After Stalingrad, with decisive help from America, the Russians regained their efficiency and advantage over the *Wehrmacht*. The illusions of the Soviet Army's downfall, however deep-rooted in the German consciousness, were all collapsing. Many Germans started to ask themselves if they should renounce such superfluous commitments as this gigantic motorway, and construct and work with the sole objective of the war in mind, not for a post-war future of a Germany in conquered Russia.

Shortly afterward, the men in yellow uniforms with the swastika armbands and the initials 'O.T.' were transferred from the enormous motorway to create new impregnable bastions to block the path of the growing number of Russian armoured vehicles. However, even these would be inadequate in the end and were of no use.

RANCID BUTTER
AND BITTER HONEY

WHOEVER TRAVELLED along the dirt track that leads from Mijerovo and Kantemirovka to the Don in August of 1942 would never have imagined that there, in those little houses crouched in the steppe, lived men in uniform, the *Sonderführers*, entirely absorbed in their own activities that had little to do with any war operations. Even so, only a few hundred yards from there, the incessant daily traffic of German military vehicles passed by in a cloud of black dust. Theo Nabe snorted like a bull each time a dirty, tattered soldier left the dirt track and ventured into his 'realm' in search of butter, milk and honey. His firm reply, calculated to dissuade them, was always the same:

'I hope you realize that it is all reserved for the hospitals, the wounded and the service corps.'

And he said it so flatly that the poor fellows clicked their heels and left in resignation and embarrassment, but never without saluting him with due respect for hierarchy, in spite of the fact that Theo Nabe was only a simple *Sonderführer*, who had never fought in a war, or at least not in this one. If they had seen him months later, when the waters of the Don had become increasingly treacherous, they would not have said goodbye with such respect, and might even have struck the table with their fists, pointed a bayonet into the belly of this hypocrite and demanded that he release the provisions that they requested.

The wooden arrow nailed to a telegraph pole, slightly faded from the sun and rain, read in washed-out letters: *Landwirtschaft Abteilung*. It was so small that one had to look carefully to see it. The track sloped gently downwards and the cluster of white and blue houses was hidden away in a hollow. However, Yekaterinovka seemed to be submerged in a peaceful, rural atmosphere.

I entered a sort of office crowded with tables and typewriters. 'I'd like to introduce you to Mr Nabe, Mr Frolidor, Mr Bender; ah, and Mr Tamburin.'

These were the men in charge of Yekaterinovka.

Hens and ducks scratched at the earth, a dog barked out of pure habit and Theo Nabe's splendid German Shepherd wagged his tail as if we had been best friends all our lives. Two brown cows yoked to a cart brushed off the flies with their tails.

From the kitchen, the plump Frau Hofer beckoned me to come in, speaking her own form of German with unmistakable Russian origins. What with a glass of spirits and a cigarette, the time passed quickly, the sun set, and another day had come to an end. There were seven of us at dinner, and Mr Nabe insisted that I sit at his side. The other three *Sonderführer* made themselves at home along with the two interpreters Anya and Galina. They served us *borshch*, a delicious beetroot soup, with the best white bread, followed by roast beef and mashed potatoes, a tomato and cucumber salad and a dessert of puff pastry with almond paste. The fresh apples had been brought from a remote area by a commission agent who travelled between the fertile Dnieper basin and the wildest parts of the Don, exclusively for the *Sonderführer*, of course. For their own supplies, the agricultural *Sonderführe*s had unlimited access to the local resources, and they could not complain.

They pestered me with questions: what was my job in Italy, where was I from and what did I think of this damned awful world? After who knows how many cups of hot liquid that just about passed for coffee, we retired to our rooms. I had to digest that meal, and as I was not used to such large feasts, I needed some peace and quiet. Anya's and Galina's rooms were opposite mine. They were wonderful girls, quiet and hardworking, but not very satisfied with their life and less so with the way that they were spending their youth. Before saying goodnight, Nabe wanted to show me the house. He no doubt wished to receive my compliments for his organization of the place, as he was the boss, and his other co-workers hardly counted. Everything is so well engraved in my memory that, when Anya told me her story weeks later, after having fled from Yekaterinovka, I could imagine the events vividly, those underhand dealings that went on in that collective farm in the steppe.

During the dinner, Nabe had asked me for some red wine, in exchange for a shipment of butter for an Italian service corps' field hospital. However, Nabe advised me not to tell anyone about it. It was a personal enterprise, and if the *Landwirtschaft Führer* came to hear of it he would be in trouble.

At the time I was obliged to spend some time in the area in service, and was therefore able to make frequent visits to Nabe's farm. The enormous German shepherd had become so accustomed to me that instead of barking as she did with everyone else, she wagged her tail on seeing me, and made a great fuss of me. Anya and Galina welcomed me with open arms simply because I was Italian, and Frau Hofer learned how to cook very tasty *tagliatelle* to which she dedicated hours of preparation. Everything gave the impression that this 'set-up' would last for ever, and they constantly spoke to me of phenomenal projects with boundless prospects for the future.

However, the same parade of military vehicles continued along the Don trail in the same cloud of black dust, supplying the big units on the front that, at one moment or another (nobody knew when, but no doubt before the winter), would have to move to the Volga. The four *Sonderführer* were convinced of it and their faith led them to work incessantly in order to gain the maximum yield from the land and increase the reserves that the Reich was building up for the improbable eventuality of a few years of dearth.

One October day, Theo Nabe came to see me at my command post. He was going on leave to Germany, accompanied by his friend Bender, a nice young lad, a wonderful *Sonderführer* full of brilliant initiatives, and with an open mind very different from Theo's. The car, loaded up with boxes, bags and packets, looked as if it might break the suspension.

'We are off to Germany,' said Nabe, his eyes alight with joy. 'If we are lucky we will find a place on a service aeroplane and tomorrow we will be in Berlin, not far from home. We'll be back in three weeks. I have left Mr Frolidor in charge of Yekaterinovka, and he will go on leave when I return.'

They were more than satisfied with the two carafes of Italian wine that I gave them. Seeing them leave so fired up with enthusiasm, I wondered what they might have hidden in all those boxes.

The twenty-one days passed, and in the blink of an eye, Nabe was back at his post like clockwork, once again looking through the windows with melancholic eyes at the dust that marked out the route to the front.

The first rain made the track more compacted and the dust cloud less dense than during the summer. Nabe rambled on, telling himself that before he got the next leave permit, he would see the snow, the thaw leaving the military vehicles stuck in the mud, the first flowers bud in the steppe, the wheat grow high and the graceful sunflowers ready for harvest. And only then, perhaps, would another 'twenty-one

days of leave' come around. Since his recent return from his homeland, his *Heimat*, he had begun to feel spiritually removed from this
Russia in which he was alone, a foreigner in a faraway land. He was
overcome by a deep depression, and the twelve months of waiting felt
longer than ever to him.

Bender, on the other hand, did not feel nostalgia for Germany. He
had returned enthusiastically to his Marianovka, his steppe, together
with his *muzhiks* who reeked of sunflower seeds, goats and clandestine
tobacco. But he was much younger and he also had a little blonde girlfriend who made him forget his wife. This happiness of Bender's, in
that country so vast and foreign, became an obsession for Nabe over
which he began to lose sleep. It even burdened him when in his little
office, with the coming and going of *muzhiks* and more or less important *starostas*, who were also the characters in a drama in which he was
finally realizing that he was a performer.

It is said that 'opportunity makes the thief', and one night, when his
three colleagues had to spend the night in the village, a unique opportunity presented itself to Nabe. He had brought a bottle of *Steinjäeger* back
from Germany and he had no less than the idea of sharing it with Anya.
He invited her to his room, offered her a seat on the bed and a cigarette.
Incredible, but true: this sullen *Sonderführer* was presenting his interpreter with a cigarette. Anya showed her surprise at such courteous
behaviour; how much the 'grandad' (as she and Galina called him) had
changed! After the cigarette and the first drink, he poured her another,
and this continued until Anya's head was spinning and she refused to
drink any more. Nabe, on the other hand, continued to drink until his
vision was blurred and his tongue and hands began to get out of control.

That night they were alone in the house. When Anya started to leave,
Nabe, as red as a beetroot, suddenly grabbed her arm and cried, 'Where
are you going, my pretty!'

She tried to break loose from him and he, without letting her go,
insisted with feverish desire, 'Now that you have drunk, you have to celebrate with me.'

Anya was a strong girl. As soon as the impertinent old man let go
slightly, she broke loose, shut the door in his face, and ran to close herself in her room.

'You don't know what you're doing, my pretty. Think about it. You
don't know what life's about. Let me in and you'll see how everything
will change for you,' begged the 'grandad' from the corridor.

The cockerel's crow startled Anya as she lay awake in her bed and woke up the snoring Nabe in his room as he lay sleeping off his hangover.

Days later there was a party, and everybody drank a lot. Frolidor had managed to distil some vodka and he poured it freely, with the inevitable consequences. Nabe, who since the night of the *Steinjäeger* had suffered the torment of his love for Anya and her complete indifference to him, became consumed by his obsession with Bender's situation, with his far away home, with growing old in this vast land and in the happiness that he, like Bender, would have attained had Anya shared his feelings.

The consequences of the night's drunkenness were particularly serious this time. Anya and Galina went to bed early and the others went back to their rooms more or less inebriated. However, this time it was Tamburin who was looking for an opportunity, prepared to do anything for it. Two glazed doors closed off the corridor of Anya's room. Unable to open them, he decided to batter them down. He shattered the first door, and cut his hands on the glass. The second he dealt with by giving it an immense push. Faced with that wild beast, Anya could do nothing but escape through the window, and was lucky that the house only had one floor.

None of Tamburin's colleagues heard the racket that he made. The vodka had anaesthetized them. However, in the morning, things changed. Tamburin did not know how to explain his bandaged hand, and Theo Nabe understood from the broken glass what he had not wanted to see before then: the passion of his rival, Tamburin.

The incident was considered as closed, and the four *Sonderführer* would have continued with their routine, but something was constantly nagging at them, and they could not continue as if nothing had happened. Consumed by love, Nabe hated Tamburin, who was sick with the same desires. He also envied Bender for his seeming happiness with Galina, while she was infatuated with Tamburin.

No more black dust clouded the air and here and there military vehicles could be seen stuck in the mud. Since the first snowfall in November, the columns of trucks, camouflaged in white, had continued along the track. Nabe, more melancholic than ever, suffered his tormented solitude before the smiling face of Bender, happy to have returned to Russia. Anya was a stupid little girl who knew nothing of life. Galina was too much in love with other men, but with how many of them?

Nabe decided to find a girlfriend amongst the Russian personnel in his *kolkhoz*, and finally he was happy. Her name was Victoria. He called her Fräulein Victoria, but it was common knowledge that if he was not in his room at night it was because he was with his 'Vitti'. Vitti soon became the little queen of the farm at Yekaterinovka, personal secretary and interpreter to the *Kreislandwirtschaft Führer*. Nabe had to look after her very large family and he had no choice but to turn a blind eye, or rather, to oblige all of the *kolkhoz* storekeepers to do so, because Victoria pilfered such quantities of flour and honey, butter and potatoes, that it was impossible to pass it off as the amount needed for just one family.

This was the state of affairs when Anya left Yekaterinovka, unable to continue living in this oppressive atmosphere. Tamburin did not stop pestering her, and if they were left alone in the place, Anya had no choice but to run away. A little scandal put an end to the situation.

Nabe was also in charge of two tanneries. The biggest and best equipped was managed by a man named Grisha. All of the skins from the livestock in his area were given to the two establishments to be tanned and the leather was intended for the army, as it was confiscated material. For some time, the markets in the *raion*, the province, seemed to be surprisingly well supplied with leather shoes and boots, which were expensive but of good quality. There was above all a certain model of women's shoes that sold very well. For a while the traffic went unnoticed, but one day checks were made, the merchandise confiscated and the source was investigated.

Nabe was in trouble. The clandestine shoe factory had been supplied by Grisha's tannery, and the go-between had been a certain Victoria Kasakova, secretary and interpreter in the Yekaterinovka farming district. Nabe's involvement in the fraud was extremely likely, even though they could show that he was completely crazy about this woman. In the end, his connivance could not be proven. The only consequence that he suffered from this was his transferral to the north, to less fertile lands, where the *Sonderführer* lived in fear of their lives because of the partisans.

The change affected the other *Sonderführer* who were also transferred. The only one who stayed was Frolidor, the most reserved, the most serious and the most proud of the land. Anya, from whom I heard the story, ended up going in search of some distant relatives, between the Dnieper and the Bug.

It was a grey morning in December when I returned to Yekaterinovka.

I found Frolidor, who had replaced Nabe, sitting in his office with his head in his hands, downcast. He was managing the area alone since the promised replacements had still not arrived, and they probably never would. I asked him for honey and butter and he allotted me 200 pounds of each. He was so apathetic that I could have asked him for as much as I liked and he probably would have given it to me. He assured me that he would stay at his post until the end in the hope that not all would be lost. Most of his subordinates had deserted when the Russians broke through the Don front. Imperturbable to the last, the only German left amongst hundreds of Russians with doubtful loyalty, without really being a soldier nor having experienced battle, Frolidor showed integrity with the dignity of a soldier.

Two hundred pounds of butter and 200 of honey. One of my men, who had just loaded the precious cargo into the truck, summed up the general feeling:

'This is the end, Lieutenant.'

The transit of men and vehicles along the track was interminable. Everyone was retreating and behind them came the clamour of war, like the beating of a drum that announced Russia's revenge. Yekaterinovka was crouched in a hollow and the rolling steppe seemed like a sea about to engulf it.

Some German artillery sections aimed their weapons at Yekaterinovka, backed up a few yards, and flicked a switch and six incendiary rockets landed on that oasis of peace. There were a number of explosions in succession, and great towers of flames rose into the sky. The sappers continued on their course as if it were nothing, on their way to look for the next target to destroy. Yekaterinovka burned. However, on the track along which we fled from the Russians, the dust would return in the summer, as if everything had happened in the blink of an eye.

Never had butter tasted so rancid nor honey so bitter to me as on that retreat.

THE RUINS
OF STEPANOVKA

IN CHILDREN'S FAIRYTALES, there are fairies with magic wands, forests of trees that speak and everything has a soul and tales to tell. I once came across the walls of a real house that had a tale to tell.

Galina was crouching down in a field collecting herbs. She was so delicate about it that you would have thought she was afraid to harm them. In her left hand she held a little bunch of herbs that grew stem by stem. From a distance, it looked to me as if she were picking flowers, as the spring was exuberant and colours bloomed everywhere.

Galina had a blonde plait and blue eyes that showed infinite sadness. My companion greeted her in Russian and asked our location in a brusque manner. However, she was unperturbed, kneeling in silence on the grass, and she just looked up. Then, perhaps believing herself a little discourteous, she brought the bunch of herbs close to her mouth and said: '*Nuzhno kusat*,' (they are for eating).

She was so pale… She picked those herbs so carefully because they represented a large part of her diet, if not all of it. The dearth was horrendous. In their retreat, the Bolsheviks had destroyed everything. With traditional Russian hospitality, Galina invited us to her house, a red-brick bungalow in the shade of some ancient trees. In the corridor, amongst the damaged icons of saints and prints of tractors and other farm machinery, there was an old photograph that stood out, in perfect condition, picturing a group of equestrians. I looked at it with curiosity and I thought I could see the palace of Stepanovka in the background. I looked at it in the light of the window: I was not mistaken. The tops of the trees covered part of the facade, but there was no doubt about it: the photograph had been taken right there, and my imagination began to drift back many years to a hypothetical past.

The group is preparing for a gallop. They are whipping the horses, trotting beneath the bare branches, the horses' hoofs rustling the autumn leaves and the water from the puddles splashing their boots and the bellies of their mounts. They have ridden far away, but the sound of galloping can still be heard as they lose themselves in the steppe's dry and fading sunflowers.

Stepanovka was still awaiting the return of the cavalcade. Many years had passed, thirty perhaps, and all that was left of the Kosonov's fief since the violence of the revolution were those huge, solid walls. The war had finished too, and Stepanovka had stood the toughest test; it no longer feared anything.

Galina was the daughter of a Kosonov. Her mother, a quiet and digni-fied lady who strove to make us something to eat with what we could offer her, was one of the horsewomen in the photograph. Galina pointed her out to me with the little finger of her slim, white, transpar-ent hand. She was the elegant lady with the magnificent steed. Her father was at the other end, on the right of the picture. The others in the group were friends, guests and landowners.

Mrs Kosonova saw us looking at the old photograph and she came up to us shyly, ashamed of her modest clothes and the state of her house, hiding her raw hands, hardened from work, under her white apron that protected her worn velvet dress. She looked at us, smiling because the photograph was of interest to me and because I was asking her daughter about Stepanovka. She was proud that we could see her as she was before, when she lived not in a *kolkhoz* but in a house of the Kosonov's fief.

'After the First World War,' said Mrs Kosonova, 'the revolution broke out. They killed my husband but a commissar stopped them from burn-ing Stepanovka down. It had such thick walls and such big rooms that it could be very useful. They threw me out, but I didn't go very far. I moved all that I could here, over the stables and waited for Galina to be born. I looked after her and educated her myself, at the cost of great sacrifice. I made sure she studied, and we were only separated when she joined the faculty of medicine in Jarkov. She studied for two years with real dedication, until the war brought her back to me.'

At that point, Galina took my hand and led me to her room. On a small table stood some books on medicine. She spoke to her mother as she flicked through the pages of these crude books that nevertheless were full of photographs, and seemed to be an attempt at popularizing science, only costing a few roubles: the fruit of a Russia aimed towards mass production. Galina showed me the anatomical torso that she used

125

to study with: a half mannequin, badly made from papier mâché in colours that were slightly off mark.

Time was pressing, and the dusty track awaited us. A hot, suffocating wind lifted clouds of earth. Those of the sky looked like the vast sails of invisible ships, all heading along the same course: they came from the east where their whiteness was diluted, then sullied as they met the horizon of dust that tainted them red, obscuring the line of the track even further.

I took a last glance at Stepanovka and the memory of those equestrians prepared for the cavalcade. Apart from Galina and her mother, who lived over the stables, nobody lived in the Kosonov's old fief. Fragments of glass sometimes still fell from the palace windows when the wind cut through the abandoned rooms and rattled the loose frames, some of which hung out threateningly. Mould invaded everything: the hall, scattered with rubble, and the wide staircases that led to the first floor, covered with the excrement left by the Russians in their retreat in order to offend the occupying forces, forming a barrier that was hard to cross. However, on the outside, Stepanovka retained its former majesty. Before the vastness of the steppe, it was like a green island of huge gardens, flaunting its social class and perpetuating something of its history.

The car started up with a jolt. Behind us was the *kolkhoz* of Stepanovka, with its long line of tractors like iron corpses, their broken chains and their dismantled motors partially covered by a reddish cloak of rust. Galina and her mother remained among these ruins, the last witnesses to an era that had ended.

The war would return to Stepanovka but not the equestrians. Its roar filled the steppe and made the ancient trees tremble and the rusted carcasses of the tractors shake. But that bygone world was not resuscitated and Mrs. Kosonova never put away her white apron or her worn velvet dress.

AFTER STALINGRAD,
CHAOS

A ROMANIAN non-commissioned officer headed a detachment, apparently made up of disbanded soldiers, who were dissuaded from any attempt to escape by the escort's rifles. On that cold February morning of 1943, the escorts and the troops were dressed in the same khaki uniform as the Romanian Army, and wore fur hats that only just revealed their eyes, tortured by frozen tears that turned to minuscule stalactites on their lashes. Poking from between their limp walrus-like moustaches were acrid-smelling cigars and cigarettes made from dried leaves and newspaper.

'*Fahnenfluchtige!*' (deserters), shouted Major Ruben tersely, looking at me fixedly as if to underline the gravity of the word. '*Fahnenfluchtige,*' he repeated, turning his opulent torso in the car in order to follow them with his gaze, as the sad procession faded into the distance.

I would have liked to refute this, but I held myself back because we had arrived at our destination. In the little village it was very busy: Romanian, Italian, Hungarian and German soldiers were walking up and down the one main street that cut the village almost exactly in half.

'We have arrived,' said the major, inviting me to get out of the freezing metal cage that was his car. '*Ortskommandantur*' ('Area Command'), read a well-planed wooden board, painted yellow and black in the typically polished German fashion of sign posting. After introducing me to his co-workers and showing me the command post, in a room full of maps Ruben showed me the route that I had to follow in order to get to another village near the Black Sea, according to orders that I had been given. Just as I was about to take leave, a Ukrainian militiaman entered announcing to the major, who was the garrison commander, that a Romanian non-commissioned officer, a certain Michele Lubescu needed to speak to him urgently. He was passing through with some survivors from Stalingrad and was requesting supplies.

They showed the non-commissioned officer in. He was under 30, his eyes an intense black, as was his hair, his forehead was wide and he wore a frank, pleasant expression. It was quite strange that, despite the long march, his uniform was in a good state, but this, on the other hand, made the major more inclined to help him.

He could make himself understood in German and knew how to present the problem. He requested a hot meal for his men and enough provisions to get to Mariupol, the detachment's destination. General Antonescu had ordered the reorganization of the disbanded Romanian Army, which had been obliterated on the Don by the Soviet units, along with the Italian Eighth Army, the Hungarians and the Germans. As soon as I left the building, I saw the detachment of disbanded soldiers and could see the kind of men that this young officer had to lead to the regrouping centre. It was not a task to be envied. The villagers must have been used to seeing this kind of spectacle, because they walked by without even looking at them, contrary to the German soldiers who spared no effort to mock them, laughing and making comments such as '*Fahnenfluchtige!*'

The weeks passed and I was already 60 miles from that village, on the coast of the Black Sea, when Michele Lubescu turned up unexpectedly at our command post. He was asking for a hot meal and provisions for 70 disbanded soldiers from the First Romanian Army whom he had picked up wandering in the steppe where they had survived on what they could find or steal. He had learned some Italian and he showed me a document with the letterhead of the Romanian Army. It outlined precise and detailed orders for the recovery of the disbanded soldiers. I asked him where the men that we had to feed were, and he hastened to show me another document listing 70 names.

We had no extra supplies and were obliged to save what we could. I asked him where these men were, and he told me that only a few of them had come with him, and the majority of them were in the station with the munitions convoy that they were escorting to the regrouping centre. Satisfied by his answer and unable to verify his story, I gave orders for the supplies that he had asked for to be taken to him.

On another occasion, Lubescu appeared with another Romanian, but since the provisioning had been passed to the German authority, I did not have to take care of his request and he left again with his contingent of disbanded soldiers.

However, one day, a Cossack officer named Georgi Fiodorovich, who

The author with his '*Parabellum*'

One of the many windmills used for flour in the Ukraine

BELOW
The author with the chief of staff of the First (Armoured) Army and other German officers

Two scenes from
Rikovo theatre.
Maestro Zeiss
from behind and
Katia close up.

Mr Schwarz, *Sonderführer* and *Kreislandwirt schafter* – director of several *kolkhoze*s in the Ukraine

BELOW The author with Valentina – see 'Madame Antonina's "Headquarters"'

The author between
two *Sonderführer*

BELOW The author in
a two-horse open sleigh

Urgent transportation of supplies to the Don front,
by a column of emergency Fiat trucks under the author's command

Engineers Weimann and Ploke inspect the Soviet sabotage of some railway lines

A *muzhik* like those of 'Katiusha's Well'

The Ravenna division on the move

ABOVE Displacement of workers in Briest-Litovsk

OPPOSITE TOP German soldiers in a street scuffle in a Ukrainian town

OPPOSITE BOTTOM Russian prisoners waiting to be counted. See 'The obsession'

RIGHT Nina the interpreter with the author, taking a break in the sunshine

Colonnello S.M. F. Kraemer - Pz.A.O.K.1

OBERST i.G. F. Kraemer - Pz.A.O.K.1

Staff Colonel F. Kraemer of the First German (Armoured) Army.
See 'Preparing for "Operation Citadel"'

DUE GENERAZIONI E DUE POPOLI.

Two generations, two nations

OPPOSITE TOP The Italian soldiers'
melancholic return to the west after
the Don front was broken

ABOVE Rikovo's steelworks

OPPOSITE BOTTOM Women working for
the Todt organization in the construction
of the Berlin–Dniepropetrovsk motorway

Re-provisioning with civilians and horses on the Donets front

Soviet soldiers give themselves up in a field of sunflowers

was working for us, grew suspicious of him and had him arrested. I found out about this by chance from a captain in the German secret police.

The chief of police who took Sergeant Lubescu and his companion into custody handed them over to the Central Commissariat in Gorlovka. The investigations and interrogations revealed that Michele Lubescu had disappeared from the ranks a year beforehand and nobody knew whether he was dead or had deserted his regiment of sappers from the Romanian First Army. Distinguished for his courage when faced with the enemy on the front, he had participated in the capture of Odessa, a glorious chapter for the Romanians. During a short stay in a small village in the rearguard he met a girl and fell head over heels in love with her. He then failed to turn up to resume the march with his regiment. So many disappeared, either from receiving a gut full of '*katiusha*' fire, or from mines and bombings. They took him for lost and that was the end of that. However, he could not live without doing something, so Lubescu opted for what seemed to him under those circumstances to be the most simple and profitable idea: to pose as a sergeant and pretend that he was the commanding officer of a lost garrison from the Don. Of course, for his plan he needed the complicity of some survivors. Alone he would have aroused suspicion, but a modest contingent of soldiers would give the appearance of authenticity to a dramatic pseudo-retreat from Stalingrad. There were four nationalities amongst the troops on the Don front – Germans, Romanians, Italians and Hungarians – and therefore, the communications in four languages made co-ordination by telephone or radio practically impossible. At the time, tens of thousands of soldiers from the four forces of the Axis were travelling along the dirt tracks of the Don. Thousands died of the cold or from bombings, or by falling victim to the Russian armoured vehicles that pursued them. In order to survive, fugitives killed horses and all kinds of livestock, and stole what they could from the *kolkhozes* that had been destroyed by the fighting.

It was under these circumstances that Michele Lubescu began his subterfuge with his small detachment. With the winter campaign and the consequent destruction of the Romanian Army, the chaotic conditions were ideal for his operation: the disbanded Romanian soldiers, exhausted by the hard battles in which they were always defeated due to lack of adequate weapons and troops, had no choice but to steal and ransack in order to survive. Michele Lubescu travelled between the cities along the southern front, collecting the remains of Romanian units amongst the confusion. Instead of asking for supplies for the numbers that he had, he asked for more than he needed, hoarding great quantities of food and selling them on the black market, thus earning thousands of roubles.

The agricultural *Sonderführer* did not know how to cope with that chaos, and not a day went by without the disbanded soldiers attacking some *kolkhoz* or another, killing a couple of animals or damaging something in the farm buildings that were already suffering under the Russian counter-offensive. However, Michele Lubescu perceived the weaknesses stemming from the defeat and knew how to make use of the situation. Wherever he showed up he was received as a benefactor: a Romanian sergeant dedicated to locating deserters and disbanded soldiers fallen to plundering, and he was always welcomed. Every door was opened to him and hardly anyone objected to his demands. The sooner he could gather up this rabble of deserters the more willing people were to sign his chits for provisions from the service corps or the *kolkhozes*. Sergeant Lubescu certainly knew how to spread out his requests and move to a new area rapidly in order not to arouse suspicion.

The investigations into his unit bore no results, but it was the first step to discovering the fraud. Apart from the pretty Ukrainian girl, teary-eyed from Michele's arrest, nothing interesting was revealed. It was obvious that Lubescu had taken precautions and had hidden the fruits of his 'commercial enterprise'. The captain of the German secret police finished his tale:

'Sergeant Lubescu is awaiting the verdict of the Romanian war court in Mariupol. He is also charged with usurping the rank of a commanding officer of a detachment.'

My visit to the German civil servant arose from the fact that Ukrainian policemen were assuming authorities that they did not have and had arrested five disbanded Italian soldiers that morning. They held them in a little village in the middle of the countryside between the Don and the Donets. This is where the five of them had founded a 'republic', enforcing their own rules of occupation. These shrewd Italians, so as not to become enemies of the local population, and so that they could live with their women undisturbed, had not bothered any of them. They had plenty of food and they were careful not to be discovered. Their needs cannot have been a burden on the locals, otherwise this autonomous 'republic' would not have lasted all these weeks.

This was one more episode in the indescribable chaos that followed the collapse of the Don front and the fall of Stalingrad. I tried to play down the incident, but the reaction of the German captain was very different from mine and he gave me a long lecture about military duties, implying that such things did not occur in the German Army. With the example of this incident he began to allege that the tragedy of Stalingrad had been considerably aggravated by the incapacity of the Italian Eighth Army and the Romanian First Army. Luckily I did not have to lose my temper. It was a German sergeant who silenced him by entering the room.

'What is it?' asked the captain, annoyed at the intrusion. As he had just walked in, the sergeant never imagined that the Italian officer in his superior's office could understand German.

'Captain, the Ukrainian Militia has brought some *Wehrmacht* deserters. This is all the information I have for the moment. All I have been given is three *Soldatenbuch*' He brought the captain the three military identification cards. These little books that resembled passports were in a terrible state. With these words he had placed the Romanians, the Italians and the Germans on an even plane, bringing the long-winded speech that his superior had just given to its knees. The officer, visibly annoyed, handed the identification cards back to the sergeant and sent him away brusquely. As a parting shot, I said '*Fahnenfluchtige*,' and left, with a point in my favour.

Days went by and the chaos grew. Hundreds of thousands of soldiers and civilians who had collaborated with the occupation forces were retreating from Stalingrad and the Don front. One day, an old man approached me. Giuseppe Padovan was one of the many thousands of human beings who had been displaced by the conflict. Despite his 80 years of age, he had walked over 20 miles in order to reach our position. He seemed like more of a museum piece than a living being, but he still had enough breath in him to explain himself.

All he wanted was a ration of butter and flour from the Italian command.

We were already making preparations to move. Who was going to take care of this ailing old Italian from Friuli? I suggested that he come with us to the Dnieper, from where he could get on a troop train to take him back to his native town in Italy. However, Giuseppe Padovan answered unfalteringly in a mixture of Friulian dialect and Russian with a Ukrainian accent that he did not want to go. He had lived in that black fertile land for half a century and he did not intend to leave, no matter how difficult the times of the Bolsheviks had been. He had an ailing wife as old as he and a son in the Red Army. Perhaps the boy would come back one day, and what would he do if he could not return to his old parents? Giuseppe Padovan would not leave Russia; he had also been a 'deserter' in his day. He had come to Russia as a very young man with an Italian theatre company, and instead of returning to Italy with his colleagues, he had stayed in Russia to be with the woman with whom he had decided to spend the rest of his life.

THREE DAYS
WITH THE
RUTNIKOV FAMILY

AN OLD LADY was vigorously massaging the bruised and swollen feet of a soldier in tattered uniform, lying on the kitchen table. She brought hot water from a metal container on the stove and used it to bring back the circulation to his almost completely frozen legs. The Italian soldier rested his head on a goatskin. He looked as if he had fainted. Just from the state of his uniform, his unshaven face and protruding eyes, you could tell that he was one of the survivors from the Italian Eighth Army's tragic retreat on foot over hundreds of miles from the Don to the Donets.

The woman was so intent on saving him that she barely even looked at me. My beard had also grown, my coat was ripped and I too was looking for shelter. I tried to hide the revulsion that overcame me as I walked through the door: the unbearable stench of must and dirt made me wish I had a gas mask. The *hata* windows were sealed with mud from the first autumn rains to insulate the house against drafts, so that the only form of ventilation was from opening and closing the door. The little house had one of those enormous stoves that are always lit, with a bench next to it reserved for the most important family member to sleep on.

The old woman urged me to help her hold the 'patient's' body straight. This was my first day with the Rutnikov family.

The following morning, two comrades-in-arms came to pick up the soldier. They loaded him onto a truck with some other wounded and freezing men. On this second day, God chose to give me a tangible sign that Providence favours those who do good deeds. I offered the old lady a bread roll and she accepted it with immense joy and gratitude. She told me that she had not eaten bread made with flour for almost three months, since her son, an electrician in the mines, had gone with her grandson to the River Kuban in search of wheat.

'I am old, and few soldiers stay in my house. There are plenty of places with pretty girls where they can go, so why would they want to come here? And without the soldiers there is no bread. I had hoped that my son and my grandson would be back, but now I have lost all hope. They left without a safe conduct pass, hidden in a military convoy heading for the Caucasus. I am sure the police have discovered them and sent them to Germany or to a factory in the Urals, or else they are digging trenches.'

Suddenly she fell silent. A young girl had just entered and she spoke to me in a very forward manner.

'My name is Tatiana Ursina, *gospodin Ofizier*,' she said.

She told me she wanted to escape before the Russians won back the area: in the village they knew that she had put up a lot of soldiers on their way through and she was sure they would shoot her as a spy. In this little village, I thought to myself, her painted nails and red lipstick gave away her profession. I told her that I was afraid it was not within my power to help her, but if she feared the Bolsheviks so much, she could do what so many other civilians were doing: find herself a sleigh, load on the bare essentials and leave. However, Tatiana Ursina knew that she was in possession of an almost infallible weapon and she was not going to give up easily. She went on to say that she lived nearby and tried to persuade me to change lodgings: in her house I would find a clean room and white sheets. Rutnikov the electrician's house was a shack in comparison to hers, which had been built by her husband, an engineer. From the doorway she pointed it out to me. If I made up my mind to come, I could easily move there the following morning.

Just as she was about to leave, two men dressed in goatskins arrived, worn out with fatigue. In the moonlight I saw Tatiana's eyes linger for a moment as they met those of the older man.

'See you tomorrow,' she whispered to me as she quickly left after this unexpected encounter. I did not know then that fate had just put two sworn enemies face to face, at one of the most tragic times of their lives. Without knowing who these two men were, I guessed that they were the old lady's son and grandson. She could not believe her eyes when she saw them and had to hear them speak before she would believe that it was true. Then she threw herself into their arms.

Their joy gave way to a few simple words and then they fell silent. The new arrivals threw off their *shapki* (sheepskin hats), took off their padded jackets and sat down on the bench next to the stove to warm up.

The lady took the oilcloth off the sleigh and picked up a half-empty sack, letting it fall to the ground with a heavy thud.

This was the fruit of their three-month journey.

She looked at me with a deeply lost expression and the words were stuck in her throat only to come out as an unintelligible stutter.

'Mrs Rutnikova is trying to tell you that this bag you see here is the result of their three-month voyage,' translated the interpreter.

When Rutnikov heard him he laughed nervously, while his son, with his head leaning on the table, began to snore. His father turned to me and exclaimed, 'You don't understand. You can't understand. How can you understand that a man can go in search of wheat for three months, only to return with less than 100 pounds of the stuff? It's ridiculous. I don't understand either, how God can allow the Rutnikov family, who have always worshipped the Lord Almighty, to starve to death, while Tatiana Ursina, that woman who was talking to you when we arrived and who has always been an adventurer, has more than enough wheat. She is not only able to sell it, but she speculates in it, taking advantage of others' misfortune. Think of it – 7,000 roubles. Months and months of sacrifices and savings, hours and hours climbing electricity and telephone poles under the searing heat of the August sun and in freezing winter gales... From here to Rostov, hidden like robbers in a flatcar and from there to Mariupol, fleeing the Russian offensive. Then from Mariupol to here with a column of Cossacks, pulling the sleigh like animals, trying to get here with our four bags of wheat before the Bolsheviks cut off the road. And finally, when we were only a few miles away, almost home, the Ukrainian police stopped us, and because we had no passes they took the wheat and left us with half a sack. It's just pitiful!'

Rutnikov fell silent for a few minutes. In the intimacy of his home and the warmth of his hearth I was not the enemy. He was getting this all off his chest and speaking to me as if I were one of his compatriots. He was aware that any man who suffers knows what injustice is all about. In my position I could not be that different from him.

'Tatiana Ursina! Tatiana Ursina!' he muttered through gritted teeth. 'The Rutnikov family will not starve to death. God cannot want us to perish from the lack of a travel permit. It can't be God's intention that Tatiana may go to the Don whenever she pleases, and that when the soldiers come from there each day they offload pounds and pounds of wheat at her house in return for her "hospitality". It cannot be God's will that to top off all her sins she refuses to sell me her wheat "because it isn't winter and the price is very low", according to her reckoning.'

I listened to Rutnikov's soliloquy in silence. I was nobody to talk. Judging from his expression, his protest was deep-felt and the police's unjust course of action did not come from a desire to enforce the law. He was adamant that there was more than one 'Tatiana Ursina' who travelled to the Don whenever she wanted to, and not out of necessity but to speculate. Throughout the upheavals that Russia was enduring, there were people who took unfair advantage of others' misfortune. Perhaps, since God was not remedying the situation, the only way to stave off death, according to Rutnikov's modest philosophy, was to take justice into his own hands where Tatiana was concerned.

Old Mrs Rutnikova stored away the meagre fruit of the long journey in a dry place. Her grandson was sleeping, propped up in the same position, and Rutnikov the electrician remained silent, perhaps dwelling on his declaration: 'The Rutnikov family will not starve to death.' It was already late and I had to leave early in the morning. I lay down on my sleeping bag that served as a mattress and fell asleep warmed by the stove. This was my second day with the Rutnikov family.

The first thing that the electrician said to me the following morning, with the help of the interpreter, was: 'The Rutnikov family will not starve to death.'

In a hiding place in the little kitchen, he showed me three and a half sacks of wheat. I looked at him in astonishment, waiting for an explanation. He closed the door so that nobody could hear us and went on to say:

'God has not allowed the Rutnikov family, who has always respected His holy commandments, to starve to death. The Rutnikov family has never gone against the word of the Lord and trusts in heaven's protection. When you were asleep last night, *gospodin Ofizier*, Tatiana Ursina's lips were tormenting me, the very same that I saw speaking to you last night on the doorstep of my own home. I felt the blood rush to my head and my heart was beating as if it were going to leap out of my chest. All I could see was bags and bags of wheat before my eyes, and all I could hear was the cursed voice of that woman. Three months before I left for the Kuban I asked her if she would sell me 650 pounds of wheat for 7,000 roubles. She said that you couldn't call that money, winter was on its way and I would be coming back to beg her for it then, ready to pay more than double that. Last night I turned this over and over in my mind and I could not sleep. Was it God who was filling me with such worry? Suddenly a mysterious voice induced me to go outside, and before I knew it I was standing in front of Tatiana Ursina's house. I knocked at the door and she opened it herself. She must have been expecting company because she was exuding perfume. When she saw me she tried to slam the door in my face, but I stopped her. I was overcome by a wave of desire and I lost my mind.

'I grabbed her around the waist and pulled her against me. She resisted and tried to scream, but I stopped her by forcefully pressing my mouth onto hers. I lustfully rubbed my dirty beard against her delicate, fragrant skin that she had carefully prepared for love-making. I grasped her in my arms, pushed her inside, shut the door with my foot and fulfilled my desire. I wanted to fight back with the same weapon that she had used to monopolize the wheat and humiliate me. When I felt I had taken enough advantage of her, I let her go, but I covered her mouth with my hand. But when I saw her face, as white as a sheet, and silent, I was afraid for a moment that I had suffocated her. Her lipstick was smudged and her face looked like that of a clown. I shivered, terrified that I had killed her. "Tatiana Ursina, say something, answer me! It's me, Rutnikov the electrician. Three months ago you refused to sell me wheat for 7,000 roubles. Of the four sacks we managed to get from our whole trip, the Militia left us only half a sack because we were without a permit, and because Rutnikov the electrician can't bat his eyelashes at the police like you. Listen, Tatiana, Rutnikov the electrician doesn't want to hurt you, but if his family dies, you and your son will be damned." I turned to go. I hoped that I had made an impression on her. I knew that taking the wheat from her by force was not God's will. The bread from it would have given me indigestion and led me to an early grave.

'Finally, Tatiana Ursina came round and pulled herself together. She must have thought that if a man could take advantage of her as he pleased like that and then leave voluntarily, almost at dawn, without having harmed her, it must have been a sign from God. She got up, although a little shakily, took my hand and led me to the garden. She made me dig in the frozen ground and take out some boards that covered a well, full to the brim with wheat. She gave me four empty sacks, which she helped me to fill and then lent me her sleigh to take them home. We covered the well with earth and she said goodbye to me, adding, "Forgive me Rutnikov. Your family will not starve to death." As we said goodbye there was very little moonlight and I couldn't see her smudged lipstick. She looked very pretty, too much so for a man of my age.'

This was the tale of Rutnikov's night raid. There were the four sacks of wheat. His mother and his son were still asleep and I had to leave without saying goodbye. However, before I left, Rutnikov the electrician said to me:

'I will not tell my son what happened last night in Tatiana Ursina's house. She is a very dangerous woman. I will tell him that it was Providence that made the police return what they had taken from me unjustly.'

This was my third day with the Rutnikov family.

SATURDAYS
AT NINE

BETWEEN THE PAGES of an old notebook of mine I came across a very faded and almost unrecognizable photograph of Michael Bebdur, *Hauptsturmführer*, chief of the SS assault troops in the department of Stalino. The date: November 1942. The inscription was hardly legible, the usual stuff, praising the 'camaraderie of the Italo-German brothers in arms and the infallible victory'.

For a moment I could see his severe face, looking out with the air of a conquistador over the flat land of the steppe, laid out like a canopy whose colours merged into the sky at the horizon.

A Mercedes enveloped in black dust stopped outside the *hata* where I was temporarily lodging, a few hundred yards from the main track to the Don. There was no sign indicating our presence there and the track was in a terrible state for such a luxurious sports car. I thought that it must have been a high-grade officer who had got lost. I leaned out to take a good look. I was wrong: a skinny little man covered in dust got out of the car, wearing a uniform with the insignia of the SS. Taking off his glasses, he brought me a document addressed with my name, surname and the destination of my unit. It was an invitation to dinner for the following evening at nine. As I was reading it, I could not help noticing that there was a beautiful young girl sitting in the Mercedes. Seeing my curiosity, the messenger said:

'*Kleine Marusja. Unsere Dolmetscherin*' (little Marusja, our interpreter).

She smiled and gave a slight nod. She was wearing a dusty white headscarf, which she took off before straightening up in her seat and holding out her hand to me.

'Marusja,' she said in a soft voice.

The introductions had been made, and I accepted the *Hauptsturmführer* Michael Bebdur's invitation.

The dinner at the SS headquarters had been laid on with no expense spared. In the pretty little building which housed the headquarters of the Officer's Club they had cleaned and plastered the rooms and furnished them well.

'Our Officer's Club,' said the *Obersturmführer*, the colonel in chief, on receiving me. 'Since we are going to be here for some time, it is worth requisitioning the best that this *verfluchtes land*, this accursed land, has to offer.'

Michael Bebdur welcomed me himself and introduced me to his guests. The women seemed ill at ease, and I searched in vain for the pretty Marusja. Finally, when the three musicians had resumed their entertainment, the interpreter appeared on the arm of a coarse grey-haired officer who, unlike his companions, was not wearing his tunic, and had his shirt open. The evening was quite pleasant. For me, in any case, this was an unexpected occasion and an unbeatable one in terms of meeting this privileged breed that wore the much feared double S on their uniforms. *Hauptsturmführer* Bebdur had me sit at his side and told me all sorts of things, finishing with high-flown praise of the 'great Mussolini', who had recovered the empire for Italy and was leading it, at the side of Germany, to a stunning and infallible victory.

There were plenty of toasts drunk, the first of which were accompanied by florid speeches, as if we were at an official ceremony. Soon, however, my fellow diners had lost their faculty for coherent speech and the toasts drifted towards the exaltation of feminine beauty, both present and absent. The dishes came, one after another, in succulent variety and abundance. The servants came and went from the kitchen to the dining room, perspiring from their efforts. The dancing continued until the early hours of the morning. However much effort I made, I could not adapt to this horde with which I had nothing in common. I tried two or three times to approach the pretty Marusja, wanting to get some information on those who had been invited, but I could see that she was reluctant to converse with me, so I exchanged a few words with the sergeant who had delivered the invitation instead. As I bid him farewell and thanked him, Michael Bebdur told me, on behalf of his companions, that during my service there I had a standing invitation, as a representative of the great Italy, to their Saturday evening parties. This was when, as far as possible, they celebrated the end of the working week.

When I left in my car at about 2am, the party was still continuing in the SS Officer's Club. We had to slow down as we came across a column of tanks that were leaving for the front. Two armoured cars with anti-aircraft machine guns aimed their four cannons at the sky and fired at the Russian planes, bringing me back to reality. A battalion of sappers in combat gear marched past. A few miles on we met a column of ambulances that were transporting the dead and wounded to a field hospital.

I arrived at my quarters just as the sun pulled off its ashen shroud and greeted the new day with its weak light. The first news came with reports that a new offensive seemed imminent and that we should prepare ourselves. Units of *bersaglieri* on motorcycles rode noisily along the Don trail, battalions of Blackshirts were on the move from the barracks to the front line; the roads in the immediate rearguard were like a feverish anthill, while *Hauptsturmführer* Michael Bebdur's SS were probably continuing with their party in their respective rooms, and in good company.

Just as the news had predicted, a barrage of artillery fire gave the signal of the imminent advance, so I did not have the chance to take up Bebdur's invitation. Many days went by and the front began to move towards the east. The dead, both civilians and soldiers, came to thousands. The Donets front, with a powerful thrust towards Stalingrad, stopped at the Don and, meanwhile, a German armoured army attacked in the Caucasus. After a few bloodstained weeks, I had to contact Bebdur again on military matters. He was not at his command post when I arrived, but they told me that he would not be long. The pretty Marusja welcomed me. She was busy with the translation of some files from Russian into German. I took the opportunity to have a chat with her, alone, and away from her jealous boss. Marusja told me that we Italians were different from the Germans and that we had not gone to Russia to make war against the civilians, against families, against everything. She told me this in a very low voice so that she would not be overheard, because in that house 'the walls had ears'. She had learned her modest Italian from a soldier in the cavalry, 'a wonderful boy' and one of the first men to enter Stalino. One day he turned up at her place to clean the mud off his uniform. Marusja even remembered his name, 'a name full of music, just like Italy'. Her ashen eyes were lost in pursuit of his name, beyond the walls of that narrow prison that incubated denunciations and suspicions. Then she started to look nervously at her watch and to count the minutes. Her boss would not be long in returning. He had only gone for a short meeting, otherwise he would have taken her with him: he was a possessive man and he did not like to leave her alone. Jokingly I asked her if she would not prefer to leave without waiting for her boss. She said that if she came with me, the major would undoubtedly discover where she had run away to.

'And one day, Marusja *kaput*, for sure, and nobody would know who nor why. *Kommandant*, very jealous of Italians.'

She had become an interpreter for the SS because she had declared that she could speak German. If she had not accepted, she would have ended up in a labour camp in Germany. This would have finished off her mother, who had nobody else in the world.

Heavy footsteps approached and Marusja assumed her usual expression. She arranged her papers, put out the cigarette that I had offered her and bent her head, going back to her work. Michael Bebdur came in, humming to himself. He wore no belt, and his tunic was unbuttoned. They cannot have warned him of my arrival, and he could not help but look somewhat surprised at my presence. He collected himself immediately and, with some embarrassment, expressed his satisfaction in having me as a guest once more.

Once we had dealt with what I had come for, he asked me for the latest news from the front and whether it was going to continue to shift towards the Volga. He was fully convinced that the Russians would 'use their last cartridges' that very same year. He rejected my protests against his view and shrugged his shoulders with a jovial smile. He knew the Russians perfectly well, these '*verfluchtes Brüder*', these accursed brothers. He kept enough samples of them in his prison to make any anthropologist envious.

'They are all without culture, ideals or homeland: an inferior race that wanted to crush Germany, and European culture and civilization.'

He renewed his invitation for the following Saturday, but I had to continue on my journey. The track was almost deserted. Since the front had moved towards the Volga, the roads were literally empty. The German Army and its allies, ourselves included, had moved so far away from the supply lines that if the Russians ever breached any of the sectors, they would be able to camp at their ease and attack us from the rear. Bebdur and his friends were calmly enjoying their Saturday nights for the time being, satisfying their every desire with good food and alcohol, with nobody to ask them for the bill. They laid down the law, and they could do as they pleased. They entirely trusted in victory and exalted the Führer and Mussolini, never doubting eventual triumph, even if the war had to last for years.

A man wearing a black oilskin cape bent over to enter the door of my shelter. He was dripping water all over. His hood covered his face, and in the weak candle light of my room I did not recognize him. Then he took off his hood and looked at me with a sinister glint in those steely eyes of his. Michael Bebdur? What was he doing in the Don? His strong handshake and metallic voice with laboured breath settled my doubts. His large rubber boots were muddy up to his knees, his tunic was torn to shreds, there was a big rip in his trousers and the blood from a wound stained his right hand.

'Bebdur, what happened to you? What are you doing here?'

It was four o'clock in the afternoon and it was already dark outside. Looking down at his ruined *Hauptsturmführer* uniform, he held his wounded hand up to his forehead as if recalling a bad memory.

'I have been searching for this place for hours,' he said. 'Nobody knew how to direct me here, nor did they seem to care about the state that I am in. Your Italian soldiers did not even answer me. They didn't understand German. None of them ' He paused to catch his breath. 'The Russians fired a machine gun at my car and poor Karl is dead. The petrol tank caught fire and the vehicle burned, with Karl inside. I found myself completely alone, the only German surrounded by so many Italians, who acted as if they did not care, indifferent to my state, as they struggled to get their trucks out of the mud. I began to shout, curse and give orders. Nobody paid any attention. Nobody! Can you believe it? Is this how your army is trained? Are these the men that Mussolini forges in Italy? Is this their idea of camaraderie with their German allies? My car is a burnt-out wreck and I was lost and alone in this vast terrain. I knew the river was only a few miles away and that the Russians could cross it during the night and take me prisoner. I cursed at your soldiers and then I turned back to find a firmer stretch of the track where it was easier for vehicles to pass, until I finally met an Italian worthy of Mussolini who stopped his car to give me a ride. I asked him to take me to a German command post, but from the signs that he made I understood that there were almost none in that section of the Italian Army. The nearest one was several miles away and the track was impassable. We went to an Italian command post where, after giving your name and with the help of an interpreter, I found out that you were not very far away. How lucky I was to find a friend amongst so many strangers.'

The following day, having calmed down a little, Bebdur was waiting for me at the camp hospital where he had been medicated and cleaned up a bit. He felt like a fish out of water; alone and surrounded by foreigners, powerless and unable to communicate because no-one spoke his language. Distressed, he was observing the Don steppe with inquisitive eyes, watching the Italians coming and going. He was in such a state that they would have a hard time guessing that he was a German officer, let alone from the SS. The next day, I found someone to accompany him to a German command post. He asked me if I could let him know whether he could recover the charred remains of his friend, but I dissuaded him from doing this. The Russians were pounding the road with long-range artillery and we were answering their fire. It did not take a lot to convince him: he was in enough of a hurry to get back to his own kind, change his uniform and sleep on a feather mattress, safe and sound and away from the Russian patrols that crossed the Don by night to make raids on our rearguard. Before going, he asked me a favour. He really wanted to have a photograph taken of him on the banks of the Don and, if possible, taken from above so that the course of the river could be seen behind him, as long as there was no risk of being hit by a sniper. I could not deny him a photograph, so I took one right there, although I did not manage to get a panorama behind him. In order not to waste time and to dissuade him from this, I warned him that to approach the river was like looking for his death, and it was not worth risking it for a photograph.

When he finally got back to his headquarters, Bebdur's adventure spread like wildfire. It was a rude awakening for everyone. Good heavens: those accursed Russians! They still had enough artillery and air force to threaten the communications, so that there along the Don, the war was really serious… Was there any news from Stalingrad? Poor Karl had died at his first contact with the front! Karl also worked for the SS and so that everyone would know that he had died along the Don, they raised a kind of tomb in front of the headquarters upon which they placed his helmet with the eagle emblem with outstretched wings holding the swastika in its claws. This was the first thing to catch my eye as I entered the SS command post for the last time. I had brought the photograph with me and gave it to Bebdur. He was delighted, but insisted on taking the negative and giving me the photograph with an inscription on it. Before saying goodbye, I asked after Marusja and he told me that, given her age and her doubts about continuing to work in this command post, he had entrusted her to a recruitment inspector who had promised to send her to help his wife in his country house in Germany. As for him, he would no doubt leave the command post, because things were not going as well as had been expected. There was to be a reduction of personnel in the political police and, as senior officer, he would most likely have to be the first to volunteer for the front. Michael Bebdur had lost his proverbial optimism. He had received his first blow in the Don with the death of Karl. They no longer held the Saturday night parties. The atmosphere had changed.

A faded photograph with an illegible autograph: an enthusiastic face from when the war did not directly affect him and he was able to sit with his men on Saturdays at nine before a richly laid table. The *Wehrmacht* and the SS were two bulwarks of Nazism but, above all, were two armies; and furthermore, were two breeds of men taken over by latent heartless antagonism, within the armed forces of new Germany.

HE, MARSHAL
TIMOSHENKO

FROM THE MEMORIES OF
DIMITRI ALEXANDROVICH

ThHE GERMAN GENERAL entered the *hata*, the *Wehrmacht*'s Division 298 counter-espionage headquarters. Lieutenant Dimitri Alexandrovich stood to attention and hastened to help him off with his thick goatskin coat. The general hung up his astrakhan *sapka* on a nail, stamped his black felt boots a couple of times to get the snow off them and warmed his gloved hands over the red-hot fire of the stove, before sitting down.

A *babushka* came in to stoke the fire. Once her task was completed she left with a bow.

'Lieutenant, what are you expecting to get from tonight's prisoners?'

Lieutenant Dimitri Alexandrovich shook his head and answered:

'There is only one Russian officer, and I don't think he has any information of interest to us. I have reason to believe he is just a good soldier of peasant origins, and I don't think I'm wrong.'

The lieutenant had been a second lieutenant in the tsar's guard and had had veterans and austere Cossacks under his orders before ending his career and becoming an interpreter for the *Wehrmacht*. He did not lack experience. The general focused on the man's grey hair and pointed beard and exclaimed, smiling, 'You can't complain! For a 50-year-old lieutenant you beat the record of the subordinate officers of my division.'

He changed his expression and went on:

'We need to get information… as precise as possible. If we don't get any really useful information from today's prisoners, I will have to order another raid on the enemy's battalion on the opposite bank. I suspect that they have armoured units that are very well trained. Crossing at this stretch of the Don with the bank on our side void of vegetation, unlike that of the Russians, is dangerous and I don't want to risk any more men. It will be the last attempt.'

Lieutenant Alexandrovich tapped twice on a piece of rusty metal attached to the low ceiling and gave a brief order to the soldier who appeared. Moments later, a Russian prisoner was brought in, escorted by two soldiers wearing helmets and with bayonets fixed in position.

The general gestured to the lieutenant to begin his interrogation, while he looked at the captive, scrutinizing his badly made black boots, his trousers and his tunic with no sign of rank or service corps, and his lack of a weapon. Lieutenant Poskov was obviously of peasant origin: although he boasted indifference and disrespect, his rough hands gave no respite to two little acacia twigs, showing a justifiable and natural nervousness.

Without losing any more time, Lieutenant Alexandrovich peremptorily read in Russian his rights as a prisoner in compliance with the International Convention. A German commando had captured the officer, an infantry lieutenant, the night before along with his detachment. Their heavy fire from the opposite bank of the Don had been a constant threat. The interrogation was meticulously transcribed. They took the prisoner out and the lieutenant commented·

'General, this Poskov knows nothing about the Russian deployment. He is a lieutenant in Division 350, under Timoshenko. Just like any other soldier under this Marshal, he does not say a word more than necessary and I have not been able to get him to change his mind. He only made a show of sincerity when I asked why the big Russian units remain in the rear of the front. "It's not the first time," he just told me, "that our Chiefs of Staff abandon the so-called cover units in order to keep their plans secret. Isolated, they have no choice but to resist until the last while they still have supplies and munitions, and then die fighting. Marshal Timoshenko knows that his soldiers prefer to sacrifice themselves rather than be dishonoured. This is this only way we will save Russia. "'

The general listened without blinking to the reply from the peasant of the Volga who was prepared to save Russia, but he could hardly hide his admiration. They continued their interrogation of his soldiers, one by one, but no interesting information came out of their ignorance. Once the protocol was concluded, the general turned to the lieutenant who was handing him his fur coat and said :

'Well. We will have to find out about what kind of deployment is being prepared on the other side of the river in whatever way we can. This Timoshenko is changing the destiny of the southern front. It is the first time that I have heard a declaration like the one that we have had today. Before, we caught tired, disillusioned officers and soldiers, who did not believe in the recovery of their army, whereas he, Timoshenko, not yet backed by his general staff, is helping to save Russia... by retreating.'

The general shook the former tsarist official's hand, got up into the *troika*, covered his ears with his scarf and threw a big blanket over his legs. The horses set off and the sleigh sped away swiftly as if it floated on the frozen surface, until it disappeared into the mist of the blizzard. The jingling of the horse's bells slowly faded away in the distance.

Lieutenant Alexandrovich stayed a moment in the hallway of the *hata* contemplating the hazy silhouette of the low sloping straw roofs. He took a deep breath, felt the lash of the snow on his face for an instant and then carefully opened the door, letting the ice-cold air into the entrance. He slammed it shut and went over to the warmth of the stove before sitting down at the table. He took a little metal coffer from the floor, opened it with a little key from his pocket and looked carefully through some papers until he found a tiny photograph. He looked around cautiously and went to the window. With the portrait cradled in his hand, he reminisced with admiration over the figure of a dignified and elegant second lieutenant of the Tsar's Imperial Cossack Guard. He read in a low voice, 'Prince Leonid Svenvitch Kimenhoff, second lieutenant of the Tsar's Cossack Imperial Guard, Moscow, 1914.'

Then, standing to attention before the shallow window frame, staring at the invisible horizon of this white December night, memories of his life flashed through his mind. He looked down at his thin hands, scored with thick blue veins. He felt the grey-green cloth of his sleeves, rubbed the silver eagle and swastika on his lapel and whispered through gritted teeth, '*Herr Oberleutnant* Dimitri Alexandrovich, interpreter, in the general staff of the *Wehrmacht*'s Division 298, former Prince Leonid Svenvich Kimenhoff, second lieutenant of the Tsar's Cossack Imperial Guard,' as he ripped up the photograph and threw it into the fire of the stove.

When the general came back the following morning, Lieutenant Alexandrovich was awaiting him anxiously.

'I promised you a development for today, and your general has kept his promise. We have new prisoners and I have given orders to the escort to leave us alone with them during the interrogation.'

They led a Russian officer in. He held his hand up to his visor, and the two German officers sitting opposite him returned the salute. The Russian introduced himself:

'My name is Dimitri Yakovlevich Resmilov, born in Astrakhan on 2 February 1909. I am a colonel in the Soviet Army to which I owe my loyal duty as a Russian, a soldier and a Communist. I serve under Marshal Timoshenko. I hope to have saved you time in the preliminaries of this interrogation. Neither pleas nor threats will get any further information from me. I have thought about what I have just told you and its possible consequences, but this is what Marshal Timoshenko wishes for Russia.'

Then, true to his word, the officer put up an obstinate silence from then on. The general, to whom Lieutenant Alexandrovich had translated word for word, stood up and retorted:

'As a soldier and gentlemanly adversary, I salute him as an honourable inheritor of the Russian military tradition. The interrogation is over. He will be held in my division's prison camp. Good luck.'

When the two soldiers came back to escort the prisoner away, Lieutenant Alexandrovich, with his notebook in hand, said:

'General, since we have arrived on the Don I have noted down over 100 desertions and only four of the interrogations have been really productive. From this long line of deserters, four were Ukrainian, two from White Russia and the rest a whole bunch of badly equipped troops, mostly Mongolian, with obvious hatred for Russian officers. If the Soviet Army has many Marshals like Timoshenko, I would venture to say – contrary to the opinion of German high command, who believes that Russia does not have many worthy men – that we are in a very tricky situation. The Volga's industry, now transferred to the other side of the Urals and to Siberia, is working non-stop.'

In the days that followed, not a single occurrence worth mentioning was recorded in Office 1 of the division, although the coded messages indicated large concentrations of armoured resources in two sectors along the front. The east bank of the Don was covered with scrub and vegetation. Apart from concealing and facilitating the adversary's manoeuvres, this hindered the quantitative aerial observation that would have enabled the adequate deployment of our troops, which were quite dispersed and badly equipped. The scouts along the section of the front covered by the Torino and Pasubio divisions crossed the river each night and went several miles into enemy territory without running into any interception patrols. They dropped packets of leaflets calling on the Russians to desert, as they did with us, even to the point of calling the officers by name! This was a strange and dangerous mirage of a war of positions that could not last. It was foreseeable that the Russians, unmanning that section, would plan to concentrate their efforts on other points and at some moment unleash a strong attack in order to break through the front somewhere else. They could allow themselves this luxury in the knowledge that our divisions would not cross the Don and embark upon such a dangerous risk. Especially as Stalingrad had already been turned into a raging incinerator of men and resources.

During that waiting period and guessing at the imminence of the siege, in the ingeniously equipped ditches and trenches, protected and well supported, our troops stayed alert: long beards, tired eyes, and faces marked by the interminable vigils in polar conditions. The men went in and out of these dens every ten minutes, as it would have been impossible to be on duty for longer periods than that throughout the night. The frozen winds from the Urals lifted little whirlwinds of blistering snow. The studded wooden soles of our trench boots with their goatskin uppers, obliged us to move forward on all fours in order not to slip on the frozen surface. When the flares lit up both banks as if it were day, it was important to stay down and not breathe. For camouflage in the snow, the patrols were dressed in white and had to keep as still as statues. Whoever garrisoned the trenches on the banks had to run to their posts along the communication passages, grab their weapons, remove them from the bonfires that kept them warm, fix them in position, load them with the shells so icy that they 'burned', arm the gun and wait for the signal to fire: a pistol shot. Those who suffered this the most threw muffled curses, and there were those who crossed themselves, entrusting themselves to God.

The Russians launched the attack one night in December. We fought in the trenches for several days, one against ten, like wild animals, but the enemy breached the front. Orders and counter-orders were received until the communication lines were cut and the divisions were abandoned to their own fate, and the retreat had to begin.

There was a lack of petrol for the prisoner trucks: to take them on foot in columns would be dangerous. An extreme decision had to be taken: to eliminate them! However, before giving this order the German general had Colonel Resmilov appear before him. Through Lieutenant Alexandrovich he told him that due to war developments, they were not in a position to transfer the prisoners, unless he gave them information that would allow them to retreat to a secure position and thus take the prisoners with them with no risk of escapees.

Alexandrovich told me that the Russian colonel refused to do this and, according to his notes, he answered:

'It is better for Russia to lose 200 prisoners than for a colonel of Timoshenko to betray his marshal. We prefer to die in silence for the free Russia that we desire.'

At the end of August 1942, after the capture of Voroshilovgrad, a peasant from the Donets basin at whose house I was staying the night showed me the picture of a horseman: the young face of a handsome soldier, leaning over the graceful mane of a galloping steed. He noticed that I did not understand what was written at the foot of the picture and he repeated the name written in Cyrillic two or three times to me:

'Timoshenko, Russian general Timoshenko,' and taking me outside, he turned to the west, and then to the east, gesticulating and muttering something in Ukrainian that I could not understand. Nevertheless, I remember that he accompanied that arc from east to west with another phrase:

'*Rokossovski, drugoi bolshoi ruski general!*' (Rokossovski, another great Russian general!)

One day in April 1943, when passing along that road again, I remembered that peasant and I wanted to find his house. I searched in vain. Nonetheless, his words had been engraved in my memory and even more so his gestures, so that I relived the scene in my mind. That was when I finally realized what he had wanted to say to me:

'He, Marshal Timoshenko, had won the battle of the Russian retreat to Stalingrad. The other, Marshal Rokossovski, had reaped the fruits of the great Timoshenko's delaying tactics, and months later had managed to win back the Dnieper.'

In fact, the Ukrainian peasant knew that the Soviet Union, retreating towards the Volga, was only concentrating its forces and gathering itself in order to make a push to regain the lost terrain.

Some heavy German tanks passed alongside us, churning up the snow and earth. Their disrespectful glances showed they were convinced of having the most powerful war machine in the world, and were sure of a victory.

Lieutenant Dimitri Alexandrovich, who travelled with me and had told me the story of Timoshenko's officers, stroked his pointed beard two or three times and, as they drove off into the distance, mumbled in subtle Russian irony:

'Unfortunately, that lot don't believe in a Marshal Timoshenko.'

THE OBSESSION

AN ENDLESS COLUMN of men, still smelling of trinitrotoluene from the bombs, meandered slowly through Slaviansk. The straw roofs of the little houses burned menacingly and a warm wind from the south, carrying the steppe's black dust, fanned the flames and spread new fires along its course. It was a black day for that pretty city in the upper Donets.

A few miles away, the Russians continued to fire medium and heavy artillery, with the back-up of a powerful armoured convoy. From a disused rail track, amidst the mishmash of uprooted rails and twisted iron, sporadic explosions sounded from the wagons of munitions.

In the city, surrounded by tall acacia trees and miraculously intact, stood an Orthodox church, raising its golden dome to the heavens. Some Ukrainian soldiers in *Wehrmacht* uniform watched curiously as others escorted Russian prisoners. They greeted us awkwardly and embarrassed.

The occasional sudden spray of machine gun fire sounded, like a drum roll, briefly speeding up the column's slow, tired march. It did not last long though: fatigue, open wounds, malnutrition and the dulling of the senses were all stronger than their fear or survival instinct. The prisoners were of all ages and nationalities – some were civilians, black sheep from a multicoloured flock, all walking at the same pace and with the same expressions as their escorts in khaki uniform. They all advanced like robots, but where to?

The German sergeant who accompanied me glanced at the wretched rabble with contempt and, turning to me, he said, '*Nichts Kultur*' – uncivilised.

'What are those civilians doing in amongst those troops?' I asked him.

'Partisans!' he answered laconically, lumping the whole lot of them together, reflecting how war distorts the mind.

'Partisans?' I contested. Such a generic term did not convince me, and I wanted a more detailed explanation.

'Maybe not all of them,' he went on, surprised by my scepticism, 'but most of them, of course. There are Russian soldiers who had time to change out of their uniforms before surrendering, and others who did not enlist. You know as well as I do what happens in a battle. Each man falls to his lot, and those who hid in this miserable country's disgusting huts pay for all those that tried to outsmart us. Furthermore, the less riff-raff there are, the fewer problems we'll have.'

This did not convince me either and I insisted further, 'Are they all going to be detained in the same prison camp or are the so-called "partisans" separated from the regular troops?'

'*Ach woh*? What are you saying?' he exclaimed unhesitatingly. 'Do you think there is time to take such care in Russia? They make a list of names and catalogue them all as workers. The real "partisans" or snipers or whatever you want to call them, it makes no difference, have already had what was coming to them. When the column reaches the internment centre the first selection will have been made on the battle field. Most will survive, and keep their hope of freedom alive. But do you know how?'

He looked around cautiously before going on:

'We don't have enough men to keep watch over hundreds of thousands of prisoners. You see those men over there?' he said, pointing to some soldiers who were marching alongside the endless column, armed with machine guns. 'You see them? They have the white armbands with the Miliz or Ukraine label and uniforms identical to those of the *Wehrmacht*, but without the German eagle on the tunic breast. They cannot be mistaken for our soldiers, by their faces apart from anything else. *Nichts Kultur*. These men are in charge of guarding the prisoners. When the centres gather large contingents like these, just two German officers will take care of this rabble, with a few *Panzer*. These Russians, you see, what with Bolshevism and the war, have become really stupid. In a nutshell, very few of them have tried to escape or taken advantage of the fact that we have so few resources to guard them.'

He became more talkative with the cigarette I offered him.

'Look, the Ukrainian prisoners have special privileges. The *Wehrmacht* has a provision that states whoever can prove they have experience – in industry, farming or in any profession – will be freed and can go back to work in the profession they had before the war. Their family members prepare the paperwork for this, but whether true or false, all of the papers are forgeries. *Alles Schwatz*, all fakes. For a few hundred roubles the *starosta* and the chief of the Militia will provide them. The workshops need workers, not prisoners, and so it's all quickly dealt with.'

He paused before going on. 'It's seven o'clock. Staying here is dangerous. The Russians are usually on time and any moment that cursed armoured convoy that we haven't managed to silence yet will start giving us trouble. To tell you the truth, these damned Russians aren't short of equipment since the Americans have been supplying them.'

We got back into the armoured car and continued on our way towards where the column had disappeared. Behind us the tremendous explosions fired from the Russian convoy had started again.

An officer of the *carabinieri*, accompanied by a former Russian officer who had been a prisoner and now acted as an interpreter, was moving towards a thousand or so prisoners standing in formation. Their uniforms were so tattered that it was difficult to see for whom they had been serving. They were standing next to the ruins of cheap little houses of the kind that were commonly built for labourers in Russia. Although they were watched over by a detachment of guards, during the night, under the shelter of darkness and torrential rain, there had been a mass flight. In the hope of putting a stop to the escapes, the commander of the camp was announcing through the interpreter that due to the flight of prisoners, they were now forced to resort to severe measures and he had declared their decimation. There was a gasp of astonishment all round. The instinct for survival knows no bounds, nor is there a regime in which it can be suppressed. They had a roll call and the separated 'chosen' ones were to be taken away. The commander ordered the interpreter to warn them that if anyone else tried to escape, whether alone or in a group, the whole lot of them would be punished. The commander hoped that this means of dissuasion would stop the haemorrhage.

The condemned men were not resigned to their fate and they desperately began to pray loudly, crossing themselves repeatedly, commending their souls to God. Some even fell to their knees and beat their foreheads to the ground.

Amongst them was one man, bent with age, who had been captured with a fighting unit and was therefore taken prisoner like the others. The hand of Providence unexpectedly saved him when the group not chosen, shouting loudly, pushed a political commissary out of their ranks, and he was put in the old man's place.

The condemned, contrary to what had been announced, instead of being shot were taken to another camp about 60 miles away. Later they were transferred further away in the hope that no one would find out: the Italian commander hoped to frighten the prisoners but also to save these unfortunate souls from death. No matter how far they were taken, however, it was not far enough to keep it a secret. A few days later everyone knew that those who were taken had not been shot, so the escaping started again. The only one to be severely reprimanded was the commander.

The victorious *Blitzkrieg* continued, with whole armies being encircled and over a million Russian prisoners taken. There were almost more prisoners than there were combatants. They could be seen all over the place, marching down the dusty tracks. In summer their faces were caked in sweat and black dust, in autumn they were covered in sticky mud, and in winter they were unrecognizable in their tattered coats and rough beards, battling against the piercing wind and sub-zero temperatures. They were forced to dig ditches in which to bury the dead, to load munitions and pull sleighs. They diligently gathered up any pieces of wood they came across so they could light a meagre fire to rest in front of through the night, while still dressed in the same old rags. They were always ready to accept a cigarette or a crust of bread, holding out their empty motor-oil cans for a morsel of hot food. Then there were those who were executed immediately upon capture, by both sides, due to the lack of resources to guard, feed and house them.

I had just got back from Kamensk, alive and well after a narrow escape from violent bombing, when I was ordered to go to Nikitovka. A column of prisoners under Italian escort had got lost and failed to find the German internment camp. Time was running out, the escort was sparse and they had not slept for two nights. They had no provisions left and the weather was bitterly cold. I reached them on the Konstantinovka trail, amidst a monstrous mass of armoured vehicles. It was one of the indescribable traffic jams that the German First Army created on their retreat from the Caucasus at the end of 1942. The camouflaged tanks sliced up the ice. In those latitudes the German soldiers in their colonial uniform seemed surreal: they sat in the turrets of the tanks, astride the motorized artillery cannons, perched on the running boards of the trucks, at the wheel of big *Zundap* or BMWs and crammed into sidecars.

Low-flying 'Storks' skimmed over the dirt tracks constantly, like gliders, almost headlong into enormous flocks of black crows. The din being made on the ground drowned out the noise of their engines.

The column of prisoners which I had finally found had prudently stopped off to the side of the track not far from the camp. We finally arrived before nightfall. Coincidentally, the German sergeant who was to take charge of them was the very same officer who had spoken to me about the prisoners at Slaviansk. This made matters easier to deal with, although he was not at all happy to take on even more prisoners since he had just had to release thousands of them in Stalino the day before. However, some German soldiers and another twenty Ukrainian militiamen who had escorted our column would be able to give him a much-needed helping hand.

I was already preparing to leave when an Italian officer, exhausted after the trip with the prisoners, came to confide in me. He wanted to report a very delicate position, and it was in everybody's interest that it not be left unattended. A few months previously he had caught a civilian transmitting information to the Russian Army from a radio in a basement in Voroshilovgrad. The civilian identified himself as a lieutenant on a mission for the Red army. Due to the rush of events that followed his capture, nobody had taken care of the matter and he had passed unnoticed into the crowd of prisoners. He had then started to organize them and actually improved the way the camp operated by doing so. His praiseworthy behaviour was noticed by the commander, who made his record disappear from the files and thus saved his life. Now that he was being handed over to the Germans, the Italian was concerned that if the details were gone into, there was a risk that the Russian would be killed in strict accordance with the rules. I thought it would be best if I listened to the prisoner himself.

'I am Lieutenant Sarkov of the telegraph corps. I never knew my mother or my father. I am a son of the steppe, I don't know where I was born and I believe that I must be in my thirties. The Communist Party took me in and I got a degree as a mining engineer in 1938. I got a job in a big iron mine. With the invasion of Poland and Russia, once our army was routed by the German attack, the commander of my unit asked who was willing to sacrifice himself for Russia. I volunteered and, dressed as a civilian, I hid in a basement in the suburbs of Voroshilovgrad with a clandestine transmitter. A while later the Italians discovered me and took me prisoner. I knew they could shoot me for being a spy and I resigned myself to this fact. My country and the revolution had given me everything and it was only logical that I sacrifice myself for Russia.'

Muffled shelling continued in the background as I deliberated over the facts. My instinct was to spare him. The Russian lieutenant knew that the transfer of prisoners to the Germans had been concluded and he probably had very little time to live. I took a daring decision and I dismissed him without further ado, on the condition that he promise me on a handshake that he would continue to show the Germans the same respect as he had shown us.

My Italian colleague, a silent witness to this decision, breathed a sigh of relief and shook the lieutenant and me by the hand. I never saw them again.

However, my thoughts about my decision did not stop there. The Volga, the Don, the Urals and Siberia ran through my mind. I felt defenceless in the middle of this atrocious cold that descended upon us from the Urals and flooded the plains of Siberia. Terror sent shivers down my spine: if it came to it, would I also be shown mercy by a *starosta*, or be given a pass to get back home? Or, more likely, would I end up before a Russian officer who would execute me without a second thought?

ALARM IN LISISCHANSK

HALF BURIED BENEATH the snow opposite Irina Semikobina's house, the silhouettes of giant OKW trucks from the *Wehrmacht*'s high command announced the presence of a German detachment. Although this should have deterred me from going in, I knew that Irina would welcome me with her usual hospitality, something that had become well known amongst the Italian troops. I caught her in the middle of her household chores and she begged me to excuse her while she went to make herself more presentable. In the little lounge where she left me to wait were a large sofa and some nice armchairs, along with some paintings and tapestries in pretty bad taste. In pride of place on the table stood a large photograph of her husband, an engineer and the source of all of this unusual comfort.

Irina reappeared, transformed, wearing a translucent black silk dress and stockings. She had brushed her hair, put perfume on and painted her lips. Only her hands, still red and swollen, gave away the fact that she had been doing the cleaning. She then began to tell me about her recent misfortune. She had not had any rest for almost a month, attending to the uninterrupted flow of Germans passing through, some of whom had heard that her house was very clean and welcoming, and that the lady of the house was attractive and friendly. As soon as one lot had left, the next lot arrived and they were never satisfied. They were so demanding – clean sheets, basins to wash in, everything had to be spick and span. At night their demands were brought up a tone and poor Irina had no choice but to go and sleep elsewhere. Her house, so pretty and tidy, had been transformed into a *Heim*, or quarters for the *Wehrmacht* to rest up for the night, in good company if possible.

We were chatting like this when a German non-commissioned officer showed up, very annoyed at my presence. These men were particularly bothered by the Ukrainian women's preference for Italians. His trousers were held up by a pair of braces over his half-open shirt that revealed his large stomach. On his feet was a pair of rough old wooden and canvas clogs. He muttered an excuse and left. Irina had gone pale. I was pretty sure that as soon as I left the German corporal would make things difficult for her because of my visit. He had plenty of ways of doing this at his disposal, there was no doubt about it. I reproached myself for having come, as I had not wanted to create problems for her. She would not give in easily, but I promised that I would drop in on my way back from Konstantinovka in case this brute had done something to trouble her.

A few days later I kept my word and returned. Irina had been counting the moments, because they had arrested her brother Igor, who lived with her. He had been reported to the police by the German corporal who claimed to have heard him transmitting secret messages by radio. This was an economic disaster for Irina, because they only managed to survive thanks to Igor's job as a railwayman for the Germans. Without Igor she would be obliged to give in over the one thing that she had been denying her German guests until then, just so that she could continue to feed her already undernourished children.

Without further ado I went to testify in the Semikobin family's defence before the town's Ukrainian police. I managed to get them to reopen the case. They asked for information from Monakhovo where Igor worked and they found out that he had a very good record and that the confiscated radio in question was not in fact working. So they set him free that very afternoon. Irina was overcome with joy and would have done anything to show me her gratitude. However, the German, seeing Igor free, while unaware of my involvement, decided to seek his revenge.

It was a dark night. The snow fell like petals onto the wide, empty Donets–Don trail, and it seemed as if the war had ended. It was easy to imagine the armies, having given up their fighting, taking refuge in the intimacy of a cosy house and a comfortable, clean bed. Before I succumbed to sleep, I spent a moment enjoying the white silence of this cold cotton peace that had been granted by heaven. Everything was enveloped in a deep slumber. Who could disturb this tranquillity?

Little did I know, on the other side of the frozen waters of the Donets, thousands of Cossacks were getting ready to awaken the village brutally. Irina's brother woke me up with a start. There was a strange light filtering through the frosted glass of the little ground-level window, coming from a reflection on the snow. The railwayman leaned over and whispered to me that the Cossacks had crossed the Donets, and we had to flee as quickly as possible from there. His source of information was 'Radio Steppe', the fastest and most trustworthy of sources.

I jumped from my bed and went out without making a sound in order to gather together the thirty soldiers staying in lodgings nearby. I got them into the trucks, whose engines ran both day and night so as not to allow the diesel fuel to freeze up, and set off to join the division right away. Igor thought it wise to leave Irina and the children sleeping: if they left the house it was likely they would lose it. His sister had no reason to fear reprisals as she had honestly defended her honour as a mother and a Russian, and the Cossacks would undoubtedly know this. He, on the other hand, had to escape with us. His job with the Reich transporting convoys of troops, supplies, munitions and fuel was a betrayal to his brothers, and the commissar would not pardon his treason.

Igor was in the first truck with the interpreter and me, and he offered to guide us safely through the regions of Alexandrovka and Kagamvische. We had to stop in Figarovizka though, because the road became impassable. We heard shelling, machine gun fire and isolated gunshots. Then everything went quiet and we became snowed in.

It did not remain quiet for long. Suddenly the sky was lit up for an instant with a bright red flash of light and we saw enormous flames rise up into the sky. When the snow falls in the steppe on nights when there is hardly a breath of wind, the senses become easily confused, but Igor was used to the tricks that the steppe played, and asked me to order the men to be silent so that he could listen more closely. Soon, after a few brief outbursts, we heard a mysterious muffled noise: it was the hoofs of the Cossacks' horses. We manned our stations as best we could, weapons at the ready, with our only heavy machine gun protected behind the snowed-in trucks. It crossed my mind that Igor had led us into a trap – a diabolic abomination considering I had helped him gain his freedom – and my hand went instinctively to my pistol. However, I did nothing, but waited to see what would happen.

The muffled sound of horses' hoofs became clearer, but it was difficult to judge where it was heading until it seemed to be coming straight for us. It was nearly daybreak and if we were caught there it would surely be the end of us. The Cossacks had numbers far superior to our own and would annihilate us. Suddenly we heard a violent scuffle to the left of where we were. It went on for a few minutes and sounded like firecrackers going off. At the same time, there was a red glow that lit up the whole area, followed by a sudden blaze that made our frozen, terrified faces glow with a strange red light. Igor told us that the danger had passed.

The Cossacks had passed our flank by just a few yards when charging on Messaroch. They must have come across a German garrison next to the *kolkhoz*, and eliminated this obstacle by burning it down, as they were renowned for doing.

Igor advised me to make use of the situation and advance towards the west before dawn broke upon this scene of fighting. He showed me the fastest road to Krasni Liman. We started up our engines and at the quietest possible speed we passed Messaroch. Meanwhile, the noise of the skirmish, distant and muted, sounded like the dispersed echo of a pack of hounds about to catch their prey. Igor did not come with us, though. Happy to have repaid his debt to me, he wished to return to the village to see what had become of his sister and the children and, as far as possible, to Corporal Halter. Only then did I remember that as we hastily left, the two enormous OKW trucks were not in front of Irina's house. That cursed German! Out of spite he had not told us of the order to retreat that he must have received from his superiors.

In Krasni Liman everything was in disorder. The people were overexcited, speaking of nothing but the Cossacks and exaggerating their numbers: six, eight, ten thousand. Many civilians had loaded their sleighs with household belongings and were preparing to flee rather than be liberated by their Russian brothers.

They did not come though: the *Wehrmacht*'s tanks overwhelmed the horses and sleighs, driving back the intrepid medieval cavalry that fought in 1943 as they had in the times of Genghis Khan. I was ordered to go back to where I started from, taking the same track we had left so as to avoid being surrounded by the Cossacks. I was greatly surprised to find Irina's house intact. The only evidence of the skirmish that had taken place near her house was a few dead horses with frozen Cossacks in their stirrups. I approached the dead with respect and trepidation. They lay like fallen statues, petrified by the frost in horrific poses. A young, blonde Cossack lay there, as peaceful as an angel, still wielding his sabre, with his eyes turned towards the heavens as if following his soul.

Irina Semikobina smiled at me on my arrival as if nothing had happened, welcoming me with her usual cheerful hospitality. Igor was back at work in Monakhovo station and now that the Cossack attack had been routed, Corporal Halter was also back at her house, insolently strutting around in his braces as if he owned the place. I went on my way the following day, leaving Belogorovka for ever. The war's luck was now on the side of the Russians, though, not Irina's, and one morning in March her house was burnt down in the fury of battle. Corporal Halter was not amongst the survivors. Who knows if Igor, to take revenge, had not killed him on the threshold of the house?

After some time I found myself near Berlin's 3rd Division command post near Gorlovka. I remembered that this was Halter's unit and, to rebuke him for his behaviour or at least to find out what had happened, I asked for news of him and the OKW transport detachment from Lisichansk. The quartermaster on duty looked up the details in his records and told me that the corporal must have perished in a partisan ambush. He did not know where exactly, but he believed this had taken place in Belogorovka, near Lisichansk, during the division's relocation. In the confusion that followed, nobody noticed Halter was missing. The following day, when his absence was noted, they could not go back in search of him because the Cossack cavalry had taken over the village, this time reinforced with tanks. The quartermaster asked if I could fill him in on any other details, but I avoided hypothesizing. It was not important: one more or one less of the thousands of disappeared soldiers, it was all the same to him.

I left, however, convinced in my heart of hearts that Irina's brother had not been far from where that particular death had taken place.

My chain-tracked vehicle moved across the trail of snow and mud, mud that announced the arrival of spring. We were leaving behind the winter and the memory of the Cossacks passing through the village of Lisichansk in blood and fire. Suddenly I seemed to see before me the figure of Corporal Halter coming towards me wearing his braces and strutting arrogantly. Next to him was the vision of Igor, with his railwayman's coat, covered in grease and coal dust, the stoker of a locomotive for the Reich... As we moved forward along the track, they seemed to become more and more real to me. Was Igor trying to explain the end of the story to me? He seemed to be saying something, but suddenly his image faded. Perhaps it was Halter who was trying to say something, but then his bulky figure also disappeared.

Abruptly I was brought back to reality and here nobody could help me to learn the truth. The image of that fallen blonde horseman in his stirrups, like an angel on horseback looking up towards heaven, took the place of that other mirage of those two enemies. I thought to myself that he was the one who was still alive, whereas Igor and Halter, independently of their final, reciprocal culpability, could not exist unless I brought them back to life in my story.

The bloodstained blanket of snow now covered both Igor and Corporal Halter of the OKW. In my mind's eye, thousands of Cossacks on horseback crossed the foggy horizon singing their war anthem, while in Belogorovka the war had moved on.

IVAN SAMOJLENKO,
A STORY

THE LIAISON OFFICER brought me an envelope marked 'confidential'. I quickly leafed through its contents. The German high command was calling for a list of White Russians volunteers from the Ukraine, specifying the age limit, with conditions of service, rank and pay comparable to those of the German armed forces of the *Wehrmacht*. These were not simple battalions of auxiliary services with chauffeurs, cooks and so on, but fully armed and equipped units. The Ukrainians were being called to sacrifice themselves for the sake of 'the Ukraine's liberation from Bolshevik oppression'. They used the argument that the German invasion was a step towards Ukrainian independence. No man fit for service who longed for the freedom of his country should show indifference at this crossroads in the country's destiny.

There were specific and detailed explanations on two other documents that complemented this notification, stating that Germany's allied armies should show respect for the new recruits in their role in the 'anti-Bolshevik crusade'. It must be said that there was no shortage of incidents between the Germans and the local militia due to the opinionated attitude of the Germans towards these 'uncouth ex-peasants from the steppe' who dressed in the same grey-green uniform as the *Wehrmacht* but were unable to speak German.

This 'confidential' document was no concern of mine. However, if Major Von Brandt had sent it to me, he must have had a reason. I found out what this reason was one morning in September of 1942 when Captain Hase, a subordinate to Von Brandt, came to see me. He had orders to recruit and instruct a battalion of Ukrainian volunteers. With 500 men about to arrive, he had still not managed to find the ideal place to quarter them. This was a major factor in the training of these men, but he told me that he would make do with a few small buildings instead of one big one if necessary, as long as they were close together. The few houses available at the time were in ruins, with no glass in the windows and no washing or toilet facilities. Although this was not such a problem in summer, the men could not be housed in such conditions in winter. The only glass factory around was in Konstantinovka and the Russians had done so much damage to it in their retreat that all the Germans had managed to rebuild made only a few hundred square yards of glass per day. What is more, there was such a heavy demand that a request for glass was unrealistic. Captain Hase had heard that there were still a few buildings under Italian juris-diction that were just about acceptable for his needs. He asked me to go with him to Krasnii Gorodok to take a look at number 7, a building that could possibly serve his purpose.

The building turned out to be fairly well preserved. It was an indus-trial school built on a hill, and the captain thought it would be adequate quarters for his Ukrainian recruits. A short while later, the volunteers, all very young men, were settled in. There were major problems involved in the military training of these civilians, since it was impossi-ble to judge who could be trusted. It was only to be expected that many of them would see their enlistment as an economic incentive, with a privileged position above their compatriots, as well as a good way of escaping forced labour in Germany. Of course, it was not to be forgot-ten that if the situation changed and the Russians returned, they would pay for their collaboration with the enemy with their lives. It was important to consider these factors when training the battalions. The Germans' intention was to structure them organically, assigning them a command and administration from the *Wehrmacht* and recruiting exclusively Ukrainian non-commissioned officers and troops.

One of the first to enlist was Ivan Samojlenko, an extremely young district head of the Militia at Malojvanovka. He was promoted to lieu-tenant and was assigned to instruct the 1st Company. He was intelligent and friendly, with bright eyes, not very tall but strong as an ox. He spoke passable Italian and German and demonstrated the makings of a military man. I wanted to know more about him, and he told me that his father had been deported to Siberia for the simple fact that he was a member of the well-to-do bourgeoisie. This had wounded his mother terribly and left him scarred for life. From that moment onwards there was only one thing that motivated Ivan: revenge. He had nursed that one obsession for years and now he had the opportunity to seek his revenge and make his enemy pay with their blood for the suffering that they had inflicted upon his family and for his unhappy childhood. The intensity with which this boy told me his story showed me that he had an iron will and would take his revenge at any price. He was convinced that a Bolshevik victory would signify the perpetuation of something hateful. He wished to save Russia, but never to bend to a revolutionary regime that took away the essence of his homeland. That symbol of the hammer and sickle brandished by the men who broke into his house to take away his father would remain nailed to his heart for ever. In his desire for revenge, he would fight against it without mercy wherever need be, even at the risk of losing his own life. Captain Hase had evidently found himself a courageous man. Ivan was a diligent collaborator, an audacious and intelligent officer, and a natural leader who could be entrusted with the delicate responsibility of training those troops.

I returned to Krasnii Gorodok three months after Hase's battalion had moved into the school building. The recruits were training under Samojlenko who had zealously dedicated himself to the job. A freezing cold wind swept the hillside, but neither he nor his men seemed to notice. He insisted that I stay a while longer with him and 'his boys', recruits into whom he had instilled his anti-revolutionary ideals for the independence of the Ukraine.

'I trust these volunteers completely. I hand-picked them one by one and I would swear on my life that they are loyal. I rejected some that I did not find convincing. Captain Hase gave his approval and he will not regret it,' he said.

Afterwards, he accompanied me to the command post where Captain Hase and his officers met me. We talked almost exclusively about the training of his battalion, the difficulties that they were overcoming day by day, and the risks that they faced. He said they had already been entrusted with a few important missions such as the surveillance of two railway bridges, some industrial installations and the scouring of areas where partisans were operating. They were replacing the *Wehrmacht* troops very efficiently.

That day in December was the last time I saw Hase's battalion for a while. The next time I was passing through Krasnii Gorodok they had left the industrial school building and nobody knew why they had moved to new quarters. No one had any news about the Ukrainian battalion. A German non-commissioned officer who was defending a 6 mile stretch from cavalry infiltration with only three tanks said to me: 'Look, we have come from the Caucasus and I assure you that we have better things to do than worry about a battalion of Ukrainians. They will more than likely have passed over to the enemy with their arms and equipment, like all the others.' And with this he plunged back into the top of his 'tin can', muttering swear words through his teeth which chattered in the freezing cold. When the early thaw brought on a truce, giving the exhausted soldiers a chance to rest from the winter battle, Krasnii Gorodok found itself behind enemy lines and was already a distant memory for me. However, Hase and Ivan Samojlenko's men were still putting up a disciplined fight in the area of the steppe still under German control, without many desertions. When the winter thaw was over and the ground was awakening to the first signs of spring, I bumped into Hase's battalion near Kristovka. There was a longing for renewal and freedom in the air. The blinding snow had been banished, the grass was turning green and the leaves were budding on the trees. This was the scenery in which the unexpected meeting took place. Hase thought I had disappeared in the siege of Mijerovo and I thought he had been swept away by the retreat to the west of the Donets. I scoured the troops for Ivan Samojlenko, but I could not see him anywhere.

'Who are you looking for, Samojlenko?' asked the captain. 'Ivan has left us for ever,' he said, knitting his thick black eyebrows and biting his lip. 'We left Krasnii Gorodok with the Russians at our heels. I had been instructed to keep the town until the Soviet advance guard arrived and then to retreat at the last minute. The command needed to know if I had full confidence in my men. If I hadn't they would have ordered a retreat under the control of *Wehrmacht* units. Ivan Samojlenko dispelled any doubts of mine and I decided to stay. The sector had to be defended against any possible Russian infiltration that might obstruct the retreat operations of other units. I gave orders to the team of explosives experts under Samojlenko to blow up the buildings and the barracks, while we carried out the retreat.

'I never saw him again. There were some who escaped and reached us when we were already far away, who told me that he had died in the ruins of that Party building in the centre of town. You may remember it: that concrete monstrosity crowned with the hammer and sickle carved out of stone, which had remained intact, despite being riddled with bullet holes. Ivan had expressed his desire to knock that symbol down many a time. It was not easy to reach because it was on top of a kind of hyperbolic pinnacle.

'When we were ready to leave,' continued Hase, 'I saw Samojlenko with a great big box of explosives that he told me he had saved a while back for the grand occasion: to blow up the hammer and sickle on the Party headquarters. Those were more or less his last words before he wished us goodbye, sure that he would be seeing us later on during the retreat.

'But we won't be seeing Ivan again. It was like a voluntary suicide in which he took the lives of a few of his best men. They must have been just about to demolish the building with the explosives, and we don't know what happened, but the charge must have gone off before it was meant to. We have lost a good officer and a group of élite soldiers.'

Hase looked at the clearing in the woods where his men were setting up camp as if he were looking for the thickset figure of the lieutenant. My eyes followed his fruitless search.

'We owe him our lives,' he added. 'The desertions from our battalion can be counted on one hand, unlike in others where they have been disgraceful. Major Fonsted's battalion, for example, changed sides in its entirety, after having killed the commander and officers. The only thing that Germany has achieved with these battalions is to arm the enemy with equipment and combat units.'

He fell silent, looking at me as if he wanted me to draw my own conclusions from this. Then we chatted about the ill-fated winter campaign, which sent so many of Germany's hopes to the dogs. It was already nightfall by the time I left, and his men were mounting guard. The open campfires projected strange red flickers of light onto the black earth and the stormy sky, the shadows of the hard-working soldiers were lengthened to disproportionate dimensions, and their silhouettes stood out against the scarlet flames. The acrid smell of dirty men, of soldiers recently out of the trenches, filled the air in that small clearing surrounded by bare trees and plants unfamiliar to me. At dawn they would take up their march once more. Perhaps, one day, we would bump into each other again, in the immensity of the steppe or on the streets of a big city.

ELENA KUDINA
TELLS HER STORY

4 FEBRUARY 1943

A FREEZING WIND blew across the vast orchards of Staropetrovsk and snow swirled around the ice-covered branches of the apple trees that stood in endless rows like a garland around Schwarz's *kolkhoz*. The Stalino *Wursterei Gesellschaft* was moving the herds from the great complex to a safer area near Mariupol. The *starosta* of Staropetrovsk offered to be head shepherd. He was a German from the republics of the Volga and one of Schwarz's main assistants. Just like the beasts that he herded towards the west, he too felt hounded. Friederich Enz, the well-known slaughterman from Nuremberg transplanted to the heart of Russia under the unquestionable order from the *Wehrmacht*, had left too. This arbiter of thousands of animals' destiny had to pack up his belongings, load them as best he could on a sleigh and head towards the west, hastily abandoning his little yellow house on the corner of *ulitsa* Bolnichnaya. And just as the good mechanic Alexei Shimienko had almost finished his car, after three months patiently assembling a mosaic of bits and pieces he had managed to procure!

Schwarz had also gone. As he said goodbye, he told me that he would be back before long, and asked me if he could exchange a large amount of petrol for diesel fuel. Now that he had abandoned the complex organization of *kolkhozes* and *sovkhozes* that he was in charge of, everything had gone to pot, like an army abandoned by its general.

We moved into the outbuildings that up until then had been used by Russian workers in the German farming administration. Staropetrovsk was a former fief of the Russian nobility, and although the Bolsheviks had converted it into a state farm, its architecture and spatial distribution still reflected its original glory. They had changed the livingrooms into barns and warehouses and turned the bedrooms into offices. The Russian administrators who had retained their jobs under the Germans did not come to work that day. They knew very well what awaited those who had collaborated with the Nazis now that their proletariat comrades had crossed the Donets and they had only two alternatives: to disappear or to follow the *Starosta* Kontiurov's herds along the road to Mariupol or in the tracks left in the snow by Schwarz's car.

The silos were full to the brim with wheat and sunflower seeds, and civilians who came intending to pillage had no choice but to turn back when they saw our troops mounting guard. The snow continued to block the track to Makeyevka despite the fact that more than 300 workers had been trying to clear it for three days. The snowstorms just formed new white drifts that were as capricious as the sand dunes of the deserts under the simoom. An officer of the grenadiers was working miracles with his exhausted men, organizing the deployment of tractors and sleighs to help the blocked or broken-down trucks.

It was not a good idea to start off yet. It would be better to wait... the Russians permitting. They would be there in three or four days if they continued at the present pace. I was serving with the last Italian units in the area, and part of my assignment was to look after certain civilian issues, an unpleasant duty that had been passed on to me by the last German commander before heading for the Dnieper.

I moved into *Starosta* Kontiurov's office. Office? How had we got used to saying things like this? This office, for example, now that the Germans had abandoned it, seemed more like a woodshed than a room. Its furniture had been broken up by looters. You could see that the *starosta* and his men had not spared their effort before leaving: they had ripped out the electric wiring, taken out the windows and hacked the doors to pieces. The furniture, tables, chairs and shelves were smashed to smithereens. There was even human excrement on the mattresses of some of the beds. However, we had to pretend that the organization was still working, and carry out the civil inquiries.

An ancient little old lady who had come from far away brought me two fat white capons to influence me into making the Italians or the Germans set her grandson free. He had been taken prisoner, but she knew neither how nor where. 'What difference does it make?' she said. All I had to do was give her back her grandson, and she would give me these chickens. I patiently explained that this was not the right time to deal with such problems. She would not give in, insisting that her grandson was a good boy, he was 17 years old and she had brought him up herself. He had never wanted to go to war and was happy at home, because before the war there were plenty of capons like these that he used to eat, the poor dear!

Next came a girl who wanted to know the current location of an Italian unit that she wished to join at any price because her boyfriend served in it, a corporal from Verona, who had promised he would marry her and take her to Italy. I was powerless to help her either and she left, terribly disappointed.

Next entered Elena Kudina, as slim as a gazelle. I thought I recognized her. Elena noticed that I was straining to remember and she helped me:

'You got my father out of prison, Lieutenant sir,' she said in passable Italian. I could not remember it at all though, since so many people had filed passed me during those months of the war. 'It was Major Ansani that pleaded before you to grant my father his freedom.'

The name of the major in the Alpine corps with whom I had spent a few days in July, brought back the memory and I began to recognize Elena's features as she explained her case to me.

She wanted to reach the Dnieper with her father, and was afraid of being caught and arrested if she left without a safe conduct pass. It was almost 200 miles to the Dnieper by the most direct route and she needed what the Russians called a 'passport', an obligatory document or identity card. She no longer had it, though: the NKVD of Boguchari had it, which complicated the issue. I asked her to give me the details. Each civilian who came from enemy lines had to undergo a thorough interrogation, and Elena Kudina began her story in her own style of Italian, which was then transcribed by an excellent interpreter:

'At the beginning of November, when my father was freed from Rostov prison, we did not know what to do to stay alive and were desperate for food, so I decided to go to the Don. I knew that the time to go looking for wheat had ended and that the winter's hardships would accentuate the difficulties posed by the journey. I also knew that the police had become very strict, but I decided to leave anyway. We had to survive somehow. My neighbours had already gathered their provisions for the winter months, while I was walking to Rostov, and I had no choice but to make up for lost time. I had been warned that the peasants in the Don had become much more tight-fisted and that whereas once you could get ten roubles for a dress, for example, now you got no more than five. So I had to make do and sacrifice my little Swiss gold watch, that had belonged to my poor mother, in exchange for a sack and a half of wheat. Fortunately a friend of mine came with me, even though she had already made the trip, because she wanted to supplement what she had obtained the first time. At the beginning we were quite lucky. We did the first part of the trip in military trucks, thanks to the warm hearts of the Italian soldiers who took pity on us when they saw us alone on the track with our modest sleigh, freezing to death.

'We found wheat between Mijerovo and Poltava. My friend took me to the house of some peasants with whom she had dealt previously. They gave me a sack and a half of wheat for my little gold watch and I was very pleased. We were preparing to make the journey back when the police stopped us and took our pass away, preventing us from going home. If we had gone on we would have risked arrest, interrogation and imprisonment in a concentration camp, the precursor of deportation to a factory in Germany. We had the wheat and my father was waiting. What could I do? The only option was to wait. We went to the command post of the Italian garrison in Medovaya in the hope that they would provide us with a safe conduct pass, but they told us that the permits were temporarily suspended. They said that we could make use of our time spent waiting by serving as interpreters, because in Medovaya they had found no one who could speak Italian.

'We were delighted to accept: in this way we would avoid ending up in Germany. However, we had only just begun to work when, on 19 December, the Italians received an order to leave the village quickly. We went with them, dragging our sleigh. A very tall, strong lieutenant colonel commanded the column. I think he was a little deaf in his left ear, and he spoke Italian with a Russian accent. The other officers included five majors and many others of lower rank from the "Torino" and "Pasubio" divisions. We went on foot, and one day we came across a Russian soldier with a horse dragging a sleigh loaded with munitions. They called me over to interrogate him. He claimed to be from Yurovka and he was taking the munitions to Karlovka, 3 miles away from Yurovka. We asked him if there were Russians in Yurovka, which was only a mile away. He said there were not many. The men asked the colonel what to do and he ordered us to continue as far as Yurovka because he was convinced that there were no troops there and that the Russian was lying. We arrived in Yurovka and we found the village empty, with just one Russian soldier walking down the street with a gun. He claimed to be a Ukrainian militiaman in military uniform, and nobody took any further notice of him. Then the colonel gave the soldiers permission to look for lodgings and to rest before continuing their march the next day. Half of the troops stayed in Yurovka and the other half went with the colonel to the village of Alexeika-Losovskaya, just over the hill from there. Less than an hour later, when we were already settled in our lodgings, we heard shots being fired on the Alexeika side of the village. We were alarmed so we went to join the others. It must have been almost nine in the evening. The colonel was calm, saying that it must have been German soldiers shooting in some skirmish or another, but no sooner had he said this than a whole load of Russian soldiers piled out of some bales of hay, shooting with automatic rifles and machine guns. The Italian soldiers answered their fire shouting 'Savoia!' but the colonel ordered them to cease fire, wrenched the rifle from a soldier who was just about to shoot and threw it into a fire that they had lit to warm themselves by. They all protested that they should not give themselves up without having fired a shot but the colonel said that without automatic guns they could not defend themselves. He took a white handkerchief, tied it to a rifle and waved it in the air. Some soldiers near to me and my friend, Tamara Samoilenko, advised us to ask the colonel to say that we were Italians, if we fell prisoner, so that they would not kill us.

'We did this and the colonel replied: "I don't know you and I don't intend to say anything." So we moved away from the soldiers, and slipped off to eat something in a house where there were more Italian soldiers. No more shots were heard. A little while later an Italian soldier came in shouting: "The Russians! Run, they are killing everyone inside the houses!" The Italian soldier put his hands up and a Russian snatched his gold watch immediately and took him to a group of prisoners. As soon as we came out of the house they captured us and took us away with the rest. The Russians gathered up the arms, threw them into the snow and led the column to the main street of Alexeika-Losovskaya, where they had their command post.

'Thirty or so Russians kept watch over us with machine guns that held seventy-four shots. Some Italian soldiers who had *Tre Stelle* cigarettes broke open the packets and threw them to the ground. A Russian picked one of them up, looked at the symbol on it and said, laughing: "Why are you throwing away this tobacco? Because they carry the fascist wheat sheaf? We aren't killing you because of this. Are you killing us because ours carry the red star?" The Italian soldiers wanted to know what they had said and I translated it for them. Some other soldiers tore up photographs and German marks, and a Russian lieutenant who saw it said: "Why are you destroying these photographs? Aren't they your loved ones?" I repeated this in Italian and the Russian lieutenant asked the soldiers if they understood some Russian. "*Da, da*", they answered smiling. The lieutenant smiled also and said, "*Harasho, harasho*, very good." A Russian captain shouted the order for all of the officers to come out of the lines and then took the colonel and the majors to the command post. The captains, lieutenants and second lieutenants were separated from the group and the non-commissioned officers and soldiers were left in the column. Turning towards my friend Tamara and me the captain said, "You Russian traitors have been working with the Italians." I responded, "My father was on the front and he fell prisoner. The Italians helped to have him set free and come back home to work. They have always treated us well, not like you do." The captain wanted to grab his pistol and shoot me, but the lieutenant stopped him, saying that it was not a good idea to do something like that in front of the troops.

'Then they took us to the command post without letting us take our sleigh of wheat with us, so we left it with the Italian soldiers. The captain turned to me and said, "You were an interpreter for the Italians, now you can do it for us," but I told him that when it came to very complicated issues, I was not very able, so my friend Tamara offered to do it. At the command post, in a little room in one of the village houses, sitting at the table, were a Russian colonel and a major, and at the door stood a sentry. The Italian colonel and the five majors were standing to one side. The Russian colonel asked him for information on how many troops there were and the Italian colonel told him that he commanded 360 men and he did not really know how many other men there were because there were different units involved. The Russian colonel wanted to know what German forces were in the area and what equipment they had, and the Italian told him that he did not know exactly, but he knew they were considerable. This is how the interrogation ended. They put us in a German vehicle, the colonel, the five majors and six of us girls, as they had caught four other prisoners the previous day in Mankova. They took us to another command post where a 15-year-old boy from Rikovo was acting as interpreter, after having fallen prisoner with the "Torino" division.

'After almost an hour's drive in another vehicle captured from the Germans, they took us all to Boguchari. Here they separated us from the officers and took us to the headquarters of the NKVD, where they kept us from the 23rd to the 26th without giving us anything to eat, locked up in a room with a sentry on guard. On the 26th they interrogated us for the first time. A major from the NKVD asked us what had caused us to work for the Italians. We told him that we had no other choice, as otherwise we would have been sent to Germany. The major's judgement was simply, "You are Italian soldiers' women," and they kept us in the Militia building for another ten days with 300 grams of bread and a glass of tea once a day. On 6 January, the major and a captain interrogated us once again and the next day they made us work and scrub the floor and we ate two meals. On the 23rd they came back to interrogate us again.

'The NKVD was only a few hundred yards away from the house where we were confined. They took only three girls at a time to be questioned. The Russian soldier who escorted us told us that he had been an officer and had fallen prisoner under the Italians. At the concentration camp they had treated him very well, but when the Russians freed him they demoted him to a private as a punishment for having been captured. He thought it wrong that the NKVD should convict us for having worked with the Italians and he was prepared to help us to escape. He pointed out the house of a lady who would exchange some clothes with us so that we would not be recognized. When the interrogation was over the major made us sign a statement. We asked him what would happen to us and he told us we would go on trial before a war tribunal for treason. When we got back to our prison, our three companions were no longer there. The soldier who had suggested escape advised us that in the evening an inexperienced 17-year-old militiaman would be guarding us, which would make it easier for us. At four o'clock the young lad came on guard and my friend Tamara and I asked him if we could go out to the lavatory. He did not know that it was his duty to accompany us, so as soon as we were outside, we slipped away through a wooden gate and went straight to the house that the soldier had pointed out to us that morning.

'The woman was waiting for us. Tamara gave the woman her wristwatch in exchange for a jacket, a shawl, a small sled and 60 pounds of wheat. We slept at her house and at dawn we headed towards Medovaya, crossing Racetskoie and Kantemirovka. Along the road we met many Italian trucks driven by Italian prisoners serving in the Russian Army. Without more ado we reached the Donets. In the village of Trebisino we met some civilians who had come from Dniepropetrovsk, Stalino and Rikovo on their way to the Don in search of wheat, but had been blocked by the Soviet offensive. Some Russian tank drivers who were staying in the same house as us for the night told us: "Wait a few days for us to throw the Italians and the Germans out of your village and you will return with us triumphant." The landlord did not think it as easy as that, though. He was an elderly man with three sons fighting in the war. Like so many others, he had not heard news of them for months and he knew better than to be too optimistic. When we were alone, he showed us how to get to Sokolniki, a village less than 3 miles from there in the middle of a wood. There we would find woodcutters who crossed the Donets each day for work, and we could go with them so as to avoid more trouble getting home.

'We followed his advice and we met a woman who was chopping wood and trying with difficulty to pick up a heavy trunk. We helped her, loaded the trunk onto the sleigh, and together we crossed the frozen river. She told us that another 3 miles away, in Kripaki, there were Germans, and we could travel as far as that unhindered. In Kripaki we saw the first Germans. They asked us where we came from and if we knew where the Russians were, and they told us which road to take in order to get back to our village. Finally we got back to our families in Siergov and Debaltsevo.'

Elena had finished her story and she breathed a deep sigh. Having gone first of all to Rostov to get her father out of prison and then to the Don to look for wheat, it was a relief to have finished her tale of all her misfortunes. But her story was just an everyday occurrence in those days of the war and I cannot think why I had the patience to listen to her. 'How complicated men are!' she seemed to be saying as I took note of her last words. 'I have to explain all this in order to get a safe conduct pass?'

Basically all she was telling me was that she went to the Don to look for wheat, was travelling between November and February and came back with nothing, in a worse state than when she left, in tatters and minus her mother's wristwatch. Her father had been waiting for her for three months, he knew what it was like between the Don and the Donets and she was the only thing left to him in the whole world. It would be so wonderful, having lost all hope of seeing her again, for her to appear there before his eyes.

She added no more details. To me, 'the Commander', her private life was none of my business. There was a long column of vehicles from the *kolkhoz* outside, waiting for me to give the order for them to start up towards the Dnieper. There was surely a small space in one of these vehicles, she said, despite their heavy load, for her and perhaps one day her father as well, wherever it may be, even on the radiator if necessary. The Dnieper! She held her breath as if to diminish her presence and leave me alone with my thoughts. How could I deny her a safe conduct pass? If Elena wanted to seek her salvation on the other side of the Dnieper, which was not possible here, having worked for the Italians, she should be able to follow that voice that called her towards the west. This voice would not betray her!

'I was born on the 9 May 1925. I'm 18,' she told me.

I completed the pass with her details, a scrawl and a stamp. Her life was safe and her happiness ensured for that day at least. I could not give her the go-ahead to travel in one of the trucks: the vehicles were full up, and any space left was always kept for a soldier so that he could cover hundreds of miles of frozen steppe on four wheels and not on foot. Yes, she had lost her sack and a half of wheat, but she had obtained the piece of paper signed and sealed. In the ledger of her life, 4 February would not be a blank entry but a plus on the income side.

When I was finally alone in the ruins of *Starosta* Kontiurov's office, the whistle of the freezing wind from the Urals, bending the bare branches of Staropetrovsk's apple trees, was even more piercing and prolonged, strengthening my desire for the end of the war, so that I could go home.

THE WAX MASK

ZENYA WAS 17 YEARS OLD. I met her by chance one night in May 1943 in Dniepropetrovsk. We were waiting for a train to take us north to Gomel, in order to join our Eighth Army, or, with any luck, be sent back to Italy.

We were waiting on tenterhooks for the high command to make their decision. We knew what was awaiting us in the cities and the great forests of Russia: violent air raids, terrible living quarters, continuous attacks from bands of partisans numbering some 40,000 men. The days we spent in Dniepropetrovsk were heaven-sent, and during our time there we tried not to think about what the future might hold. And there were girls here too – German girls in the army and air force auxiliary services, and Russian girls who had escaped deportation. The placid waters of the Dnieper, the clear blue sky and the budding of spring on the acacia trees that lined Karl Marx Avenue made us think of love again.

I had been wandering the streets for hours looking for accommodation when I came across a little cottage, locked up and seemingly uninhabited. I went to ask someone in the next-door courtyard and came across a courteous elderly lady sewing some black fabric. She immediately understood what I wanted and without saying a word she led me down a narrow hallway cluttered with furniture. This opened out into a room, faintly lit by the little sunlight that filtered through a thick blue curtain. There I saw another wizened old lady slumped in a wicker chair. Her sunken eyes scrutinized me closely, as if they were eating into me. I stepped back to elude her gaze and in my haste I knocked some books off a wooden stand. My hostess led me through into a spacious room whose windows were covered with blue lace curtains through which filtered a strange light.

The woman huddled against the door in silence, as if waiting for me to say something. As my eyes became accustomed to the dim light, I saw that the room was almost entirely empty. As I tried to lift the curtain, the lady made a sudden movement as if to stop me. I could tell she was upset, but this house was so strange, so mysterious, that I had to explore it. Behind the blue lace curtains were panes painted in the same colour.

I could not check anything else out because the electric light did not work and I did not have any matches. Deciding to make do with what I had seen, I had my baggage brought to the room. On the left wall there was another door and I started towards it, thinking that some other soldiers could be housed there. This time the old lady leaped in front of me barring the door and gesturing with her hand that I was not to enter. I thought she was guarding some hidden treasure, grain or money perhaps. I tried to explain to her that I was only interested in lodging a few men. I reassured her that we would respect her belongings and give her time to move them out of there. However, her eyes filled with tears and her sewing fell to the floor. The black cloth made me suddenly think that there may have been a death in the family. Perhaps the forbidden room had belonged to the deceased and was sacred for its memories, so I insisted no further.

Mrs Kashirina was greatly relieved when she saw that I had given up and although, in the false light of the room, I could not see if the colour had come back to her cheeks, at least her hands had stopped trembling. Nevertheless, her eyes shone strangely and the tears were still there. A ray of white light filtered through the window revealing her expression. I understood that she was weeping with gratitude. With that, an end was put to our silent conversation conducted through gestures. We had met as enemies, but had now suddenly become friends, each reading the thoughts of the other.

I arranged my things in the room, the grim encrusted windows were cleaned and thrown open to the fresh air. The condensation from the ceiling dried out, the sparse furniture was arranged and still nobody dared to break the prohibition by opening the mysterious door.

The soldiers were lodged in nearby houses and we had nothing to do now but wait for our orders to ship out. I would have liked to solve the mystery of the closed door, but I concentrated my curiosity on the other members of the family. I got them to open the door onto the street again, to avoid the ordeal of having to pass in front of the wizened old lady's disturbing gaze. However, I often saw Mrs Kashirina, busy at her housework. I guessed that the family must have been well-to-do, because there was always a pot on the fire that gave off an appetizing aroma.

With Mrs Kashirina lived a teenage girl. She was pale and weak and marked by the signs of tuberculosis. She was well dressed and her hands were delicate, despite the rough chores that she carried out. She told me that the lady of the house was the old woman slumped on the wicker armchair, from which she said she would refuse to budge 'until the war is over and the Holy Ghost has come down upon the earth'. Mrs Kashirina was her daughter and the widow of a wealthy man from Dniepropetrovsk who had died during the revolution. She had been left with a daughter, who was now 18, married and with a new-born child, the only one to break the rules of the family, crying at the top of his lungs, especially during the air raids. The young husband came home only at curfew. He earned quite a bit of money selling watches in the market.

There were just two mysteries left to solve: the forbidden room and a man dressed in mourning who always came to the house at the same time every evening. He arrived on a bicycle along the acacia-lined avenue, entered the courtyard where our military trucks were parked, and leaned his bike against the wall. Then he exchanged a few words with Mrs Kashirina and left soon after, but never without casting a glance at the tightly sealed windows of the mysterious room.

Then one night in May, not far from the house, I met Zenya.

We went for a walk to the top of the hill where the university stood, now closed due to the war. We stopped in front of an enormous Mineralogy building that had been converted into a German field hospital, and sat down beneath a romantic old tree. Below us the river meandered lazily among the factories of the industrial zone and along the peaceful, sandy banks in the centre of town. A ceaseless flow of military vehicles and trains streamed over the two long bridges. Rockets swept through the sky and the dogs in the suburbs barked furiously.

Nearby, a tram jam-packed with passengers screeched as it turned the corner, just like trams everywhere in the western world. I do not know why, but that busy city scene that seemed so European made me think Zenya must be different from the other Russian girls I had met. She had been born and raised in Dniepropetrovsk. The war had swept through the city quickly as the front rushed eastward. A girl who had lived in a large town would not have suffered the same things as the girls from Rostov, Slaviansk, Kramatorsk or Rikovo. The trams were still working at ten o'clock at night and there were few signs of destruction here, so perhaps this was why Zenya seemed more European, less Russian, not as unfortunate as other girls her age who had been caught up in the whirlwind of war. Here I tell her story, just as she told it to me under that tree that was planted when the city was still called Yekaterinoslav.

Zenya was in her first year of medicine when the war interrupted her studies. With the university closed, the students and the professors were recruited or put into auxiliary organizations and rearguard services. Many of her friends had decided to remain faithful to the revolution and along with a large portion of Dniepropetrovsk's population, they followed the exodus with the Red Army. Nevertheless, the evacuation was not as total as the Supreme Soviet would have liked. The commissars had begun to lose their authority once people heard the catastrophic news that deserters brought back from the front and soon it was obvious that the invaders had such formidable weapons and fought so hard that any hope of recovery was vain. Vast roundups of thousands of Russian soldiers were carried out each day and the tragic watchword was, 'retreat, retreat, retreat.'

Zenya's father and elder brother were on the western front. Her younger brother had gone to Siberia for military training and her mother had died a few years before. Zenya had escaped two orders for recruitment into the *Arbeitsgehörde*. She had no intention of leaving her home or her city; she had few belongings, but if she abandoned them, no one would protect them from looters. Moreover, her father had made the dreadful mistake of marrying just before being shipped out to the front, and her stepmother was a grasping woman who had already threatened to sell part of the furniture to buy food and clothes. She had earned her living by showing her legs on stage as a cabaret artist and, with her terrible wild eyes, she had brought strife into the family of Afanasi Vasilevich. Zenya held out, sure that her father would come back one day, but in the meantime her stepmother had dropped her thin veil of hypocrisy and turned the house into 'lodgings' for soldiers so that she could live well without working. Zenya's protests had been useless: the woman had threatened to report her to one of the most regular German visitors to her 'house of lively soirées', and Zenya was forced to bite her lip.

Day after day Zenya's friends disappeared as girls of her age were kidnapped for forced labour. Some committed suicide rather than face a life that the few survivors had described as torture. Others had opted to cross the River Bug to reach the Romanian lines, because it was rumoured they would be safer there.

'Some of my friends encouraged me to try it,' continued Zenya, 'especially once the Germans gave the order for all Russian girls born in 1924
and 1925 to report to the labour bureau and be sent to Germany. They
would not even exonerate the interpreters. I did not want to leave my
house in my stepmother's hands, so I stayed here, and now I am alone.'

Zenya seemed to be speaking more to herself than to me, and I did not
want to interrupt her, so I kept quiet. I wondered though, why she was
telling me all this. Was she sincere or was this evening's walk a pretext to
coax some precious information out of me? Dniepropetrovsk was full of
Russians working as spies for the Germans or the Soviets. The way we
had met said nothing in her favour, and she could be making it all up. In
the darkness, in the faint light of my burning cigarette, I could read
nothing in her eyes. I struggled to make out her expression by the light
of the tram's sparks as it struggled up the hill. Signal flares momentarily
lit up the imposing architecture of the university.

Zenya wanted to take the last tram home. In the bluish light of its
lamps I could finally satisfy my curiosity: from the sound of her voice
and in the faint glow of my cigarette, I had imagined her differently.
What I now saw was a typically Russian face with high, prominent
cheekbones that gave her a wholesome look. Her round eyes had a
childlike sparkle; her black, curly, well-brushed hair framed her oval-
shaped face; her small mouth, with its brilliant smile, showed off pearly
white teeth; her hands were well manicured and she had a graceful
figure. She did not appear to be a deceitful woman. This was even more
reason to be careful, since espionage was expert at picking beautiful
young informers.

We got off and began to walk down the avenue of acacia trees under
the starlit sky and Zenya took me straight to her house. We went
through a heavy metal gate and entered the courtyard. It was a comical-
looking addition built onto the wall of a large building, a 'cross-breed'
that was common in Russia. She urged me to walk on tiptoe so as not to
wake up her stepmother and led me by the hand to a room where she
left me alone for a moment. A tiny bulb in a large crystal chandelier lit
up an Imperial-style living room with two big gold-leafed mirrors. A
Caucasian rug lay on the parquet floor. It was a complete contrast to the
grey monotonous Soviet interiors that I had come across so far.

Zenya offered me a seat on a green satin sofa, treated me to a cigarette
from a silver case, lighting it with an elegant cigarette lighter, and asked
me to excuse her for a moment while she went to change.

While I waited I leafed through a photograph album that was sitting on a little table. I only noticed that the girl had returned by her heady perfume, and the sound of her voice caught me by surprise.

She had put on a long, white, embroidered dressing gown that hung off her almost bare shoulders glimpsed through a transparent blue lace nightgown. Her pale cheekbones set off her black hair and her brown eyes. Sinking down beside me she lit a cigarette, then took the photograph album from my hand and looked at the photograph that had caught my attention. It was the face of a young woman framed by a classic red headscarf in the Russian style. The perfectly regular features and the eyes veiled by long dark eyelashes made the picture look more like an oil painting than a photograph. Zenya saw that I was impressed and leafed through the pages of the album, showing me several pictures of the same woman.

'This is Elizaveta Grigoreva, my best friend,' she said. For a long moment Zenya's gaze followed the smoke spiralling from her cigarette to the ceiling 'She killed herself four months ago to escape being deported. She was on my course at the university: one of the brightest, and a real beauty too. She was well-paid by the famous artists who she modelled for and could afford to buy elegant clothes that made her look even more stunning.'

In 1941 her friend had met Grigori Michailovich, a famous sculptor from Dniepropetrovsk. They fell madly in love and were soon married. When the war broke out and the order was given to retreat to the Urals, they stayed hidden in Dniepropetrovsk. During the first months of the occupation they lived quite well. Grigori opened a studio in Karl Marx Avenue with a notice that advertised 'Portraits, sketches and caricatures', and he attracted a good clientele of soldiers. His workload increased and with it their income. When Elizaveta had a miscarriage she lost her exemption from labour service. The Germans went from house to house in search of women. Tormented by the idea of deportation, Grigori seemed about to lose his mind. He stopped painting and started work on a mask of his wife in coloured wax to be placed on a dummy in a coffin in a secret room as if she were dead. The idea was to make it look like a funeral chamber in order to trick the Ukrainian police if they came to arrest her. By working day and night he managed to create a perfect replica.

'The picture you are looking at is a photograph of the mask,' she told me. 'Elizaveta told me everything. How she laughed when she saw the shock on my face on seeing the macabre scene! Grigori proposed to help me too, and a few other survivors, and he started to model our faces. However, one night he had one of his epileptic seizures and while his wife was taking care of him the police raided his studio and discovered his workshop. They continued to search the house and found the funeral chamber. They thought that he must have been mentally unstable to do such a thing. Later it came out that the informer had been the wax supplier. Two days later they came for Elizaveta. She knew she was tubercular and preferred to put an end to her life rather than face deportation. Grigori's grief was indescribable. I suffered my own grief, feeling guilty for having accepted her help. If only I had chosen to cross the Bug...' and she breathed a deep sigh. 'Well, who knows, even if I had, maybe they would have tried to help other girls.'

She dried her tears with a little silk handkerchief and closed the album. Her story seemed a little suspicious to me, but then she made a last confession that cleared up all my doubts.

'Now that Elizaveta is at rest beneath the flower beds in the garden, all Grigori has is a replica of her face, the creation of his artwork. He has not had anything to do with anyone since. Every afternoon, dressed in mourning, he rides his bicycle down the acacia-lined avenue, leaves it in the courtyard of his mother-in-law's house and goes to a blacked-out room where nobody is allowed to enter: the "funeral chamber". He stays there for a while, quiet and alone, and comes out just before the curfew. In the four months since Elizaveta died nobody has wanted to occupy that house, and not because of the lack of soldiers looking for lodgings. It is because when Mrs Kashirina gives in to their insistence and opens the dark chamber, they all leave, scared stiff.'

I got back to my lodgings at dawn. Everyone was asleep. The idea of a mask in a coffin in the adjacent room kept me from sleeping. The very next day Zenya asked for my help: she wanted to go to Italy or to be taken to the other side of the river Bug. She no longer had the strength to wait for her father and brothers to return, but neither of her requests was possible, and I tried to tell her as gently as I could. When I brought her a present of 40 pounds of wheat that had been confiscated from a *kolkhoz* during the Russian retreat, it was her stepmother, a good-looking and beautifully dressed woman, who opened the door. Zenya had gone out, so I left the sack with her, telling her that I would be back. However, that afternoon our orders for repatriation were confirmed, and I was so busy getting ready that I had no time to say goodbye to Zenya. I was happy to leave the quiet house, with its funeral chamber and the wax mask.

It was only when I had left Dniepropetrovsk far behind that I dared to tell my comrades about the secret of the forbidden room; the old, mummified woman, Madame Kashirina's tears, the blue curtains, the window panes painted blue and the mysterious evening visitor. I was no longer thinking about Zenya in the euphoria of my return home, when two *carabinieri* in the little station of Transinistria found her stowed away in one of the trucks on our train. She had managed to convince one of our men to let her and a friend hide there so they could try to reach Italy. I saw them, dirty and shivering, as they faced the colonel who was questioning them, and I wanted to put in a word for them. It was not necessary though. The colonel did not have the slightest intention of handing them over to the Germans, but instead planned to assign them to our command post in Leopoli (now called Lvov), and if they could not be employed there, he would take them with him. The men in Leopoli promised to help them and our convoy went on its way, leaving the two girls waving farewell with their handkerchiefs, their eyes brimming with tears.

THREE UNFORGETTABLE
RUSSIANS

1 ALEXEI,
A MAN OF GOOD
INTENTIONS

ELENA'S HUSBAND was an engineer and an outstanding member of the cadres of the Communist Party in Gorlovka. He wanted to sabotage the German invasion from his workplace and therefore had not followed the Russian Army in its retreat. However, he had miscalculated and both he and his wife, whom the neighbours called the 'deputy Communist', had many enemies. One of these reported them to the German police, and during the investigation he was arrested. Elena and their 15-year-old daughter were not touched, but their house was requisitioned.

As fate would have it, two of my colleagues and I went to lodge in that very house and soon we realized that Elena was a fervent Communist and suffered from hysteria. She also had a weak heart and I witnessed one of her heart attacks: she was lying in her bed, gasping, in the arms of her daughter who was crying desperately, as it was impossible to obtain oxygen and medicine. We managed to get them some drugs and this made things smoother between us so that we could establish a more cordial relationship. However, our friendship with Alexei, a likeable Ukrainian mechanic who advocated independence and had his workshop opposite Elena's house, rocked the boat, making living together in harmony impossible. Alexei was a good father and had a big family, which left him no choice but to repair German military vehicles whenever the opportunity arose. He was keen, intelligent and honest, and he loved his work. He earned enough to keep his wife, three children and a sister who never left the house for fear of possible deportation to Germany.

Alexei's privileged financial position made Elena green with envy and, during a heated discussion, she even said to him that if the Russians won back the city she would report him for being pro-Nazi. Alexei, who did not mince words, said that he would not forget what she had said, but that she had better warn her friend Stalin not to send the

Russians back there. It was to be expected that such close neighbours, who were irreversible enemies, spied on each other. The destinies of each one depended not only on the result of the war but also on the movements of the front.

In all of this rivalry, what fate awaited Elena's young daughter, Vera? I did not dare to ask Alexei when he spoke to us of his cruel intentions, but I saw unshakeable determination in his eyes. He was a mild-mannered man, but he was perfectly capable of doing harm, and he would not do anything by halves: allowing the daughter to live would be laying himself open to revenge.

Our efforts to re-establish peace between the two families were in vain. The moral policy that the Communists had instilled into the people prevented civil coexistence and this superseded any other viewpoint. When we left on 12 April 1943, Holy Thursday according to the Orthodox calendar, Elena did not even bother to say goodbye. The air was still, the sky was full of stars and the half-demolished church near the cemetery had opened its doors to the faithful. Men, women and children flocked in, either in small groups or single file, holding candles and muttering prayers. They looked like souls from purgatory in Dante's *Divine Comedy*.

The military column started its long march by making a detour around the multitudes so as not to disturb them, and the troops crossed themselves as they passed the packed church. Our Easter Sunday would be 25 April, when all the churches in Italy would sound their bells to celebrate the resurrection of Christ. I hoped that perhaps Elena and Alexei would be reconciled that day. However, Elena was this 'deputy Communist' and an atheist. A squad of Russian bombers with detection devices located our column and machine gun fire rained down on us, as the 'souls from Purgatory' stood with their candles trembling in the half-demolished church. These were three factors that made the miracle of that reconciliation rather problematic.

In Stalino we joined another long column of trucks heading towards the Dnieper. We were already far away, but Elena, Vera and Alexei were lying in wait in their houses, opposite each other, watching for the moment of tragedy to arrive. A few days passed by and the front stabilized, mainly because the spring thaw made it difficult to move. The tanks advanced like sick elephants and the wheels of the trucks spun in the mud without going anywhere. Nature had stopped everyone and the weapons were silent.

Many civilians fled in panic from the cities being won back by the Red Army and even the *Sonderführer* retreated towards the west. One of the consequences of the *Wehrmacht*'s retreat was that it left Alexei without a job.

He loaded everything from his workshop that he possibly could into his truck, got a safe conduct pass from the German command for his family and headed to Dniepropetrovsk, where the units that had survived the winter battle were concentrated. Far from Gorlovka, and above all from Elena, he was able to set up his workshop again. I would like to believe that he examined his conscience and repented his murderous plans. I prefer to imagine that Alexei the mechanic, true to his principles, ended up behaving like a man of good intentions.

2 SIXTY KOPEKS

Nadia Shpakova came to see us. They told her that we had gone to Kuzminskaya, Dniepropetrovsk's freight train station, to catch a train that would repatriate us to Italy, and she wanted to do her utmost to come and say goodbye. There were a few miles between Dniepropetrovsk, where she lived, and Kuzminskaya, but it did not matter, even though she had to walk and it would take her a long time. The convoy would wait, because God would not allow me to leave without seeing her. How could God let me leave Russia without a keepsake from Nadia?

I was already settled in the wagon with an eight-day journey ahead of me when I saw her appear, soaked to the skin with her face full of anguish. The locomotive let out a high-pitched whistle that sounded like a mournful howl in the dark stormy night. In the half-darkness of the platform, the coming and going of soldiers speeded up and loud voices were interlaced with curses. A sudden jerk made the compartment's oil lamp sway. Two big teardrops shone in Nadia's eyes. She knew that in no time at all we would be far away and she would be left all alone, crying on this station platform that joined Russia to Italy, the object of her aspirations.

The gruff voice of a German railwayman could be heard outside as he inspected the wagons' breaks along with two Russian workmen. I offered her something to eat. She shook her head. She had no appetite and a lump in her throat stopped her from speaking. She took a small box out of her purse and gave it to me. It was a present from a little

Russian girl for an Italian who had treated her well: wrapped in cotton was a ring with a stone that was mounted and cut like a diamond.

'Thank you, Nadia,' I said.

She tried to put it on, and finally managed to place it on my little finger. She took my hand and looked at it, satisfied. She was no longer crying. Instead, she smiled joyfully and serenely.

'A keepsake from little Nadia for the rest of your life,' she said, hugging me strongly.

'Why did you go to the trouble?' I said, gently scolding her. 'You shouldn't have. You aren't rich.'

She bowed her head and sank it into my sheepskin coat. Offended, she frowned.

'Nadia doesn't need to eat when you gone. The Germans know that you, that all Italians gone to Italy. Now all the girls left in Russia have to go to Germany. There is no point in eating any more. You must eat, to live, to go back to Italy, to your family, your home.'

The second whistle sounded, longer and sharper. Another couple of jerks and the locomotive started up. I was wearing an old watch. I took it off and put it around her thin wrist.

'This is a little keepsake for a courageous Russian girl. May it soon count happy hours for you too.'

She cried no more. She looked at the luminous sphere and the watch hands. It was about to turn midnight. The train was already moving when she jumped onto the platform and disappeared. A railwayman from the freight-loading bay shut the door in my face. I pulled down the window and peered out into the darkness. Trying to catch sight of her was useless.

Nadia, with her little black dress. Nadia, with her little face like an orphan's. Occasionally a tangle of tracks appeared under the signal lights. The drizzle continued, monotonous, haunting. The 'tacata' of the wheels on the rails accelerated until the sound dominated everything. I sat down and thought about this Russian world that I was leaving for ever, and about Nadia, who embodied it with her soul and character.

'Nadia! Nadia!' I shouted through the window, until I went hoarse. 'Nadia! Nadia!'

Nobody heard, nobody answered. Then I saw her little purse... She had forgotten it. Dare I open it? I took three objects out of it. The oil lamp would not stop swaying, the train whistled again and the rain continued to fall.

Three things. An icon, a photograph and two coins. Sixty kopeks.

'Nadia! Nadia!' my trembling lips wanted to cry out, as the welded seam of the metal and cut class ring – representing all her money minus sixty kopeks – broke because my finger was too big.

The train whistled, my thoughts turned to the poor Russian people as my fingers turned over the sixty kopeks...

3 DOCTOR SAREZKII'S DIAGRAMS

Anna, a cheerful young blonde girl with an infectious smile, had suddenly died from an unknown disease. If the truth be known, she had tried to abort on her own, too ashamed to ask for help from Doctor Sarezkii, a specialist in abortions. Her own remedy had failed. Poor Anna; she was so unpretentious and pretty.

I had not yet recovered from the news, when Nadia turned up at the door of my office to see if she could speak to me urgently. Not yet 20 years old, Nadia was all nerves and temperament. She was so thin that you could see her bones. She liked to let her hair cascade over her face, hiding the deep green eyes that I couldn't look away from when she gazed into mine.

She knew that she could count on me to give her brotherly advice.

I had met her at her house, with her father and sister. When I occasionally passed by to say hello, her father was always in the same room, wearing the same clothes and the same tired smile, the same expression of inconsolable sadness and resignation. He seemed not like a statue, but more like a painting; his body so flat that it gave the impression it was 'stuck' to the damp, blackened wall. He made an effort to greet me politely, saying:

'*Pojalista, gospodin! Nadia zdies!*' (Please, come in sir. Nadia is over there.)

Always the same sentence.

Zoya, her older sister, a draftsman engineer, was also always in the same place, studying with the same notes spread over the same table, as if she were disconnected from the world. Nadia languished in her room for fear of going out and being caught by the Ukrainian Militia and deported to a labour camp in Germany.

Without Nadia, her father and her sister would not have been alive. Her mother had died from typhoid, and with her death the house had become even colder, her father more silent and her sister more withdrawn. They could not live on air alone and no one gave them alms. Work had to be found, and Nadia found it.

She came to see me that day to say that Doctor Sarezkii was giving her work in his laboratory, so she needed an exemption certificate from labour service. Only I could get this for her. Her job consisted in looking for herbs from which to make vital medicines that the Russian factories no longer produced. The good doctor had employed many herb collectors and now he had her, a former student in medicine.

Nadia's eyes lit up with joy as she told me. She would collect the most exotic herbs and then, in Sarezkii's modest laboratory, they would make some fantastic remedies so that poor people like her mother would not die such slow and painful deaths.

I remembered Anna's livid face, as she lay in her coffin. There before Nadia's expressive eyes I could not help but promise her to do my utmost.

Once Nadia had her certificate, she enthusiastically commenced her 'scientific expedition'. The team of collectors was out gathering herbs when the secret police raided Sarezkii's laboratory, convinced that they had discovered an important centre of scientific espionage. They turned everything upside down. They pulled the books off the shelves to scrutinize them carefully, moved the equipment and examined things under a magnifying glass. The good doctor was arrested and subjected to endless interrogations.

It is worth recalling his statement here. The inspector who let me read it would not let me take a copy, but I tried to memorize it, and this is as close as I could get to the original.

Sarezkii stated that he did not know why he had been arrested. He put it down to his involvement in abortions, which broke the law, although nobody really respected this law anyway. The occupying forces had enough concerns over matters that directly affected the war without worrying about things that did not. However, in order to clear his name, Sarezkii argued his defence in a very well structured and eloquently written document, both from a scientific and a social point of view

The first page had some diagrams with numbers and a few words, illustrating the abortion rate. During the first phase of the German occupation abortions increased rapidly, and then subsequently dropped abruptly, before coming to a total standstill from the moment the Germans decreed that pregnant women were exempt from forced labour up until the child's second birthday.

On the second page he had traced a very interesting graph on the moral and psychological development of Russian women in the first stages of the war. As a result of the first 'contacts' with the occupying forces, almost always unsolicited, several had fallen pregnant, with the consequential problem of bringing a child into the world who was the result of carnal violence. The solution was abortion, to which they were forced to resort and which became a daily occurrence.

After this preamble, the accused claimed in his plea that due to the occupying authorities' disinterest in the abortion issue, he considered himself tacitly authorized, from a health and safety point of view, to assist the unhappy pregnant women who wanted to stop their gestation in time. Therefore this was social work that he had carried out, motivated by his conscience and a humanitarian desire to do good, because leaving them to their own devices risked them cutting themselves and bleeding to death.

At this point in his defence, Doctor Sarezkii spoke at length about the methods he used and, the medication that was needed and prepared specifically, and he gave a few typical case studies, documenting them with technical health-care data.

He ended his statement by stressing that these pro-abortion activities could be considered to have ended the moment that the above-mentioned decree was published. From then on he had concentrated all his efforts into the study of new medicines obtained from herbs and, true to his responsibility as a doctor, his intention was to ease the suffering of his poor sick compatriots. This is why he had started to carry out a series of complicated experiments in his laboratory.

When I finished reading, the German inspector smiled and said that Sarezkii was a good doctor and that he could well stay with his test tubes discovering new medicines for his 'ragged' compatriots. The mentality of this German, with his one intent being to discover wrongdoing, did not even reach an understanding of the importance of that Russian man's statement. He had understood that the women had aborted out of their own choice, that the doctor had helped them within his medical abilities and that the laboratory was not there for abstract experiments. How far that simple police officer was from guessing the true and terrible meaning of those curves and axes of co-ordinates and seeing the grave accusation that they represented!

Sarezkii was set free and he returned to his world. He put his laboratory back together with a great effort, as the inquisitors had destroyed everything, believing that it was all to do with the partisans. Since abortions from then on were not only out of fashion but were avoided as much as possible, very few patients came for consultations, which allowed him to work in peace, observing the preparations under his microscope and waiting for his herb collectors to return with the fruits of their harvest.

With a lot of hard work he managed to set up a small shop to sell the remedies he prepared, and with these he made quite a bit of money since they were in great demand. He was kept so busy that he did not even have time to read the thank-you cards that came to him from miles around.

The Russian counter-offensive intensified and the Red Army got closer and closer. The Soviet attacks were incredibly violent. To flee, or not to flee? Nobody could escape this question at the time, including Sarezkii. What would happen to him if the Bolsheviks re-entered the city? He examined his conscience deeply and decided to stay. He could rest assured: the Russians were not going to investigate the abortions. Instead of fearing them, he almost felt he deserved a medal. His medicines would also be needed by the Russian Army, as there was a shortage: his little store of drugs would be a modest contribution to the victory.

It was a little store, but not so little as to escape the notice of the battalion of German snipers in charge of destroying everything the enemy could make use of. He did not shed a single tear, though, or demonstrate his affliction. The Germans left nothing but burnt earth in their retreat. Sarezkii had too much to cry about; his work, the sweat and toil of years, was reduced to ashes.

I never heard from that doctor again, nor from Nadia. The Russians won back the city, which became isolated as if surrounded by an insurmountable wall. However, I kept going over Doctor Sarezkii's diagrams in my head. When I saw the livestock wagons loaded with human beings headed for Germany, my skin crawled with the thought of the misfortune of so many people being carried away like the remains of a shipwreck. I guess it was better to have the courage to bring an innocent child into the world, even if it was conceived with a stranger. This was the conclusion I drew from Sarezkii's diagrams, and which would be arrived at by anyone who had eyes, but also the mental faculties and the sensitivity not just to read them, but more importantly, to interpret them thoroughly.

THE STORY OF
A *VOLKSDEUTSCHE*

IN April of 1943 Dniepropetrovsk had hardly recovered from the memory of those cruel battles that had broken out so close to home and as far as Pavlograd and Novomskovsk. I will never forget that day in early spring when the city seemed to be flooded with sunlight, magically peaceful, and the waters of the broad River Dnieper reflected the intense blue of the sky. It was also as if the soldiers' uniforms, now they had returned from the front and spent a few hours in the city, had lost their encrusted mud and snow from the trenches and had curiously acquired the appearance of fabulous, festive regional costumes, as if an exclusively masculine crowd had come from their different villages for a big gathering.

The black uniforms of those who operated the tanks struck the only discordant note in this festival of colours, where the khaki uniforms of General Antonescu's Romanians with their large moustaches rivalled the blue of the air force, the red of the Cossacks, the grey-green of the Italian and German infantries, the crimson billowing trousers of the German staff officers, the yellow of the party leaders and the green and brown of the gendarmerie.

Our *carabinieri*, guarding different buildings of the Italian command, had on their marvellous three-cornered hats. The round and disproportionate hats worn by Antonescu's officers, the rectangular pointed hats worn by the French soldiers and the light caps of the seamen from the Black Sea were no match for them. The troops of the Croatian legion, with their little metal shields on their right sleeves, were few compared to those of the other armies, but they also contributed something with their Balkan personality, as did the small French, Czechoslovakian, Dutch and Hungarian contingents.

The streets of the city centre were full of life when the offices closed at midday, and at five o'clock, at which point almost all of the personnel of the command posts were off duty. This also coincided with the arrival of the military columns in transit who made a stop to enjoy a walk in the 'metropolis'. Dniepropetrovsk was very strange during those few days. I felt like I had been invited to a big military contest commemorating something or celebrating a recent victory.

I walked aimlessly in the unreal atmosphere of the upper-class neighbourhood of town. I was contemplating the mirror-like surface of the languid River Dnieper, when I caught sight of two women waving scarves at me from the window of a very tall building. They were insisting I wait there for them to come down. The building was too high for me to see their faces, so I waited for them, curious to see who they were. I was wondering if they were two of the many pretty girls from the city, perhaps employed in one of the German command posts. The prettiest of them were recruited in the Italian services, so I hoped they were perhaps calling to me due to my uniform, and they were maybe a couple of 'our' beauties. I was disappointed to find that instead of two Ukrainian beauties in their prime, it was Mrs Frank, not looking at all well, and her daughter Liudmila. They greeted me like a brother, and I wondered how they had arrived in Dniepropetrovsk and found lodgings in that luxurious building in this stylish part of town. I thought back to the recent past and of the modest but important role that Mrs Frank had held in the events of the war in this part of Russia, and I recalled how I had met her in December 1942.

I was commander of a column of trucks on our way to pick up munitions at Artemovsk's powder magazine that was set up in the tunnels of the immense local gypsum mine. Lieutenant Ruber of the *Wehrmacht* was waiting for me. The cold was intense. He invited me into the mine to have a look and asked if I would like to see the 'Tunnel of Blood'. I accepted, intrigued. They had started to fill the camouflaged trucks, under the supervision of a German sergeant who was an explosives expert. He noted everything down. There was a continuous coming and going of wretched Russian prisoners from the tank missile warehouse, located in a tunnel to the right. There was no electric light, so the Ukrainian guard spent his time striving to get the slackers and stragglers out of their hiding places, where they were resting to catch their breath.

The flickering shadows of the prisoners stooping under their load in those gloomy tunnels made me think of the damned from Dante's *Inferno*. The guards' impatient shouts and insults echoed around the rock walls of the tunnels like the evil yells of devils inflicting eternal punishment on the sinners.

Our oil lantern projected our gigantic shadows onto the white walls, forming strange deformed silhouettes of our winter hats, our large fur coats and enormous felt boots. It was in that old mine that I first heard about Mrs Frank.

We finally arrived at the end of the Blue Tunnel, renamed the 'Tunnel of Blood', which was different from the others due to a heavy wooden hatchway that narrowed down its entrance let only one person pass at a time. We continued for another couple of hundred yards until we got to the other end, where the wall was formed in part out of natural gypsum and in part out of cemented rock. Ruber hung up the lantern and waited for it to stop swaying so that the flame was still. The white gypsum walls were splashed with huge bloodstains. In some places the clotted blood was dry and almost peeling off the wall. The successive sprays of machine gun fire could be seen in the lines of holes chipped out of the rock above one another. Ruber drew the lantern to the wall and told me to take a closer look: the whiteness was discoloured with this shocking stain at intervals along the wall for dozens of yards. When I told him, horrified, that I had seen quite enough, he stepped back, telling me not to move. He took out his pistol and, without giving me the time to react, he unloaded a whole cartridge of bullets at almost point-blank range. The shots echoed around the empty tunnels, both absorbed and amplified by the cavernous acoustics. I stood still and, when the echo had dispersed, I heard him say:

'When I arrived in Artemovsk and they ordered me to prepare the gypsum mine to store the gunpowder, the Russians had only just evacuated the city the week before. We came into the deserted tunnels to explore and when we came through this hatchway we heard strange noises. We continued with extreme caution, in case there were partisans or perhaps even Jews. But the horrible spectacle that emerged under the light of our lanterns froze our blood and a horrendous stench made us choke: piles and piles of corpses. However, amongst the dead bodies there was a slight noise like a death rattle and it looked as if something were moving. We shone the searchlight across the heaps of corpses to examine the hundreds of bodies, as they lay twisted and intertwined in a dreadful spasm of death. They were of both genders and all ages. The first to have been shot dead were almost expressionless, but the faces of many others had grimaces of terror, as they must have known what fate awaited them before their death. The searchlights picked up the walls where there were splashes of congealed blood and bits of brain. Our

Ukrainian guide told us straight away that these victims were civilians of German origin from the Volga republics. They were the so-called *Volksdeutsche*. This macabre spectacle overwhelmed us. The ill fate of our brothers at the hands of the Bolsheviks made us feel compelled to go and pray, but we could still hear that faint moan amongst that mass of dead meat, so we began an immediate search. There, half buried amongst the dead, we found a woman who was still showing signs of life. She was the only survivor. There had been other victims who had only been wounded by the machine gun fire, who fell down mixed in with the dead in the hope of escaping once the Russians had gone. They never imagined that there would be Russian guards hiding in the tunnels waiting to finish off any survivors.

'Mrs Frank was indeed the only one who managed to survive; the only witness to the massacre. She had been wounded on the shoulder and had fainted, but thanks to her incredible stamina she had managed to survive this horrendous killing. We took her out into the fresh air. She was emaciated, covered in blood and stank of death, after a week of having had nothing to eat or drink. After a few days in hospital she was in better condition to tell us in detail what she had lived through, and the doctor was amazed at her lucidity after having experience such an atrocity. She said that this slaughter of the German ethnic minority from Artemovsk had been the work of the *Gosudarstvennoie Politicheskoie Upravlienie.*'

Lieutenant Ruber's eyes lit up with rage. The German revenge promised to be more ferocious than their adversaries'. The horrendous massacre in the gypsum mine was just one of many brutalities inflicted on the German minorities in Russia. If Lieutenant Ruber had taken the initiative to speak to me about this tragedy, he must have had a motive, as it was not a good time to digress from duties of service. At the time the battle was raging along the Don and the the Volga, and its outcome was the officers' only concern, because they knew that they had no way of standing up to an attack by the Russians in mid winter.

Lieutenant Ruber had been crippled and exonerated from service on the front. He told me that he would gladly have come with me and my column to join the fighting, and take revenge for the German ethnic minority. Ruber was one of the huge majority of people unaware of what was taking place with the Jews in the concentration camps in Germany and Poland.

When we came out of the mines the trucks were already loaded and ready to leave. The engines were running as usual so as not to let the oil freeze and the drivers were warming their hands at the exhaust pipes. The temperature was at minus 25 degrees Celsius, and the prisoners were also waiting in formation for the chief escort to authorise their return on foot to the concentration camp, their only home, but one they were desperate to get back to. There they would light a little fire to warm themselves by using pieces of wood and a bit of coal fallen from a sleigh on the track that they had gathered.

Suddenly Lieutenant Ruber asked me if I could take a message to his fiancée, *Fräulein* Liudmila Frank who had moved to Voroshilovgrad with her family. I was very surprised by this: Ruber was promised to Liudmila Frank, the daughter of the woman they had revived. What turn of fate had saved the children from the horror that their mother had miraculously escaped? It was Christmas Eve of 1942, the cabs of our trucks had no heating, there was no time to have dinner, and even if we had, the only things we had to eat were biscuits and tinned anchovies. We accomplished our mission successfully, despite the fact that half of our trucks went off the frozen track. We had to get them back by towing them with poles rather than chains – as we had learnt from the Russians – to avoid dangerous collisions.

With the *Wehrmacht*, as well as the out-and-out defence we also organized everything that was necessary for a counter-offensive, planned for immediately after the thaw. I was ordered to carry out another transportation of munitions and it was on this second journey that the lieutenant completed the story for me while the prisoners were loading the trucks. Ruber made a show of hospitality by taking me to the *hata* where he had his command post, so that I could recover from the intense cold of that dark December. He gave me a wonderful liqueur that the Germans call *Schnaps*, and showed me a few crumpled photographs of the Frank family.

'This is Liudmila!' he said with pride, as he showed me a picture of a pretty young girl, standing in front of a painted background of country scenery. 'But it was taken 3 years ago,' he added hastily, smiling.

His expression became mild and serene once more. He explained how they had become engaged and told me the rest of the story.

No sooner had Mrs Frank recovered consciousness after being taken out of the mine than she asked after her children, whom she had left in a good hiding place before the Russians started to detain the civilians with German origins. She thought that because of her age they would not bother with her, but she was afraid for her children because they were young and strong like their father, who had been exiled to Siberia seven years before. However, the police made no distinctions, and they also took her to be tortured to make her confess where she had hidden her children. She refused to say anything other than that they had left with the rest of the civilian population who had evacuated the town and she had heard nothing more about them. They gave up interrogating her after a while and took her to the gypsum mine to eliminate her.

Afterwards, when the Russians had left the city under the advance of the *Wehrmacht*, the children came out of their hiding place. The eldest, Liudmila, who spoke perfect German, reported to the German command to ask for protection for herself, her brothers and her sister and to find out what had happened to their mother. Nobody knew anything. Poor Mrs Frank, miraculously saved by Lieutenant Ruber's men, was finally reunited with her family at home weeks later. Ruber went to visit them often and this is how he met Liudmila, which led to their engagement.

When Ruber had finished his story he gave me another letter for Liudmila Frank. He explained that she had moved with her mother and brothers from Artiomovsk to Voroshilovgrad, a city full of German and allied command posts, where Mrs Frank had found a good job as a cook for a group of officers.

Before my munitions convoy set off, the lieutenant begged me earnestly to do my utmost to find the Frank family, because it was impossible for him to go to Voroshilovgrad, especially since the winter battle was becoming fiercer by the day. I promised I would do my best.

I found the Frank family, and they proved to be very friendly and welcoming. The mother was energetic and had great strength of character, despite having suffered for so many years. She was tall and slim, with distinctive features and blue eyes, which were unusually lively. The Bolsheviks had arrested her husband seven years beforehand because his German origins made him a potential enemy. They had deported him to Siberia to cut wood in the forests. He was a lawyer by profession, something the Bolsheviks could do without, whereas they needed a workforce to cut wood in the immense Siberian forests, so Mr Frank was useful to them after all. His poor wife was left alone to fend for her four children, forced to work miracles in order not to allow them to die of hunger. Later on Liudmila found work in a textile factory while her mother tried to make ends meet by working for an hour here and an hour there wherever she could. She managed to obtain the authorization to go to Siberia to visit her husband in the seventh year of his exile, and it was like going on an odyssey in order to reach the forest where her beloved was chopping wood along with the other deportees. The poor lady searched from face to face amongst those ill-fated men. Her husband was so worn out that she did not recognize him. It was he who came up to her. Under constant police supervision, in a kind of forest retreat, they were allowed to live together for just one week at the end of which they were separated again, probably for good.

As for Liudmila, whom I saw a few times after this, she said she wanted to marry Ruber when the war was over and go to live in Germany, never to return to Russia. Peter, the eldest brother, wanted to be a soldier. Karl was still too young to know what he wanted. Victoria, the third child, did not want to study German ; she only spoke Russian, and had a Russian character and features: she was the black sheep of the family.

All this, of course, was pure fantasy on Mrs Frank's part, as it did not take into consideration the Russian Army's ability to win back the area. Then the day came when the order was dispatched to the *Volksdeutsche* to evacuate the city in face of the imminent Soviet counter-offensive. They were sent towards an area to the west of the Dnieper where all the German ethnic minorities of occupied Russia were to be gathered in a city whose Russian population had been expressly removed.

The Frank family did not obey the order, as they were sure the Russians would not win back Voroshilovgrad and, if they ever did, the mother and children would leave with the German troops in retreat. Mrs Frank had already escaped death in Artemovsk and she trusted her luck.

In a matter of days the Russians, preceded by a hurricane of fire from hundreds of *katiushas*, descended upon the city. Voroshilovgrad had to be defended. Defended to the death. There was no way the city could be evacuated. Apart from all else, Voroshilovgrad had to stay in our hands at all costs because it was from here that we planned to launch the German counter-offensive, but the retreat was ordered... evacuate!

Mrs Frank had prepared to flee at this moment with her children, but it was too late now for the German authorities to take care of them. If they had obeyed the order to evacuate before, they would have been given transport and supplies. Now there were far more urgent matters to take care of: whole divisions were pulled apart, a powerful Romanian army was routed, a mountain brigade was decimated, Major General

Paulus' Sixth Army was forced to surrender in Stalingrad, and the Italian Eighth Army was on the verge of breaking up. Germany was in danger. Voroshilovgrad was about to be overcome, almost without any means of defence. The command posts had been evacuated and the few contingents that were left had the sole mission of systematically organizing the destruction of the infrastructure and buildings that the Russians might be able to use.

There was hardly any fuel left and the few vehicles available departed, packed with soldiers and equipment. Of course, there was no room for the Frank family. The horses and sleighs had gone: the agricultural *Sonderführer* had moved everything to the west and the thousands of disbanded soldiers had taken the rest: it was the beginning of the end.

I was brought back to the present by the arrival of two nurses who came out of the large building and decisively but respectfully took Mrs Frank by the arms and led her back in. She did not resist. I followed the nurses with Liudmila as far as a room on the top floor. As they sat her down on the bed, the poor lady was unable to open her mouth to speak. She remained static, looking me fixedly straight in the eye. Then, without coming out of this kind of hypnosis, she leaned back on the pillow and fell asleep. The tall building we were in was not a residence, but a German military hospital.

Mrs Frank's daughter told me the last turns of fate that their family had suffered. The German truck in which her mother, brothers and sister had travelled had been attacked by a detachment of Cossacks. Mrs Frank, once again, managed to escape with her life from the skirmish, believing that her two boys and little Victoria had also managed to slip away unharmed. But she never saw them again. They must either have fallen prisoner or perished in the hands of the enemy. Liudmila was travelling separately because she had left Voroshilovgrad with the German officer from the office in which she had worked. She travelled with him to the River Dnieper and, by some miracle, found her mother there some weeks later, although it was difficult to recognize her by then. From the moment she had been admitted to the hospital, her daughter had not left her bedside. At times her mother had moments of lucidity, but the last tragedy had been too much for her to bear, and the doctors had not been of any help.

I asked Liudmila what plans she had, and she told me that for a while the trip to Germany was impossible, even for the *Volksdeutsche*. Maybe one day. There was nothing left of that happy young girl that I had met on my visits to the family in Voroshilovgrad. Their last misfortune had marked her terribly. She did not talk to me about Lieutenant Ruber, and I did not like to ask. In all probability he would have had to blow up the gunpowder magazine in the gypsum mine, and had perhaps perished in the process like so many others in similar situations.

I said goodbye to Liudmila and her mother, yearning to get outside to breathe fresh air and return to the false festive atmosphere that I had come away from in order to find out who those two figures waving to me from the German hospital balcony were.

From the golden domes of the Orthodox churches, the peal of bells called the faithful to afternoon prayers.

PREPARATIONS FOR 'OPERATION CITADEL'

SOME 'STORKS' – the name given by the German air force troops to the FI-156 Fieseler planes capable of taking off and landing on any terrain – were circling around Gorlovka on surveillance to protect the command post of General Von Mackensen's First Armoured Army. We looked up at them with slight envy as we got out of our vehicle, which was parked in front of a tree. There was a simple wooden arrow nailed to the tree trunk, pointing to a modest house there in the city's mining district. There were just two initials painted crookedly on the sign: 'V.M.' (Von Mackensen). It was a little bungalow with a door at either end leading onto a small fenced-in garden. It had probably been a house for workers' families. The two soldiers on guard, who looked all puffed up by their uniforms that kept out the freezing temperatures, gave way to let us through.

I was accompanying the assistant chief of staff of the Italian Eighth Army in my dual role as interpreter and liaison officer with the *Wehrmacht* at the end of the cruel winter of 1943, when the cold weather seemed to be dealing its last blows before the thaw. We finally arrived in the inner sanctum of the First Army's command. They were in the process of being reorganized for an imminent German counter-offensive – as soon as the weather conditions favoured it. The co-ordination must have been complicated further by the dispersion of the commands in a series of workers' houses, but however apparently absurd this might have been, at least it meant that the enemy air force had difficulty locating them. Gorlovka was a town still inhabited by thousands of civilians employed in the reconstruction of the industries and mines that had been sabotaged by the Red Army in their retreat. Whilst the strategy after the battle of Stalingrad was being plotted here, the day-to-day fighting seemed to have taken a break.

There was not a soul in sight inside. Not even the sound of a typewriter could be heard through the doors leading off the corridor. If there had not been a grey-green greatcoat with wide red lapels hanging from a hook on the wall, we would have turned to leave, under the impression that we must have mistaken this for Von Mackensen's headquarters. Even more strangely, upon opening the kitchen door, we saw a little lady busy at her chores. Too busy, it seemed, even to bother to look up at us. Then we found out that the Germans had set up the First Army's general staff offices without evicting the civilians, in order to cover up their military activities.

A disabled *Wehrmacht* veteran explained this to us and immediately announced our arrival to the general. We knew that Von Mackensen had a brilliant service record and was a descendant of an old Prussian family with a military tradition. He received us in a room that was almost entirely taken up by a farmhouse table, upon which lay an enormous map of the Donets basin with multicoloured flags pinned all over it. In order to break the ice, Von Mackensen started by alluding to the capture of Dniepropetrovsk in the spring of 1941, when the Italian Expeditionary Force in Russia (CSIR) had fought in 'Operation Barbarossa' with the German divisions.

'Those were much more fortunate times, but we will overcome our current paralysis also,' he added.

The general was listening to our colonel, taking note of his explanations when the telephone interrupted the meeting. Von Mackensen listened matter-of-factly to the news from the front and, with the telephone in one hand and a red pen in the other, he walked around the table to reach the strategic points on the map that he was being told about. He retorted briefly over the phone as he moved a few of the flags on the map. Just as the general was giving the order to cover the front line with all available troops, his chief of staff, Colonel Kraemer, appeared. Apparently the answer that came down the phone was that there were no reserve troops, and Von Mackensen came back with the order to mobilize even the off-duty medical orderlies from the hospitals. It was impossible to gather reinforcements and there was a shortage of men, so the only option left was to start a massive intervention of Ju-87 *Junkers*, the famous and deadly dive-bombers called *Stukas*. To this he added a final order:

'Retreat, yield to the Russian advance: it is useless to resist when you can't. Let them advance and then the *Stukas* can bomb them to kingdom come.'

Once the emergency had been resolved, Von Mackensen could

continue his conversation with us. He started by bringing us up to date with the German general staff's preparations to make up for the Stalingrad defeat and regain the upper hand in the war against the Soviets. We learned that the weather conditions were halting military operations on both sides. Also, although the Soviet winter offensives had forced the Germans and their allies to retreat from the Caucasus and the Volga, losing both men and equipment, the commander of the Southern Group of Armies, Major General Erich Von Lewinski Von Manstein, had managed to contain the Red Army in the Donets and had won back Jarkov.

However, it was necessary to eliminate the large salient west of Kursk that was forcing the *Wehrmacht* to face a front line about 300 miles longer than necessary, thus posing a grave threat to their positions from Briansk to the sea.

'The short-term objective is to stop this salient with a surprise offensive, while the Red Army is in a phase of reorganization. If we can, we must fence them in to compromise their plan of attack. In order to reach this strategic objective tactic we plan to carry out a pincer operation at the beginning of May using two German armies. It is called "Operation Citadel".'

He pointed out that the new models of tanks to be used, the *Tiger* and the *Panzer*, as well as the heavy self-propelled *Ferdinand*, would contribute greatly to the success of the operation.

Our assistant chief of staff wanted to know what was planned in case of a modification of the front between Briansk and the sea. Von Mackensen replied that if we gave the Soviets time to reorganise themselves, we must expect them to put up an exceptional defence, so this had to be avoided at all costs.

'According to our espionage,' he went on, 'we estimate that Generals Rokossovski and Vatutin will have around eighty infantry divisions, ten armoured corps, over 30,000 tanks and motorized batteries, on top of 20,000 mortars and cannon and a thousand "*katiusha*" rocket-launchers, for about one million men. Moreover, for higher security, it seems that the Russian high command plan to move the so-called 'steppe front' with thirty infantry divisions, ten cavalry divisions, fifty armoured corps and two air squadrons with over 3,000 planes and long-range bombers, under the command of General Koniev. To face this vast amount of machinery, the German army will have about fifteen infantry divisions, six armoured and two motorized divisions, along with General Hoth's Fourth Army of eleven armoured and eight mixed divisions. Plus 6,000 cannon and *Nebelwerfer* rocket-launchers, and the support of about 2,000 planes, with a total of almost half a million men.'

These details left us astounded.

At the end of the meeting it was decided that I should stay with Kraemer while the colonel I was accompanying would rejoin the Italian Eighth Army. It had to be decided whether to move this army north, towards Gomel, or to repatriate it for good. While the Führer and the Duce were deciding, what remained of the Italian Eighth Army, quartered in the Don region and still operational, would be passed under the command of Von Mackensen's First Armoured Army, thus remaining grouped with Von Manstein's armies.

Despite terrible relations between the Germans and the Italians, the meeting had positive repercussions in our Eighth Army's command, because the First Armoured Army's reputation instilled confidence and security in us and perhaps also eased a few nerves.

Now that a relationship based on equality and mutual respect had been re-established, Colonel Kraemer proposed that I assume the temporary command of one of his companies that had lost all of its officers for whom they had no immediate replacements available. I accepted and found that it was not too difficult to command that unit, even though it was composed of troops of all ages.

The next day Colonel Kraemer invited me to dine at the officer's club in order to introduce me to them and put me in contact with the youngest officers. Few of them were yet aware of the *Wehrmacht*'s plans regarding an imminent counter-offensive. There was also a plan to destroy all that the *Sonderführer* had restored, especially in the Donets basin's industrial area. Since relations with the German commanders were much improved, my first meeting with this circle of officers opened new prospects for me. I moved straight from the miserable little house where I had been lodged to the surroundings of what seemed like the most select club in town. It was extremely lively and the bar never closed: we were served by soldiers dressed in white jackets and gloves in an absolutely professional manner, and it helped us to forget the war was on. The senior member announced Von Mackensen's arrival by proposing a toast with French champagne in cut glass goblets. Soon dinner was served and we went to the adjacent dining room, where our eyes met with a luxurious feast on an impeccable white linen tablecloth, porcelain dishes from Sèvres, artistic silver cutlery, leather upholstered chairs and oriental rugs. We were a total of fifteen officers. Since I was the only foreigner they gave me the seat of honour, to the right of the general.

During dinner Von Mackensen explained to me that the First Armoured Army had been transferred to Russia when they had ended the campaign in France and, although the silver and porcelain service belonged to his own service corps, the exceptional French wines were from war looting.

'*Zum wohl!*' (Cheers!) they repeated like a ritual, downing their drinks. And so that nobody cheated, after draining our glasses, we had to turn them upside down on the table to show that not a drop was left!

When dinner was over, Von Mackensen slipped away discreetly while the rest of the officers continued, determined to drown their sorrows in alcohol. In witnessed something I never would have expected to see in the headquarters of the high command of this famous German army. Despite the intense cold, some of the officers insisted on accompanying me to my lodgings, without the slightest worry about showing they were drunk in front of the sentries. I found it incredible and incomprehensible that the commanders of an army at war could allow themselves such revelry without it damaging their authority.

I put my radio on when I reached my room. Just as I was about to fall asleep I heard the sweetest voice singing 'Lilli Marlene'. I supposed they would air a news bulletin in German after the song, but I was dumbfounded to hear that the voice of the news broadcaster was Russian. I had tuned in to an enemy radio station. By then 'Lilli Marlene' had become a song that all of the soldiers on all the fronts listened to, a melody without frontiers. After a few phrases in Russian, there came a voice in German haranguing the soldiers of the *Wehrmacht* to desert and surrender themselves in order to save their lives. Next there was a voice speaking in Italian, and I will never forget his words. He repeated them several times, interspersed with Italian music. The message was the following: '*Every Italian soldier has the right to a pass allowing him to cross the Russian lines and turn himself in as a prisoner. Every soldier in the Red Army and every Soviet citizen is obliged to accompany him to the nearest Red Army command post. The commanders of the USSR army guarantee the prisoner's life and will return him to his country at the end of the war.*' The rumour spread in our ranks that this was the voice of the well-known Italian exile called Mario Correnti, who was despised as a traitor and a swindler. His programmes could be picked up along quite a large part of the front by the Italian Army.

The words were a trick though. The truth was that the Russians were inclined to wrench any greatcoat, fur or any other warm clothing from a prisoner, stripping him of the means of survival in that atrocious weather. What surprised me even more about this broadcaster was that he urged a number of officers by name to give themselves up with the units that they commanded. When my own name rang out in that list, I understood that the information must have come from prisoners that they had captured from us. Aware of the hypocrisy of that encouragement to desert, I had the burning desire to capture this Italian traitor myself.

I turned off the radio and the following day I asked permission to go with some volunteers from my company of German fusiliers in search of that voice. At the same time I would capture prisoners, since making enemies 'sing' what they knew was now part of the day-to-day war tactics. My initiative was greeted with interest.

The war had turned into a waiting game. Despite our efforts, we found no trace of the transmitter, which was no doubt moved constantly so that it could not be located. We penetrated 'no-man's-land' but all we found was a packet of enemy pamphlets in Italian. I took a sample of the most legible of them, destroyed the rest and we returned to the base with no news. The soldiers in the patrol urged me to translate the proclamation, after which they swore profusely, since we had not managed to take any prisoners.

One night I tuned in again to that broadcast, and once again heard the same voice encouraging the Italians to desert: '*This is Radio Moscow transmitting a message to all the Italians continuing to fight on the Germans' side: Surrender!*' I realized how fanciful my intentions had been. I then had a strange association of ideas: that voice belonged to the devil, with his horns, tail and trident, dressed in red, the devil that I had been frightened of as a child. I *saw* him embodied in that expatriate.

Upon my return to Italy, at the end of the war, it was revealed that the voice was none other than that of Palmiro Togliatti, who became head of the Italian Communist Party after the war. Even then he continued his demagogy of the masses, encouraging people to unite with the Communist world ruled by the Kremlin.

Many days went by, perhaps too many, according to the First Army's general staff, and 'Operation Citadel' ended with the battle at Kursk in

July of 1943, which has now passed into the history books. In that battle, hundreds of thousands of soldiers from both sides lost their lives, and a vast amount of German and Russian equipment was destroyed. The difference was that the Soviet Army, with the help of the Americans, was able to replace it and compensate for their losses, whereas for the Nazi army, this tremendous reversal in fortune led to the final conclusion, two years later, of the capture by the Russians of Berlin and their defeat.

'...ITALIANSKI
MOLODOI...'

V
OLODIA GRISHKIEVICH'S EYES were shining with joy. He took me aside and, half in Russian and half in Italian, he whispered to me in a low voice, 'Lieutenant, sir, there is an icon, beautiful, small, near here in the house of a lady I know.'

One day he had promised me a beautiful icon in return for the 'immense pleasure' I had given him by procuring a German piano for the theatre where he was a soloist.

'Thank you, Volodia. We should go and see it as soon as possible, but not now.

He looked at me, upset. It was the middle of February 1943 and the thaw would still be a long time in coming. The constant shelling and the growing rumble of battle hung in the air of the icy steppe, surrounded by blinding snow that stretched to all the horizons and prevented us from seeing into the distance. Volodia looked at me as if he was trying to see if I was really interested in a beautiful icon. Then he said goodbye with a slight nod of the head and disappeared down the staircase of the enormous industrial school where we had set up our operations with a regiment of the German 298th Division.

The telephone rang incessantly, so I did not have time to regret the lost opportunity of obtaining an icon that, if I got back to Italy alive, I thought of putting in my entrance hall to protect the house from evil, just like they do in Russia. From my office window I could see the steppe filling up with a multitude of little black dots moving towards the west: they were columns of vehicles heading towards the Dnieper. At the same time, a cascade of voices and urgent orders came down the telephone line, which were taken down on paper and passed from table to table until they reached the hands of the exhausted and frozen-stiff couriers. Volodia and the icon slipped my mind. Those agonizing days were never-ending. The Russians continued their massive advance from the east, preceded by the lacerating shrieks of the *katiusha* rocket-launchers, nicknamed 'Stalin's organ', and backed up by the Russian air force and long-range artillery. The Tartar and Siberian troops that had survived the exposed position of Stalingrad had reached the Donets and at certain sectors they had managed to cross it, thanks to their many tanks, self-propelled artillery, and cavalry. There was a danger that attacks from the front, from the flank and from the rear would cut off our retreat. They had broken through our lines along more than 600 miles of the front and it seemed useless to try and win it back, at least as far as the east banks of the Dnieper were concerned.

Miraculously, the thaw forced the Russians to stay put, and their plan to regain the south of the Ukraine as far as the curve of the Dnieper and cut off the allied forces that controlled the middle and lower Donets basin failed for a second time. I was not among the survivors who were repatriated to Italy. Instead they sent me to a large German unit where I had to fulfil a whole range of different tasks.

The snow had become slush by then and in many areas of the steppe where the ice had made its mark there were great ridges and troughs of earth. Our tank cleared a path, occasionally spraying muddy water up into the air, which hampered our vision and forced us to swerve in order to avoid getting stuck in the mud. We left the great coal mines behind us, and the buildings that had been systematically destroyed by Russian or German bombs, and we stopped in front of the Novaya Gorlovka industrial school, which had formerly been our command headquarters and, by some miracle, was still standing. There were a few civilians travelling along the roads. Only a few German all-terrain vehicles and self-propelled artillery vehicles were driving around.

I stayed there looking at the enormous deserted building. The echo of shelling did not reach this far and the war seemed relatively far away. Then I remembered the icon. As soon as I was free from service I went to Volodia's house. I was sure that he would not be there, but when I arrived I was pleasantly surprised to find a woman, wrapped up warmly and sitting at the doorway, sunning herself. I asked her if Volodia Grishkievich still lived there. She looked at me as if she was surprised to see an Italian still in the area. She turned her head and called inside to Volodia, who came outside and was very pleased to see me. The first thing he asked me was whether the Italians really were leaving Russia. I told him that this was a normal phase that happened in any war, but that the war would go on and... we had been ordered not to talk about it because any piece of news could get to the enemy and work against us. Volodia showed that he understood.

Guessing that I was still interested in the icon, he offered to take me to the Skorina family's house. He had to call several times at the door before a loud voice answered from inside. Then we heard the noise of a heavy bolt being slid across and a shrunken little old lady opened the door to us and let us in. To this day I do not know how she managed, but she slid the huge bolt back across behind us. She led us to a spacious room, full of remarkable furniture, far superior to any I had seen in other houses. The armchairs were made from leather, although they were very worn out. There was a pretty table, an enormous sofa and prints hanging on the walls. However, it was all in disrepair and must have been so for many years. Suddenly, a very distinguished looking lady walked in. She was of medium height and dressed quite stylishly with a dignified manner, although her dress was old and patched up. Volodia Grishkievich introduced us and the lady kindly offered me a seat and asked me some questions in very good French. I spoke to her cordially in a language that I knew well, and this is how I came to learn that the Bolsheviks had killed her husband in 1926 for being a noble and a landowner. She had found herself left alone to look after her daughter, a newly born child. From then on she had lived in misery with her grief, but above all she had struggled to bring up little Freda so that 'the Party' would not take her away and turn her into their instrument. When the war broke out, the Red Army in retreat had sabotaged the infrastructure and left the city without any means of subsistence. When the Italians and Germans arrived it seemed at first that they were generous. However, the Nazis then started to recruit the workforce and created an atmosphere of terror, above all with the deportation of the youngest women to Germany.

When she got to this point, Mrs Skorina went pale. Her 17-year-old daughter had managed to remain free until then, because of her job as an interpreter for the Italians in Russian and French, but the Italians were now leaving the area and she would not be able to avoid deportation. The Germans, or their Ukrainian militiamen, would burst into their house and even if they did not take her the first time or the second, they would not accept presents for ever and sooner or later they were bound to take Freda before the head of the *birzha*, who would send her to Germany. Mrs Skorina spoke to me as if I was an old friend, forgetting – and this had already happened to me before in Russia – that I was also part of the occupying enemy army.

At this point Freda appeared. She was a young girl with straight hair, parted evenly down the centre, and gathered at the back into a thin plait tied with a black bow. She shook my hand firmly and gave me a big smile.

Her mother asked me if I would like to listen to some music, and I accepted.

Freda sat down readily at the piano and very ably played a catchy Russian tune whose chorus ended in *'simpatichnie italiantsi'*, kind Italians. It was not the first time that I had heard it and I have to admit that it reflected a common feeling of mutual warmth between the Italian troops and the civilian population. In that decaying living room the melody instilled an indescribable feeling of well-being in me.

Freda ended her 'number' with a little bow. Her mother's face lit up when I applauded them. Then there was the inevitable pause and I saw that my hostess did not know how to break the ice, so I started to explain the reason for my visit.

'Madam, Volodia told me that you would be willing to sell me an icon, and it would be my great pleasure to take one back to Italy with me as a souvenir of this land that I hope to be able to return to visit once the war is over.'

She blushed and, lowering her voice, she answered:

'This must stay between you and Volodia: I was afraid that the Germans would steal it from me, so I had to hide it.'

Raising herself, she knelt on the sofa, sank her arms down between the back and the seat and took out a little bag. Wrapped in a woollen cloth was an image of Saint Nicholas with a silver cloak, embossed by hand. It was really beautiful and far superior to many icons I had seen, and I felt privileged to have this opportunity to buy it. The little bag also contained some jewels and a pearl necklace. 'I can keep this,' she told me, putting a delicate little ring on her finger, 'until I have to exchange it this winter so as not to starve to death.' And then she hurriedly added, 'If we are still alive by then.'

Before bidding us farewell, Mrs Skorina detained me for a moment to say:

'I want you to have a memento from us. It isn't the most beautiful icon, but it is one that has been passed down through our family. I did not need to hide this one because nowadays you can find ones like this in many homes. Not even the Ukrainian guards would dare to steal or touch it. No matter how much the regime has tried to crush our faith, most people remain religious deep down.'

'Thank you, madam, it is far too beautiful and precious for me to accept. Keep it. That way it will continue to protect you.'

However, she would not give in.

'This very morning they were saying in the marketplace that the Russians are very near again, that the front is not holding up and at the very best we will have the Bolsheviks back here again.' She gave a deep sigh and went on, 'The Germans will take it, or the Russians, if they return. It would be better if you take it, *gospodin*, as a friend of ours. Keep it as a memento of how a Russian family appreciated the Italians.'

Her intentions moved me, but I tried my best to convince her that the arrival of the Russians was not to be feared and that the Germans would not know what to do with an image like this. In the end, the icon continued to fulfil its sacred role as custodian of the Skorina family.

I spent several days on the Russian–German front occupied with the preparations for 'Operation Citadel', expected to be the retaliation that would vindicate the defeat of Stalingrad and eliminate the Kursk salient that lengthened the German front by about 300 miles. When I received the order to return home, I took great care to protect the little silver icon that would be my travel companion along the journey.

I had just got back to Italy when, on 10 September 1943 – two days after the armistice – I miraculously managed to escape from the barracks where the Germans had imprisoned us like the enemies we now were. After several traumatic days I managed to jump on a train heading south and find a small space in a packed third class carriage corridor. The train was full of soldiers disguised as peasants, mostly wearing rags that the civilian population had given them in order to escape from the Germans, some of them not even wearing shoes, bunched up wherever they could find a safe haven. Some were even perched on the roofs of the wagons. They were the living images of an army that was melting like a block of ice under the sun, of a nation in a headlong descent to ruin.

The heat that was almost as strong as summer, that tragic September in Italy, contrasted dramatically with the previous Russian winter that had been so harsh that our physical suffering stretched us to the limits of our endurance. The train came grinding to a sudden halt at the station, causing us all to fall on top of one another. The door opened and I was pushed out against my will. My thoughts were drowned in the whirlpool of people. On the station platform at Bologna, leaning against our piles of miserable household goods, we waited for daybreak to see if a train would come to take us on to our destination. The scene reminded me of the Russian refugees. I had nothing with me but the icon of Saint Nicholas that I had kept hold of throughout, and I am convinced to this day that it gave me help and protection.

BLESSED RUSSIA

ARIA KNELT THERE PRAYING. She was
the only living soul in that vast field of crosses with Italian helmets. The
grass was already growing, everything was germinating in the earth and
the sun caused drops of perspiration to appear on her forehead. Would
Papa Vasili come back? The hen was brooding over its first eggs and
Mama Anna took the opportunity to clean the windows of the dust and
mud that had been used to seal them during the long winter. She was
ready to bake a cake for Easter, which was not far off now. Meanwhile,
her son Dimitri, imprisoned by the Germans, prayed in his cell, asking
God in His grace to let him return home soon, because he could not
live without his family, nor could they without him.

In the German First Army, Colonel Kraemer, Chief of Staff, showed
me the route we had to take. He had marked it out with the Roman
numeral IV and a capital B. However, his blunt pencil prevented him
from following the exact course of the winding trail, the only one to the
Dnieper that could be used. The colonel did not beat around the bush:
there was no other choice but to take this route. The stunning Russian
advance meant that the German armies ran the risk of finding themselves in a critical situation that would be very difficult to get out of.
Kraemer had the added problem of fuel, and as many horses as possible
had to be requisitioned for the re-provisioning of the front line, as they
were short by a few hundred. The following day, as if that man had
supernatural powers, I saw sleighs being pulled by horses heading in the
direction of the pale, rising sun.

Papa Vasili was one of many that pulled his horse by the halter, heading to the front with provisions. Poor Papa Vasili had to leave his small
private trade in coal, or anything else he could get his hands on, to obey
the order of the 'Great German General', who had assumed command
of the front and requisitioned both equipment and people in the
process. Now Papa Vasili had also become a soldier, and if the Russian

planes gunned down his column, he would die serving the Germans. Papa Vasili was worried they would just leave him lying there, like carrion, next to his horse's corpse. He would not have had the comfort of the last rites nor a plot in the small village cemetery. He was a simple soul, Papa Vasili. He liked neither the Bolsheviks nor the Germans. He believed in God and the hereafter, and had lived an honest life and wanted to die as a good Christian.

Two Ukrainian gendarmes called at Mama Rosa's door and, after showing her a scrawl on a piece of paper, sealed with a smudged stamp, they took away her cow, her *korova*, leaving the stable empty. Now that she had no *korova* she could no longer sell milk in the market. The *korova* was all she had. She started to cry desperately, but her daughter dried her eyes, stroked her snow-white head and sat her down in front of a cup of sunflower seeds: their dinner.

The gendarmes next called at Mama Anna's house and took her *korova* too, a good cow that gave rich milk each day. It was useless for her to beg them not to, telling them that they had taken Papa Vasili to the front and when he came back he would die from old age and sickness. Without milk they could not live. Those who were requisitioning the cow just shoved the *bumaga* with the German stamp on it into her face and went off to the other houses for the few remaining cows. However, they did not take the cow that belonged to the pretty Maria, because she had thousands of roubles, earned goodness knows how, to give them as a bribe. So she kept her *korova*, continued to drink fresh milk each day and even had some left over to exchange in the market for other wares.

Dimitri, in the meantime, continued to pine away in a *Stalag*, praying to God for his freedom. He was waiting for some vital papers, and nursed high hopes because a decree from the OBH did exist, which authorized the liberation of prisoners, preferentially Ukrainians, so that they could be reunited with their families on the condition that they resume their original civilian trade. He was a rural mechanic, he knew how to run a tractor and he trusted they would let him return to his machines and his land, and his icons. However, nobody told him anything any more. Day after day they forced him to go to the station to load munitions, even now that his legs could hardly carry him any longer from the lack of food. As if this were not enough, Russian planes flew overhead as if nothing were happening. The prisoners were not allowed to take shelter, they were just hurried to load wagon after wagon as quickly as possible so that the train could leave before the bombs were dropped. Dimitri was not a coward, but it sickened him to think that the Russians could kill a Ukrainian who was forced to serve the Germans. Every night, before he went to sleep, he knelt to pray. It did not occur to any of his companions suffering the same misfortune to laugh at him. They too, even the non-believers, felt the need for something to hold on to, and God was the only thing they had. They silently searched the skies for Him through the cracks of their workers' huts surrounded by barbed wire and guards, many of whom spoke their own language. Poor Dimitri, poor Russia.

Meanwhile, the Russians won back Slaviansk and there was fierce fighting in the streets of Jarkov for the third time. From the *Stalag*, you could clearly hear the duel of the two artilleries being fought out, the explosions of the large-bore bombs and the sound of the *katiushas* riddling the woods with missiles in order to flush out German units that had taken cover there. The Russians took the station. The Germans kept the city, surrounded by Russians, who in turn were surrounded by Germans. No one knew who surrounded whom any more, nor did they take the time to answer Dimitri, who was destined to fade away into nothing, without even being noted as a statistic. His *Stalag* was moved in the desperate march towards the east, he closed his eyes for ever, begging the Lord to bless his family that he would never see again.

Papa Vasili was still travelling along the frozen dirt tracks. His horse was emaciated and he knew that the animal would not last much longer at that pace. 'Poor Iosic! You have transported so much coal and wood over the winter, my trusty work companion, you are also going to die a victim of the war! The "Great General" gives an order, and we all have to obey. My God, my God, *Bozhe moi*, why do you make poor Russia suffer so much?'

In the meantime, the Soviets piled on the pressure with bigger and stronger armed forces. Hour by hour, the situation became more chaotic. Compact columns of replacement troops travelled up the IV B route towards the Donets to reinforce the resistance in the industrial basin that the Germans wanted to keep hold of at any price. The news that we were surrounded and condemned to death spread from one village to the next and from house to house with the speed of 'Radio Steppe'. We thought that the Russians had us surrounded, besieging us from the north with contingent forces from Rostov. The agony could be prolonged, but the end seemed to be inevitable. Many civilians were frightened by this and asked themselves what the Germans would do if their retreat were cut off. They were sure that everything that was rebuilt or in the process of being restored would be burnt or stolen. The battle could turn out to be as bloody as it had been at Stalingrad. That night Mama Anna must have said to herself that it was no good if they saw her cry, and in these circumstances she should be the strong one. I came into the *hata* to thaw out a can of meat and Mama Anna came towards me shyly, hesitating as if she was finally facing the bitter truth. Maria, her daughter, sat still in the corner, deep in thought, husking cobs of corn. The only noise was the rustle of the dry corn leaves and the draught of the metal stove.

'Now that the Red Army has cut off route IV B, the situation will become irremediably worse. If we don't break through the siege we will not receive essential supplies.' That evening Kraemer had given us a bad omen, and the colonel was not one to panic. I imagined the imminent end and its consequences for the whole of the First Army and above all for our small garrison at Debaltsevo station, which we had not managed to help retreat to a less compromising position.

Mama Anna put a plate on the table for me full of the heated tinned meat and she asked me what was happening on the front. She said that she was well aware of it all and that we would end up like Stalingrad. If we fell prisoner, the Russians would take off our clothes in order to make use of our coats for themselves and would probably kill us. There were many godless commissars for whom Christian charity did not exist. And more to the point, *Voina eto* always *nehorosho* (war is always terrible). But she and Maria would save me.

Maria stopped husking her *kukuruza* and came over to us with a civilian suit that belonged to her brother Dimitri. She insisted I take it in case I needed it at a later date. She and her mother would hide me in the house of an old lady who lived alone, outside the city in an isolated spot. I was very touched by their offer and I had to try really hard to make them understand, without offending them, that this was impossible.

The following day the news was worse. The front was falling apart and there was a shortage of troops and armoured equipment. The garrison was removed from one sector in order to close a breach, only for another one to open, and there was no end to it. As if that were not enough, Papa Vasili's horse died, and there was no news of its owner. Hundreds of horses died each day from hunger, emaciated, blown up by a mine or gunned down by a Russian plane, and the few drivers that were left feigned serious injuries or pretended to be dead and hid with the hope of returning home.

Papa Vasili was one of those fortunate drivers. He managed to return home, but he died soon afterwards. An Orthodox priest dressed in a long habit, with a grizzled beard and long hair, looking as if he had just stepped out of a Tolstoy novel, entered the room and blessed the corpse.

The Russians fenced us in and the bombings increased. The nights were hellish. In our headquarters near the station, the anti-aircraft artillery answered their fire non-stop. Despite this, three bombs fell near our *hata* in a fan shape, breaking two windows, and one even hit the little house that belonged to poor Mama Rosa and her little daughter. In the morning the few smouldering remains of her *hata* still let off the acrid smell of trinitrotoluene. Amongst the many other houses that met the same fate, it was impossible to tell which had been hit last. Mama Anna and her daughter tried in vain to recover the bodies of their neighbours from the ruins. The only thing they found was an icon of Saint Nicholas in the *korova*'s empty stable.

Convoys endlessly entered and left Gorlovka station evacuating railway equipment. The tracks were laced with mines and everything, even the sleepers, were rendered useless. But the tenacious Russians continued their relentless siege.

'Tomorrow the Pioneer 70 battalion of sappers are coming to do their business,' Colonel Kraemer told me, showing me my new destination on the map. The plumes of smoke from the trains' funnels could be seen through the little window of his office as the steam engines reached full pressure. It seemed as though they were painting the sky grey to hide their activities. They rode back and forth across the switches, hooking up wagons to a convoy headed for the Dnieper. They were headed there because Grishino was still in Russian hands and in Pavlograd the fighting was fierce.

The next day the Pioneer 70 battalion arrived. The troops were all put in *hatas* in the same street and the trucks were parked under the bare acacia trees. A lieutenant received me in the office, which had a radio, maps and a typewriter.

'The chief is not here. He has gone out on a mission,' he said. 'There is a lot to do and we are working day and night.'

At that moment we heard a terrible din, a strong vibration shattered the windows and it felt as though the house had been ripped up from its foundations.

'Don't worry,' said the lieutenant. 'That is just Captain Knieche blowing up the station. We finished the transfer of the rolling stock a few minutes ago and there is no time to lose with the Russians at our heels. Any moment now they will blow up the blast furnaces and, as soon as we finish filling up with water, the city's fountains. Don't worry about your depots; one of your sappers, on his own initiative, has taken care of it.'

There was another dreadful explosion and pieces of rubble rained down on the cars parked in the street outside. From that moment on, these horrible explosions got bigger and louder. Guards and civilians ran to take shelter, as everything was being blown up behind the Germans in their retreat. After the Pioneer 70 sappers had been at work for a few hours, there were enormous flames lighting up the sky all around us. The spirits factory, destroyed by the Russians in their first retreat and partly reconstructed by the Germans, slowly collapsed to the ground before our eyes that morning, like a scene in a silent movie. In Debaltsevo the last cases of munitions, which had been hit by a Russian air raid the evening before, blew up. All of the rail links were destroyed and the land was mined, hidden from the eyes of possible witnesses by German tanks that went round the place firing without rhyme or reason to frighten the people into staying indoors. In Kaganoviska the panic spread: the alarm had been given that the Germans were preparing to evacuate the city. The men were terrified of the possibility of being recruited to dig trenches and the women of being raped. All the civilians were preparing to escape, but where could they go, surrounded by that fence of iron and fire?

The early thaw worked the miracle that saved us. An unusually hot sun started to melt the snow, reducing the number of vehicles on the dirt tracks and therefore the supplies could not reach the large Soviet units. The demolition and sabotage were stopped while waiting for a possible counter-offensive. Kaganoviska lived in suspense and uncertainty for days. When the German troops and equipment began to be moved and it seemed that the offensive could be resumed, a good share of the population was silently euphoric at the prospect of the war returning eastwards. The prices in the market went up suddenly and the morale and good humour came back. When, instead, the signs showed that the opposite was true, marks were sold off for nothing and the value of the rouble – which had been ten per mark, according to the exchange rate set by the Germans – was at par with the German currency.

When I reached my new destination and unpacked my things I found a small package with poor Dimitri's suit inside, along with a note written in Italian: 'Maria sends this because she wants to save you from the Bolsheviks. Maria cares for the Italian soldier.' What simplicity in those words, what sentiment in that gesture, without ceremony, when she interrupted her work that evening to hand me her brother's suit. Maria had loved an Italian soldier and he was buried in the cemetery where I found her praying the day that I went back to take them the suit and tell them that the war, which was now further away, would perhaps not return to her house again.

There they were: Maria praying amongst the crosses in the cemetery; Papa Vasili resting beneath a cross in his *hata*'s little orchard; and Mama Anna, during the calm of the storm, preparing the Easter cake and opening the windows so that she could finally let in the fresh, clean, spring air.

A man with a white beard was using a hammer to tap some metal cylinders that were hanging from the branch of a tree in descending order of size. They made a similar sound to the peal of bells, calling the faithful to the evening mass. Blessed Russia!

The usual traffic of supplies had been re-established along route IV B. The road to the Dnieper was open again, covered with wreckage of tanks and corpses. There was a wonderful sunset on the horizon, lengthening Rosa's shadow. She was praying in the war cemetery in front of a feathered helmet of a fallen *bersagliere*. Blessed Russia! An austere silence reigned over this temple, whose dome was the sky and whose light was the sun. The temple was called Great Russia or Blessed Russia when the war slept.

GLOSSARY

Arbeitsgehörde, Labour Bureau
Arbeitskräfte, workforce
babushka, grandmother; manner in
    which elderly ladies are addressed
balalaika, instrument similar to a guitar,
    triangular in shape
baryshnia, young lady
Befehlstelle, command post
birzha, employment office
borshch, soup of beetroot and other
    vegetables, made from a meat stock,
    to which cream may be added
    once it is served.
Bozhe moi, my God
bumaga, paper, document (colloquial)
carabiniere, Italian soldier serving
    as a police officer
Feldgendarmerie, military gendarmerie
Feldpolizei, military police
gospodin, Mr, sir
Gosudarstvennoie Politicheskoie
    Upravlienie (GPU), state political
    police
hata, small country house
Heereskraftfahrzeugen,
    mobile army depot
Heim, home
Heimat, homeland,
    native place or country
katiusha, rocket-launchers, also known
    as 'Stalin's organ' (colloquial)
kolkhoz, collective farm
korova, cow
Kreislandwirt, farming district
Kreislandwirtschafter, head
    of a farming district
kukuruza, corncob
Landwirtschaft Abteilung, Department
    for Agricultural Economy
Meldekarte, identity card or work record
molodoi, young

muzhik, peasant farmer
nagan, Soviet army pistol,
    also called a commissar's pistol
NKVD, Soviet secret police
OBH *Oberkommando des Heeres*,
    General Command of the Army
OKW *Oberkommando Wehrmacht*,
    Supreme Command of the Army
Obersturmführer, commander of an
    assault division of the SS
Panzer, tank
Parabellum, Russian automatic rifle
    with eighty-eight shots
papirosy, very strong Russian cigarettes
raion/raiony, region/s or province/s
russkii samolet, Russian plane
shapka, cap usually made from leather
    or wool
Schutzpolizei, secret police
Sicherheitdienst, security services
sovkhoz, state co-operative for
    agricultural production
Sonderführer, militarized civil servants
    in charge of the reconstruction of
    industry and agriculture in Russia
Stalag, large hut used as a dormitory in
    concentration camps
starosta, mayor
Stork, light reconnaissance aircraft
Transport Kommandantur, commander
    of transport
troika, Russian vehicle with team
    of three horses used for long distance
    transport in the steppe
ulitsa, street
Volksdeutsche, German-speaking Russian
    citizen from the German republics
    of the Volga
Wehrmacht, the German Army
Wirtschaft, economy
Wursterei Gesellschaft, sausage company

223

BIBLIOGRAPHY

Le Operazioni delle Unità Italiane al Fronte Russo (1941/1943)
Stato Maggiore dell'Esercito, Uff. Storico (2nd edition)

Erikson, John: *The Road to Berlin*
Weidenfeld & Nicolson (2 volumes)

Kurowski, Franz: *Deadlock before Moscow*
Army Group Center 1942/1943, Shiffer Military History

Cross, Robin: *Citadel: the Battle of Kursk*
Michael O'Mara Books Ltd.

Stolfi, R.H.S.: 'Hitler's Panzer East', in *World War II Reinterpreted*
University of Oklahoma Press

Encyclopaedia of World War II (ed. John Keegan)

Goodenough, Simon: *War Maps World War II from September 1939
to August 1945 – Air, Sea and Land, Battle by Battle*